CYBERSPACE RESUME KIT

How to Build and Launch an Online Resume

2001 Edition

MARY B. NEMNICH & FRED E. JANDT

CYBERSPACE RESUME KIT, 2001 EDITION
How to Build and Launch an Online Resume

©2001 by Mary B. Nemnich and Fred E. Jandt
Published by JIST Works, an imprint of JIST Publishing, Inc.
8902 Otis Avenue
Indianapolis, IN 46216-1033
Phone: 1-800-648-JIST   Fax: 1-800-JIST-FAX   E-Mail: editorial@jist.com

Visit our Web site at **http://www.jist.com** for information on JIST, free job search information, book chapters, and ordering information on our many products!

Quantity discounts are available for JIST books. Please call our Sales Department at 1-800-648-5478 for a free catalog and more information.

Also available from JIST:

Cyberspace Job Search Kit, 2001 Edition
Fred E. Jandt and Mary B. Nemnich

The Customer Is Usually Wrong!
Fred E. Jandt

Development Editor: Lori Cates
Interior Design: Aleata Howard
Cover Design: Trudy Coler
Proofreader: Rebecca York
Indexer: Larry Sweazy

Printed in the United States of America.

Cataloging-in-Publication data is on file with the Library of Congress.

04 03 02 01   9 8 7 6 5 4 3 2 1

ISBN 1-56370-808-6

ABOUT THIS BOOK

New technology has drastically and forever changed the way people find and apply for jobs. Instead of scouring the classified ads in the newspaper, people now find the best jobs on the Internet—on job bank sites, corporate Web pages, and newsgroups. And instead of printing a resume, snail-mailing it to an employer, and sitting back to wait weeks for a response, today's job seekers are zapping their credentials into employers' hands within minutes of learning of an opening, or posting them on resume bank sites that employers search for matches.

So, to find good jobs fast and keep up with everyone else, it's imperative that you

- Adapt your resume for use on the Internet, and

- Choose the best resume bank on which to post your credentials.

This book helps you revise your current resume for Internet use, or build an on-line resume from scratch. It explores the various types of cyber-resumes, including scannable resumes (for use on resume banks, in e-mail, and for employers who put resumes into a database) and HTML Web page resumes. Along the way, you will see lots of real-life examples of attention-getting resumes.

We also offer special online job search advice for new college grads, federal job seekers, and people transitioning out of the military.

Employers considering online recruitment will benefit from the detailed explanation of the resume-scanning process, as well as from the job bank descriptions in part II.

Part II is an indispensable guide to 80 of the most popular Internet job banks in the United States, Canada, the United Kingdom, Australia, and New Zealand—the places where you can post your resume for employers to search. We have ranked the sites using a five-star system, and provide all the details you will need to determine which bank is the best place to put your resume—or search for candidates.

In short, everything you need to know about online resumes is here. And because the Internet has changed the whole job search process, this is essential information to have.

CONTENTS AT A GLANCE

TABLE OF CONTENTS

PART I

CREATING AND DISTRIBUTING ELECTRONIC RESUMES

This section contains everything you need to know to get your credentials online and into the hands of potential employers:

- Chapter 1: Resumes on the World Wide Web
- Chapter 2: What to Include in Your Electronic Resume
- Chapter 3: How Resume Scanning Works
- Chapter 4: Preparing and Submitting Your Scannable Resume
- Chapter 5: Your Own HTML Resume
- Chapter 6: Specialty Resumes

RESUMES ON THE WORLD WIDE WEB

There's little agreement as to what was the first modern computer. Some people think it was ENIAC, which was built in 1944. It took up more space than an 18-wheeler's tractor-trailer, weighed more than 17 Chevrolet Camaros, and consumed 140,000 watts of electricity! Today, most people wear more computing power on their wrists than existed in the entire world before 1961.

The Internet was born a little over 25 years ago out of the problem of interconnecting computer systems at research facilities and universities. By 1979, CompuServe, the first consumer online service, was launched independent of the Internet. In 1990, the first World Wide Web browser was developed, and by 1993 the Mosaic Internet browser was developed.

Early in the 1990s, Fred Jandt, as a university professor, and Mary Nemnich, as a job-search specialist, began to track the development of job search on the Internet. In 1995, we published *Using the Internet in Your Job Search.* In this book, we wrote about electronic resumes and included only a few pages about the new World Wide Web.

By late 1996, the World Wide Web had grown to more than 70 million pages of content. By 1998, it had grown to 320 million pages. The growth of the World Wide Web happened so fast and Internet job search changed so much that by 1997, we published *Using the Internet and the World Wide Web in Your Job Search.*

Just two years later, so much change had again occurred that our third book, *Cyberspace Resume Kit,* focused just on the resume. Since then, the places where job seekers can post resumes have mushroomed. More resumes than ever can now be found in those databases, and the technology that company recruiters use to search out and store those resumes has become more sophisticated than ever. No longer is an electronic resume simply a paper resume sent through e-mail. Thus, it has become necessary to revisit electronic resumes and the many Internet databases that contain them.

After our first book, we were interviewed on the CNN program "Computer Connections." The correspondent wanted to know how many resumes were on the Internet. We gave a tentative answer of "tens of thousands." After our second book was published, we were more prepared. After doing some counting, our best estimate at that time was more than .5 million. With the publication of our third book, that number was closer to 3 million. As this book is going to press, we're now estimating more than 10.5 million—a greater than threefold increase!

Ten-and-a-half million resumes online—should yours be one of them? A quick look at the changes in the job search process may help you make that decision. One fundamental change is occurring right now, and computers and the World Wide Web have made that change possible. Job seekers can now post their resumes to job banks: They no longer have to search the classifieds and mail their resumes. Employers, in turn, search those job banks: They no longer deal with files of paper resumes that are discarded after a position is filled. And Human Resource departments also benefit: They now have recruiting software that searches resume banks for them.

Early Internet Job Search

To see how much electronic job search has changed, let's look briefly at how it started on Usenet newsgroups.

Usenet newsgroups were on the Internet before there was a World Wide Web. They were the early way of getting your resume on the Internet. Newsgroups were particularly useful for job searches limited to one city or state.

Newsgroups are very different from WWW databases. Think of a newsgroup as the electronic equivalent of a bulletin board in your local grocery store or on your college campus. Let's say your dog is missing. You can post a message about your dog on a bulletin board for people to read as they pass by. If someone has seen your dog, that person can copy down your telephone number and call you to report where your dog may be. Another person with a dog of the same breed can leave you a message to tell you about some available puppies. And because bulletin boards are visible to anyone who passes by, another person may write graffiti on your posting.

Newsgroups function in the same way as bulletin boards, and they were *the* bargain on the Internet because you incurred no charges for reading, placing, or responding to a posting—other than, of course, the regular cost of your Internet service provider (ISP).

Newsgroups are transmitted electronically around the world on Usenet (User's Network). Usenet newsgroups number in the thousands, and they are identified by topic. Some of the newsgroups are serious discussions on serious topics; others are just for fun; still others are frank, explicit discussions of adult topics. No one group is in charge of Usenet as a whole.

There are still Usenet newsgroups on the Internet, but they are no longer the most useful, efficient, or comprehensive way of posting your resume. There are lots of problems with newsgroups; mainly, they are not well maintained. In a newsgroup, you'll see the postings (also known as *articles*) that can be as recent as five minutes old or as dated as several months old, depending on how many postings the group receives. In addition to the date, each posting is identified by its subject (or title) line. You decide which posting you want to read by wading through long lists of subject lines. Despite their flaws, newsgroups can be good places to find job leads you won't find anywhere else.

Newsgroups are identified with a [word] dot [word] and [word] dot [word] dot [word] format. The words may be abbreviated, as in **biz.jobs.offered**. This is a popular newsgroup for listing business jobs.

If you have no experience with newsgroups, one place to begin is the following newsgroup, which provides articles on how to best use newsgroups:

news.announce.newusers

Accessing Newsgroups

The easiest way to access newsgroups today is through your ISP, or your Internet browser. To send your resume to a newsgroup, you must prepare and save it as a text document. Plain text has no indents, no centering, **no bold text,** <u>no underlines,</u> *no italics,* no color, no tables, no graphics, no pictures—just text. And the standard limit for the number of letters or spaces on a line is 70.

The Netscape Navigator and Microsoft Internet Explorer Internet browsers have newsreader functions. In Netscape Navigator, you access the newsreader by selecting Window, Netscape News from the main menu bar. Internet Explorer users have two options for accessing Internet News, Microsoft's newsreader. You can either use Internet News, a stand-alone program that you run by simply clicking on its program icon; or you can click on the Mail button on Internet Explorer's toolbar and then select Read News.

Some service providers such as America Online have their own newsreaders. On AOL, click the Keyword button and type *newsgroups.* This takes you to the AOL Internet Newsgroups page. On this page you will find a Search all Newsgroups button. After clicking on it, you are taken to a keyword-search entry block. If you put in the word *resume,* you are given a list of all the newsgroups currently available to you that have the word *resume* in their titles. Clicking on one of these newsgroups opens that newsgroup and lists all of the resumes available there. You also see buttons you can use to add your resume to that newsgroup. Be sure to read the terms of service and other instructions before you post anything on any of the newsgroups. Then, you can copy and paste your text resume directly into the message field, posting it to the newsgroup.

Examples of Resume Newsgroups

The Internet has many newsgroups that are dedicated to posting resumes. You can post your resume in these newsgroups at no cost. Some of the Web resume databanks post your resume in certain newsgroups when you submit your resume to them. Most of the job and resume newsgroups serve a defined geographical area or a specific industry (see table 1-1). If you live in one of the geographical regions listed in table 1-1 or if you want to work in that location, use the newsgroup that is listed.

TABLE 1-1: RESUME USENET GROUPS	
Type of Newsgroup	**Newsgroup Name**
General	
Appropriate for most resumes	misc.jobs.resumes
Countries	
Israel	israel.jobs.resumes
United Kingdom	uk.jobs.wanted
U.S. States	
Florida	fl.jobs.resumes
Illinois	il.jobs.resumes
Pennsylvania	pa.jobs.wanted
Cities	
Houston	houston.jobs.wanted
New York City	nyc.jobs.wanted
Pittsburgh	pgh.jobs.wanted
Philadelphia	phl.jobs.wanted
Portland, Oregon	pdaxs.jobs.resumes
	pdaxs.jobs.wanted
Quebec City, Canada	qc.jobs.wanted
St. Louis	stl.jobs.resumes
San Francisco Bay area	ba.jobs.resumes
San Diego	sdnet.jobs.wanted
Seattle	seattle.jobs.wanted
Industry	
Biological industry	bionet.jobs.wanted
Medical sales	alt.medical.sales.jobs.resumes
Computer programming	prg.jobs
Defense jobs	dod.jobs

Some newsgroups contain job-vacancy postings as well as some resumes. We suggest that you read the postings first to determine whether the newsgroup is an appropriate place to post your resume.

Posting your resume in a newsgroup costs nothing and takes very little time; however, this kind of posting is not as likely to result in an offer of employment as the more sophisticated resume databases on the World Wide Web. (See part II, "Resume Banks," for descriptions of the best of these databases.)

The Issue of Online Privacy

When newsgroups were the only way to put your resume on the Internet, the Internet was still small and used mostly by researchers. So privacy was not a large issue. But with the intent of some people using the Internet today, privacy is and should be an issue. Identity theft, the crime of co-opting another person's identity through records and documents such as Social Security cards for financial gain, is considered by many to be the fastest-growing crime in the United States. It is estimated that some 500,000 people already have been victimized.

There are many ways that your personal information may fall into the wrong hands. Private companies can legally use your Social Security number without restrictions for their own purposes. Many states still use Social Security numbers for driver's license applications. Americans carelessly throw away "trash," such as pre-approved credit applications containing sensitive personal information. Fake documents are easier than ever to get, and the Internet has made getting them a lot easier. There are several sites on the Web that proclaim their ability to make IDs that could "fool your mother." Because of refined software and good printers, these documents are more convincing and easily reproduced than ever before.

The fact is, though, that you put your privacy on the line every time you go online. Web sites collect a tremendous amount of personal information about you, including your name, Social Security number, date of birth, gender, e-mail and postal address, telephone, office and fax numbers, credit card numbers, education, occupation, income, and hobbies and interests. The people who control this data know who you are and may be selling detailed information about you from the data they collect.

When you go Web-surfing, many of the online sites you visit install *cookies* on your hard drive—electronic tags that track the places you go. Opening e-mail "spam"—electronic junk mail—can also place a cookie on your hard drive. Cookies can be considered both good and bad. Cookies keep track of your preferences, and so they make Web surfing easier by tailoring what you see to what your interests are. (For example, Amazon.com uses cookies to track the kinds of books you buy and to recommend new books that might interest you.) On the other hand, cookies also allow the secret collection of personal data about you, information that may be shared with advertisers or disreputable opportunists without your knowledge.

You need to be aware that data about you is being collected with every click of your mouse.

Horror stories about identity theft have caused many job seekers to be cautious, and even reluctant, to put a resume online. However, there are a few things you can do to protect yourself.

Privacy Software

Some companies make software that can shield your privacy when you are on the Web.

Anonymizer.com

http://www.anonymizer.com/3.0/index.shtml

The Anonymizer takes each Web page link you click and encrypts it. According to the Anonymizer site, "This encrypted text is decipherable only by our Anonymizer servers. When you click on one of these links, the Anonymizer server retrieves the required page from the Internet, encrypts the links in that page's code, and forwards it on to you." Anonymizer provides anonymous Web browsing for about $50 a year.

Freedom

http://www.freedom.net

Freedom is an Internet privacy product from Zero Knowledge Systems, a company that designs tools and strategies to protect the privacy of Internet users. Freedom software protects your online privacy through a number of different means. You can select a pseudonym from a list, not only masking your personal information, but also encrypting all your outgoing data and messages. In addition, Freedom Network routes your Internet traffic through a series of "privacy-enhancing detours." These detours further encrypt your data and remove all your ISP's location information. Freedom 1.0 costs about $50.

Internet Junkbuster

http://www.junkbusters.com/ht/en/ijb.html

Junkbusters is an organization whose mission is "to free the world from junk communications." They "give you the tools to stop junk." Junkbusters' Web site contains information about how to stop junk mail and protect your privacy. Its Internet privacy software product is Internet Junkbuster, a free software package that allows you to stop cookies and remain anonymous in your Web exploration.

Shielding Your Identity with Anonymous E-Mail Addresses

One good way to shield your identity and protect yourself from junk data collection while you are job searching is to use an anonymous e-mail address. Many of these, such as Hotmail, mail.com, and email.com, are available for free on the Internet. If that address becomes junked up with spam and cookies, you can simply drop it and establish another. Another way is to use a pseudonym until you set an appointment with a bona fide employer—some online sites allow you to search anonymously or by use of a synonym. And *never* put personal data into an online profile with your ISP. These profiles contain highly personal information about you that can be used by unscrupulous people to target unwanted messages to you and even enable them to *find* you!

Online Database Privacy Policies

If you choose to post your personal information at an online database, make sure that the company has a privacy policy. Privacy policies should state clearly how and when your personal information is collected and how it is used. Check to see whether the site allows anonymous access for its users. And never post personal information to a site that you don't know or trust.

> **Note**
>
> To see how some of the online resume databases measure up in terms of protecting your privacy, see our Web site ratings in part II, "Resume Banks."

A First Look at Resume Databases

In this book, we will explore many different private online resume databases. However, this fast-growing means of job search is not just occurring in the private sector; labor departments in federal and state governments are also encouraging it. Let's look at what the U.S. Department of Labor is doing, for example, with its America's Job Bank site.

America's Job Bank (AJB) is a joint effort of the Department of Labor and the Employment Service offices of each state. More than 1,800 Employment Service offices are in operation nationwide. Employment Service offices have long been in the business of linking employers and job seekers. In 1979, the various offices began cooperating with each other to exchange information on job listings. Today, America's Job Bank is the computerized network that links these state offices electronically so that the public can have a more widespread and efficient method of sharing resources.

Originally, AJB was strictly a repository of job postings. Job seekers could search for job listings geographically. Then they could use certain job-related keywords to apply for a position by following the employer's stated procedures. Unfortunately, no other interactivity was available with this early system.

Beginning in late spring of 1998, however, AJB added a resume-posting service. Two short years later, in Spring 2000, we found more than two million resumes and over one-and-a-half million jobs posted on AJB!

Most of the job opportunities listed on AJB come from the private sector and are for full-time positions. The openings are available nationwide and represent a broad cross-section of qualifications, wages, and types of work. Because AJB is run by the Department of Labor in conjunction with the Employment Service offices, no fee is charged to the job seekers or the employers. All employers who register with AJB must be verified as legitimate employers.

You can conduct job searches with AJB simply by going to the following site and selecting various alternatives to conduct your search:

http://www.ajb.dni.us

For example, if you were looking for work as an accountant in Minnesota, you would click the folder for "administrative support," then select accountant. Then, you enter your ZIP code and specify the radius in miles that you would travel. Click "search now" and you are presented with lists of job openings matching the criteria you've selected.

To post a resume at AJB, you must first register with the service. This registration consists of a fill-in-the-blank online form where you provide such basic information as your name, address, and phone number. You can also enter a profile, if you wish. You then choose a user ID and password, which you will use in subsequent searches. Remember to make a note of these two items because you can't get into the resume area without them.

After you have completed your registration, you can begin entering your resume into AJB's Resume Builder form. You can enter a full-text resume by filling in the blanks on an online form. You can submit an "express resume," which contains only minimal information. Or you can paste your ASCII-text resume into the field. When you submit it, your resume will be posted to America's Talent Bank, the sister service to AJB. You can modify your resume anytime. Resumes stay active for 60 days, but you also have the option of extending your active period. Only employers who have registered with AJB and have been issued a password can access your resume.

Besides resume posting, AJB also enables you to create cover letters to accompany your electronic resume. You can use AJB's online form, or you can incorporate your own cover letter into the form. With AJB, you can also create custom job searches. This feature enables you to save your specific search patterns so that you can call them up for subsequent searches. The site also contains helpful information for job seekers.

If this description leaves you a bit overwhelmed, don't worry. AJB is just one of 75 resume banks we describe and rate in this book. Our objective is to help you write an effective electronic resume and post it to the resume bank that will most likely result in the job you want.

What About My Paper Resume?

You probably have a printed version of your resume, complete with fancy fonts and paper. You have followed all the long-standing rules for making it attractive and professional. This paper resume, known as a *presentation resume,* was just what you needed prior to the emergence of the Internet. Presentation resumes, in fact, still serve a purpose in a job search. However, don't assume that this printed resume is what you really need in today's world.

In some cases, you need a *scannable resume*—one that has been prepared and saved as a plain-text document so that it can be scanned directly into an employer's database. A scannable resume contains no special formatting, such as enhanced fonts and graphics. In another case, you may be preparing an HTML resume to post on the World Wide Web that will include special backgrounds, graphics, and even animation. In the following chapters, we'll tell you what you need to be successful in your electronic job search.

Ten-and-a-half million resumes online. Should yours be one of them? You bet!

CHAPTER 2

WHAT TO INCLUDE IN YOUR ELECTRONIC RESUME

As with conventional, or presentation resumes, certain elements must be present in your electronic resume, and these elements should be arranged in a certain order for the information to be effective. You will most likely be preparing two types of electronic resumes: scannable resumes and HTML resumes. When we say HTML resume, we are referring to resumes on the World Wide Web that use multimedia elements, such as graphics, animation, or links to other sites. HTML resume preparation is discussed in detail in chapter 5. In this chapter, we will examine the various elements that must be included when preparing either type of electronic resume. Because the rules for preparing the two resumes differ markedly, this chapter focuses on what to include in *any* electronic resume. The rules for preparing and submitting scannable resumes are covered in chapter 4, "Preparing and Submitting Your Scannable Resume."

Personal Evaluation

Before you begin to write a resume, you must first spend some time contemplating what, exactly, you want in a job and a career. You need to focus your objective, review your wish list of desirable goals, make decisions about where you want to work and the kind of work you want to do, determine your likes and dislikes, and decide which tasks you would never consider doing. When asked what kind of work they are looking for, many applicants respond with "Anything!" In truth, there are many tasks they wouldn't want to do, so figuring out these choices in advance avoids wasting their time and the employer's.

Take Inventory

After you know what you want to do, you need to take a look at how equipped you are to get there. Review your entire work-related knowledge base. What are your skills? How much training have you had in your occupation, formal or informal? How much actual, hands-on experience have you had in doing the job you want? Honesty is key in answering this question. Did you actually perform the work, or did you merely observe others in the organization doing the work? How long have you performed the duties? Remember that six months is six months, not a year. Stretching your background is dishonest and doesn't serve either the employer or you.

Next, look honestly at your job-related strengths and weaknesses. Where do you really shine at work? Often, a correlation exists between the tasks you like to do and your greatest strengths on the job. Think about the times that you felt you really weren't giving your best. Or think about the situations when you felt you didn't quite meet standard. These points represent weaknesses, the areas where you need improvement. You want to target jobs that give you more opportunities to showcase your strengths, not your weaknesses.

Following an evaluation of your strengths and weaknesses, you should examine your accomplishments. Think about accomplishments at work and outside your job because both places serve to point out your strengths. Ask yourself how and when your contributions made a positive difference to your organization. Quantify your achievements by putting dollar amounts and numbers on your efforts by answering these questions: *How much* money did my suggestion save the company? *How many* people did I manage? *How many* items did I produce? Think in terms of comparisons. For example, did your performance outshine others who did the same kind of work?

Remember, accomplishments make the individual applicant stand out from the others. They tell an employer how well you performed on a job, not just that you did that job.

Sample resume 2–1 for Ronald A. Enomoto focuses strictly on the accomplishments of the applicant. This candidate wrote a resume targeted to a specific position. He was making a career change after having owned his own business for a long time. In this case, accomplishments are used to illustrate his experience with the target company and his strengths in areas outside his own company.

Ronald A. Enomoto

Post Office Box 85, Half Moon Bay, CA 94019
e-mail: ron@enomoto.com

Phone (650) 726-4844
Fax (650) 726-4078

Objective

To obtain the management position of Interim Director of the U C Santa Cruz Arboretum that will utilize the broad-based skills that I have developed as a successful small businessman and through very significant involvement in the University and industry nonprofit organizations.

Special Qualifications

A management professional with extensive experience in opportunity assessment, planning, and program execution. Proven ability to organize individuals, form consensus, motivate, coordinate participants, supervise staff, and work effectively with volunteers. Skilled in interpersonal relations, experienced in public speaking, public relations, media presentations, and fund development. Knowledgeable in shared leadership practice.

Selected Accomplishments

♦ Served on University of California Board of Regents for two years. Chosen as vice-chair of Education Policy Committee; Chaired Student Regent Selection Committee.

♦ Selected to receive a three-year Kellogg Foundation Fellowship in leadership development that had state, national, and international study programs culminating in a 30-day international study trip.

♦ As President of UC Davis Alumni Association, initiated and led a $4.8M Alumni Center project. Board was responsible for design, budgeting, and private fund raising. Center was completed on time and within budget. Center was largest private fund-raising project on campus to date.

♦ Developed and implemented innovative Internet marketing of roses in overnight delivery service nationwide in 1994. Increased profitability of company 30% in two years.

♦ Grew commercial greenhouse roses completely pesticide free for three years. Reduced pest-control costs 80%, improved quality, mitigated increased regulatory constraints, enhanced the environment, and removed employees from pesticide contact.

♦ Engineered and built greenhouse water-recycling system, saving 90% of former consumption. Local industry savings reduced community rationing in seven-year drought from 40% to 25%.

♦ Developed computer control for greenhouse environment, 1986. Saved 20% of energy consumption, improved quality, and increased production. System is now sold worldwide.

Employment History
Owner of Enomoto Roses Inc., Half Moon Bay, for 32 years.

Education
B.A., University of California—Davis
Kellogg Foundation Fellowship—Agricultural Leadership Program

(continues)

(continued)

Ronald A. Enomoto -2-

SELECTED ACHIEVEMENTS

These selected achievements are presented to demonstrate ability in opportunity assessment, effective planning, shared leadership, consensus building, project supervision, successful plan execution, and team success.

Served on selection/review committee to select Vice Chancellor of University Relations, UC Davis; Director of Alumni Affairs, UC Davis.

Chaired UC Regents' Committee to select Student Regent. Brought consensus in selection process among regents, faculty, and students.

Spoke at inauguration ceremony of UCD Chancellor Theodore Hullar on behalf of Alumni Association before 4,000 attendees.

Conceived, planned, and supervised installation of Alumni Contact Service in UC Davis Alumni Association. Job-referral and resource service is used by 2,000 alumni a year.

Awarded Jerry Fielder Outstanding Alumni Award from UC Davis. Award is presented to alumni for Alumni and University service.

Serve as trainer at FortyPlus, Oakland, developing individuals in personal assessment, presentation, job-search techniques, networking, personal development, and shared leadership.

Attended satellite-transmitted "Lessons In Leadership" two-day seminar sponsored by *Fortune* magazine. Participated in presentation of information from seminar to FortyPlus members.

Conceived and guided formation of Kee Kitayama Research Foundation (privately funded) to serve California Cut Flower Industry, and served as first Chairman. The foundation generated $290,000 for the endowment fund in its first three years.

Led merger of California Ornamental Research Foundation into Kee Kitayama Research Foundation, consolidating efforts and resources into a single effective foundation.

Engineered and built greenhouse water-recycling system, saving 90% of former consumption. Local industry savings reduced community rationing in 7-year drought from 40% to 25%.

Installed first co-generation unit in Northern California greenhouse, 1985. Saved 25% on heating energy costs. Installed first greenhouse heat curtains in Northern California, 1979, saving 25% in heating energy costs.

Developed computer control for greenhouse environment, 1986. Saved 20% of energy consumption, improved quality, increased production. System is now sold worldwide.

Organized and executed plan to sell roses that resulted in 6,000 repeat customers at three farmers' markets in three years. Elected to Board of Directors, Ferry Plaza Farmers' Market, San Francisco.

Chaired Roses Inc. (national trade organization) Trade and Public Relations Committee for six years. Developed and executed a program that increased per capita consumption of roses 65%.

Ronald A. Enomoto -3-

Serve on Ferry Plaza Farmers' Market Board of Directors. Currently planning for permanent market. Represent farmers' interests as well as business and community interests.

Served as Vice President and Board member of Shinoda Scholarship Foundation. Raised and granted $40,000 annually for college scholarships.

Served as Chair of Cabrillo Unified School District Advisory Committee. Advocated and initiated district survey of parents, which had never been done previously.

Led Cabrillo Unified School District Advisory Committee in effort that successfully prompted San Mateo County Board of Supervisors to fence local schools and provide funding for playground equipment.

Hosted 85 growers from throughout California and presented seminar and tour on biological/pesticide-free control of greenhouse pests. First commercial rose grower in California to eliminate pesticides in greenhouse-grown roses.

Owned and operated Enomoto Roses Inc. for 32 years. Responsible for planning, budget, personnel, production, marketing, Internet sales, and retail sales.

Have given numerous radio and television interviews representing the cut-flower industry; testified before legislative committees, and met with congressional representatives.

Designed and presented a successful property subdivision within the California Coastal Commission jurisdiction that enhanced agricultural use of the property.

Served as President of the Sequoia Chapter of the Japanese American Citizens League. Members resided in San Mateo County and Santa Clara County.

Served on UC Davis Foundation Board. Involved in friend raising and fund raising to promote the University of California Davis. Had fiduciary responsibility for fund-raising activities.

Target Your Employers

After you know what you want to do and how you are qualified to do the job, you need to decide where you want to work. Begin by choosing the industry in which you want employment. You can be an office manager in a software company or an oil refinery. You can perform customer service in a department store or a utility company. Ask yourself which environment most appeals to you. Think about the kinds of industry in which you have been employed in the past. Different industries call for different language and terminology on your resume. For example, a person who checks product quality can be known as a quality-control technician in a manufacturing environment, a quality-assurance evaluator in a service organization, or a production checker in a processing plant.

Next, make a list of specific companies—the "A" list, if you will—where you would most like to work. Before deciding whether a company should make your list, however, be sure to take the following points into consideration:

- **Geography:** Is the company within commuting distance or desirable enough that you would consider relocation?

- **Product/service:** Are you familiar with the company's product? Is it a product that you can support? (For example, if the company tests its products on animals and you are opposed to animal testing, you probably wouldn't be happy working there.) Do you have experience with the product or service?

- **Size:** Are you looking for a large corporation, a small or medium-sized business, a local or international company? Do you have more or fewer chances for advancement based on size? Are employment opportunities limited by the size of the company?

- **Pay scale:** Obviously, you need to know that the wages at the company are in line with your desires; however, you must also take into consideration such company perks as a car, profit sharing, travel allowances, and so on. Consider, too, the chances for advancement.

- **Reputation:** Company esteem and character are important. Employees who work for disreputable companies often suffer low self-esteem and high work-related stress. We tend to define ourselves by what we do. You want to feel good about the company you choose.

- **History:** Know about the company background before you decide to work there. How has the company progressed in the past? Has it been recently reorganized? Is it facing a merger? Are you catching it at the crest of its growth or on the downward slope of its decline?

- **Philosophy:** Does your target company prize individuality or teamwork? Are employees rewarded for suggestions or advised to stick to the status quo? Does the company encourage risk-taking or prefer that everyone plays it safe? These questions go to understanding the philosophy of the company—its basic orientation toward its purpose. Decide whether that philosophy is in sync with your own.

- **Mission:** Why is this company in business? What does it hope to accomplish? Do you share the same sense of purpose?

Targeting specific companies helps you to write your resume by giving you an audience. Imagine a person preparing a speech on space exploration, for example. The preparation for the speech would be quite different for an audience of fourth-grade science students than for an audience of NASA scientists.

After you decide how you are qualified and which companies you want to target, you are ready to build your resume. The following section focuses primarily on the *content* of traditional presentation resumes and the HTML resume. More detail on formatting an HTML resume is in chapter 5. Chapters 3 and 4 discuss scannable resumes.

Resume Formats

You generally have three basic resume formats to choose from in laying out your resume: *chronological, functional,* and a *combination* of the two. In educational circles, you will also find a fourth type, the *curriculum vitae.* The following sections take a look at these formats in detail.

The Chronological Format

The chronological format puts your work history in a sequence based on the period of time that you held each position. This resume format enables you to emphasize your past work history. In a chronological resume, you generally arrange your work experience by date, starting with the most recent and working backward. This resume format works best when you have had continuous work experience in the field in which you are applying.

To construct this type of resume, list the dates of employment in the left column of the resume, separated by several spaces from the body of the resume, or just above each job in the work history as shown in sample resume 2–2. Then you detail each job by listing the company, position title, and job description. Jobs are listed in reverse order, beginning with the most recent position and working backward to jobs held previously.

Employers prefer the chronological format because they can easily see where and when you attained the skills you say you possess. With this format, employers can also determine whether certain needed skills may be stale. For example, an employer who needs an employee for a word-processing job doesn't need a candidate whose most recent experience in the field was five years ago. Word-processing programs have changed dramatically over that period of time. An applicant that far removed from the labor market may have no knowledge of Windows 95, Windows 98, or Word 7.0, 6.0, or even 2.0, let alone Word 2000! How could the employer consider that person to be competitive? Of course, if the same candidate showed recent coursework in office information systems, this training would compensate somewhat for the lack of recent job experience.

Chronological resumes follow this basic pattern:

- **Contact heading:** Your name, address, phone number, and e-mail address.

- **Objective:** A brief statement of your career objective.

- **Summary:** A condensed list of your skills and qualifications in bulleted form. (A "bullet" is a short sentence fragment preceded by a symbol, such as a •.)

- **Work history:** Arranged by date, last date first.

- **Education:** College degrees and/or relevant coursework.

- **Optional information:** Memberships, awards, military service, certificates, and activities.

■ **Personal statement:** A short statement of your personal qualities that make you a fit candidate for the job.

A possible problem with chronological resumes is that you must be careful not to leave a gap of time between jobs. If such a gap exists, you may want to consider using the functional resume format instead.

Take a look at sample resume 2–2 for Andrew Simons. It contains several of the elements of a chronological resume.

Figure 2-2

A sample chronological resume.

Andrew Simons
1900 Idea Avenue
Denver, CO 00000
555-555-5555

PROFILE

Results-oriented executive with 15 years experience in Sales, Marketing, and Product Management, with expertise in many aspects of network-based services: Internet / Intranet strategic planning and implementation and interactive voice-response technology. **Troubleshooter** who can recommend state-of-the-art technology solutions and identify new market opportunities in the field of network communication and e-commerce.

- Generate practical solutions applied to complex business communication problems based on a solid reputation for creative, innovative project management.
- Positively impact the corporate bottom line by supporting companies through technical and strategic marketing changes.
- Three years of sales and marketing experience in the financial services industry addressing automated and interactive business applications: brokerage, investment banking, and international banking.

PROFESSIONAL EXPERIENCE

20XX–Present
Computer Systems Company, Northern City, CA
Senior Marketing Brand Manager for Internet Services.

- Standardize value-added bundling of Internet/Intranet service.
- Position company with industry analysts and customers through extranets and Internet solutions.
- Liaison with technical competency group to roll out training programs to sales teams.

19XX–19XX
Communications Company, Eastern City, NY
Product / Marketing Manager

- Create, develop, and manage company's Internet Directory.
- Market research and market sensing resulted in identification of 25 high-end accounts with potential to host 4,830 Web sites.
- Project manager leading teams to develop and deliver multi-Web bundled solution; responsible for growing 75% of forecast results in multiple sales channels.
- Targeted financial services community for Internet Directory links.

19XX–19XX
Another Communication Company in New York
Sales Account Executive

- Managed sales territory as Account Executive, driving sales of high-end accounts in financial services: brokerage, investment banking and mortgage companies, and retail and professional service companies.
- Earned branch recognition for 150% quota attainment.
- Noted for retention management of client relationships, with highest base retention exceeding quota objectives month after month.

EDUCATION

MBA—Western University. Graduate School of Business. Marketing, 19XX
MLS—Eastern University, Library and Information Science
BA—Eastern State College, Major in English and Education

AFFILIATIONS

A National Marketing Association
A City Chamber of Commerce

The Functional Format

The functional format enables you to focus on your skills and abilities without putting them into any time frame. This format is arranged by grouping your experiences and abilities under one or more broad skill categories, or functions. You place these categories in order of importance to your objective rather than by the dates when you attained them. For example, three basic functions to include on a business resume may be Management, Finance, and Accounting. You would use each of these functions as a heading and then detail all the skills, knowledge, and abilities you have for each major area. These broad functional paragraphs are followed by a brief employment history that shows places, titles, and dates—no job descriptions, and not necessarily in chronological order. The functional resume is often used by applicants who have been out of the labor market for a while and need a way to showcase certain skills they possess without showing how long ago they developed them.

Functional resumes present two problems. First, an employer cannot gauge how long it has been since you had experience with each skill. Remember that recent experience is an important factor to employers. Second, writing an objective is difficult when you set up a functional resume. If you highlighted three different functions, you may need three objectives—not a good idea for clarity. You may be able to construct an objective that includes all the skill functions; however, such an objective may be extremely long.

The first part of a functional resume is similar to a chronological resume and includes the contact heading followed by a summary. The pattern then changes a bit to accommodate the different purpose of the resume. Look at the following functional resume pattern:

- **Contact heading**

- **Summary**

- **Related experience:** The functional part of the resume that includes several broad skill categories followed by a paragraph of function-related terms and accomplishments.

- **Work history:** Dates, places, titles, and so on.

- **Education**

- **Optional information**

- **Personal statement**

Remember to target your resume to a specific audience so that you can choose the functions that are most pertinent to that job. Let's look at sample resume 2–3, an example of a functional resume.

Figure 2-3

A sample functional resume.

Stephanie Wood

0000 Some Street
Some City, Texas 00000
Phone: (555) 555-5555

OBJECTIVE: A challenging and creative senior position in the sales industry.

KEY QUALIFICATIONS

- Expert sales professional with over 12 years hands-on experience.
- Demonstrated ability to work effectively with clients.
- Excellent communication skills, both written and verbal.
- Life, Health and Variable Annuity Insurance License.
- Life Underwriting Training Council.
- Successful and proven ability to close sales.

EDUCATION

Some University; Some City, Some State
Bachelor of Business Administration (19XX)—Finance

BUSINESS EXPERIENCE

Sales and New Account Development

- Conceived, developed, produced, and executed advertising campaigns and promotional activities that resulted in a significant increase in new accounts.
- Conducted financial planning seminars; located perspective clients by making formal presentations to groups and individuals.
- Provided continual follow-up to potential clients to ensure future sales.
- Consistently successful in exceeding company quota.
- Ranked within the top 5 of a large national sales team.

Client Relations

- Utilized verbal communication and listening abilities to identify clients' needs and/or problems.
- Ultimately responsible for customer satisfaction.
- Established contacts in the local Chamber of Commerce.
- Developed loyal client base and increased volume through personal attention and consultative selling.
- Attained strong product knowledge and expanded client base while maintaining excellent client relations.

EMPLOYMENT HISTORY

Some Corporation (19XX–20XX)
Any Town, TX
Financial Consultant

Another Company (19XX–19XX)
Medium City, TX
Financial Consultant

A Large Corporation (19XX–19XX)
Big City, TX
Financial Consultant

PROFESSIONAL AFFILIATIONS

- Well-Known Charitable Organization
- Speaker's Bureau
- Fraternal Organization

The Combination Format

The combination resume combines elements of the chronological and functional resumes. Like the functional resume, the combination resume generally begins with a functional section, where the applicant details several areas in which he or she has expertise. In one type of combination resume, this section is followed by a brief chronological listing of places and dates where the applicant worked before. This chronology usually contains brief job descriptions as well, as on a chronological resume.

This format is attractive and fairly easy to read, but it has a problem. Although dates are provided, an employer may not be able to connect the skill in the functional section with the date that the applicant worked with that skill in the chronological section—unless the functions match the duties listed in the chronological listing.

For example, if the applicant listed Sales Management as a function, but every job listed in the chronological section was in the field of sales, the employer would not be able to tell whether the management skill was attained at the most recent job or at the job held seven years prior to that. Look at sample resume 2-4 for Sarah Marx as an example of this type of combination resume.

In another type of combination resume, the applicant lists the functions within the chronology for each job held. Examine sample resume 2-5 for Alfred Newman to see how this kind of combination resume looks. This type of combination resume is more useful to employers, because they can readily see where and when each function was attained.

Most employers prefer the straight chronological format because it is easy to read and easier still to match skills with the time period in which they were attained. Basically, the two resume formats that work best for electronic resumes are chronological and functional.

Figure 2-4

A sample
combination
resume.

Sarah Marx

XXXX Summer Street
Bossier, LA 00000
(555) 555-5555

Objective: Sales/Marketing position

Highlights of Qualifications

- Over 15 years professional experience with the public.
- Personable and persuasive in communicating creatively with thousands of customers from all cultures and economic levels.
- Proven skill in persevering to solve customers' problems.
- Self-motivated and confident in making independent decisions.
- Very well organized and able to meet deadlines.

Relevant Experience

Sales & Marketing

- Made direct presentations to retail store owners and buyers, marketing Christmas ornaments and gift items imported from the Philippines.
- Co-hosted sales seminars for potential real estate partnership investors.
- Oriented customers by answering questions regarding project details.
- Followed up by phone to verify their commitment to invest in the partnership.
- Canvassed by cold calling for contributions to a nonprofit organization.
- Consistently surpassed sales quotas in retail clothing and housewares departments.
- Persuaded 2,500 citizens to sign a petition in support of placing a community improvement initiative on the ballot.

Organization & Customer Service

- Resolved wide range of customer problems, applying diplomacy and assertiveness to delivery delays, fee and budget problems, property management decisions, airline emergencies and in-flight problems, and culture/communication barriers.
- Organized the logistics of speaking engagements and investment seminars: location - catering - seating - literature - speakers - travel.
- Maintained extensive financial records regarding individual and corporate clients.
- Successfully collected thousands of dollars in overdue or unbilled fees by thoroughly auditing billing records and persevering in telephone collection follow-ups.

Employment History

19XX–Present
Office Manager/Bookkeeper Accounting Firm, Orlando, FL
Managed financial records; general ledger; handled collections; billing and receivables.
19XX–XX
Office Manager/Bookkeeper. Investment Company. Orlando, FL
Receivables, payables, payroll; made travel arrangements; budget planning.
19XX–XX
Self-Employed, NonProfit organization, Author/Lecturer
Made presentations, organized seminars; canvassed contributors by phone; marketed services area-wide to customers.

Education

B.A., Communication Studies–Excellent University, Miami, Florida

Figure 2-5

A sample combination resume with dates attached to each function.

Alfred Newman
1111 Loon Lake Rd.
Chicago, IL 00000
(555) 555-5555

Career Objective: An entry-level position in the human service field.

EDUCATION
B.A. Sociology, Any University, Chicago, IL, 19XX

EXPERIENCE

19XX–20XX: Adolescent Psychiatric Clinic, Springfield, IL
Staff Assistant

Teaching
- Taught academic and social skills.
- Evaluated students' growth potential and abilities.
- Coordinated services with local school system.
- Planned daily objectives and assignments.

Counseling
- Counseled students, made recommendations/referrals to alternative services.
- Reviewed case histories.
- Monitored weekly support and supervision.

Group Facilitating
- Led adolescent support groups and organized activities.
- Coordinated weekly staff meetings.
- Reviewed students' physical, mental, and emotional daily performance.

19XX–19XX: Community Center, Springfield, IL
Assistant Manager

Management
- Supervised and trained new workers.
- Handled staff relations.
- Computerized and organized records.

Community Relations
- Planned and organized center activities.
- Facilitated meetings.
- Led outreach efforts.

Personal
A dedicated, sincere professional with excellent community-relations abilities and a management perspective that has provided a healthy respect for the company bottom line.

The Curriculum Vitae

One other type of resume you should be aware of is the curriculum vitae. A curriculum vitae, also known as a *CV* or a *vita,* is the preferred format for those in education or science. In other countries around the world, resumes are commonly referred to as CVs, although these are not different in significant ways from standard resumes.

In the United States, however, the CV is most often used for academic positions. CVs typically are very lengthy because they chronicle not only the work history and educational background of the candidate, but also all research projects, publications, academic awards, presentations, and teaching history. If the candidate has served internships and residencies, these are included. Any post-doctoral studies are represented. Affiliations in professional societies are listed as well as memberships on boards.

At the Harvard School of Public Health Web site, you will find instructions for preparing a CV. You can access its Web site at the following address:

http://www.hsph.harvard.edu

Then type **sample curriculum vitae** at its search engine and scroll down the search results until you see "cv sample" or "cv1994.html." A form and a sample CV for a medical professional are provided as examples of what to include.

It is not unusual for a CV to run to six, eight, or even more pages when printed. We have included a format for a CV so that you can see how it is laid out and what you need to include. A curriculum vitae follows this basic pattern:

- **Your Name and Title**

- **Office Address:** Include your department, office phone number, and e-mail address.

- **Education:** Follow the same pattern for listing your education as in a chronological resume.

- **Honors and/or Awards:** List by year, then award, in chronological order. Spell out the award—do not use acronyms.

- **Publications:** These should be listed under the following separate categories:

Papers	Works in Progress
Books	Journal Articles
Textbooks	Book Chapters
Theses	Monographs

- **Conference Presentations:** List by date, in chronological order. List the title of the seminar or conference and give a one-sentence summation of what was presented.

- **Work Experience**
- **Teaching Experience**
- **Internships and Residencies** (if applicable)
- **Post-Doctoral Training** (if applicable)
- **Professional Affiliations**
- **References:** Unlike other resume formats, CVs contain the reference contact information on the resume itself.

Resume Layout

One of the key differences between electronic and paper resumes is how they are arranged on the page. The unwritten rule of resume writing states that a paper resume should never be more than one or two pages long. Employers find it tiresome and inconvenient to shuffle through several pages of paper to get a profile of a candidate. However, on a computer screen, you are no longer held to the one-page rule. It is generally understood that a computer screen holds less information than a printed page. Thus, you have more freedom in editing your data. Employers simply scroll down your electronic resume until they are finished reading your information.

A word of caution, however: Just because you have a bit more latitude in using space, don't ramble on until the reader is forced to press the back arrow or go to the next resume in the database out of sheer annoyance. Be as concise as you can, while still including the most crucial information about your background and experience. The key is to choose only information that is germane to the position you seek and to use the most powerful and effective language to describe it.

White Space

One way in which electronic and paper resumes are similar is the white-space rule. This rule refers to how the resume appears on the page, what we call the "lie" of your resume. Generally, the more white space, the more readable the resume. Of course, with electronic resumes, the white space becomes blue screen (or green or black or yellow or...), but the idea is the same. Employers appreciate a resume that is easy to read. The more uncluttered space they see, the easier the information is to process. Use plenty of good spacing between headings and the body of the resume.

Bullets

One important factor that makes a resume readable is the use of bullets for arranging information. A bullet is a short sentence fragment rather than a full sentence. If you put all your information, including job descriptions, in paragraph form, employers have a difficult time finding the information that they need. Bullets make the job easy because employers can effortlessly and quickly scan through the most important items to find the information they seek. Consider the following example from an accountant's resume, written in paragraph form:

> Responsible for all payroll and tax records. Did purchase orders and posted to general ledger. Did all accounts payable, accounts receivable, and trial balance. Kept inventory and prepared purchase orders. Prepared daily deposits and reconciled bank statements. Used Great Plains and Peachtree accounting software and Microsoft Excel spreadsheet software.

Contrast the preceding paragraph example with the same information presented in a bulleted list:

- Tax preparation
- Payroll for over 50 employees
- Inventory control and preparation of purchase orders
- Accounts payable and receivable
- General ledger and trial balance
- Daily bank deposits and statement reconciliation
- Proficient with Great Plains, Peachtree, and Microsoft Excel

The information presented is the same, but the bulleted list presents the information in a format that is easier to read, with lots of screen space. Furthermore, the information has been rearranged to give priority to the more highly prized skills. Except for the bullet symbols, this job description is also more scanner friendly (see chapter 3 for more information about scannable resumes).

Resume Sections

For ease of reading, all resumes, electronic or otherwise, should be broken into separate parts that address each of your qualifications and tell who you are. These sections can vary, according to what you have to offer. Let's take a look at some options.

Contact Heading

All resumes should begin by telling the employer who you are and where you can be found. Accordingly, start building your electronic resume by putting your name, address, phone number, and e-mail address at the top of the page. Include your URL and office phone number as well. Employers don't want to work very hard to find you, so give them as many options as possible to make the job easy.

Tip

On an HTML resume, make your e-mail address a link so that a prospective employer can simply click on it to get to an e-mail screen that has your address in the "to:" line.

On scannable and e-mail resumes, you should left-align the contact information, because this format works best with scanners. With HTML resumes, you have several options as to how you arrange your heading. The classic style places the name, address, and phone number centered, letter-style, at the top of the page, as follows:

Name

Address

City, State, ZIP Code

Phone Number, E-Mail Address

Another variation is the left-justified heading. This heading is the preferred choice for a scannable resume. In this style, all the lines of the heading are aligned on the left side of the page, as follows:

Name

Address

City, State, ZIP Code

Phone Number, E-Mail Address

Another variation splits the address and phone information and puts them on opposite sides of the page, below the name, which is centered at the top:

Name

Address	Phone Number
City, State, ZIP Code	E-Mail Address

Yet another variation puts the name on one side and the balance of the information on the opposite side:

Name	Address
	City, State, ZIP Code
	Phone Number
	E-Mail Address

As you can see, you have many choices in arranging the contact information when you prepare an HTML resume.

Some resumes have a demarcation line that separates the header from the body of the resume. With an HTML resume, you have several style choices for your underline. You can also put a graphic as a break between your header and the body of the resume or as a decorative top border.

Sample resume 2-6 shows Kristofer M. Pierson's resume with a graphic of an airplane for a break. When viewed online, the airplane's propeller is animated, so it looks like it's spinning. The underscored elements are hyperlinks for the Web.

Figure 2-6

The HTML resume for Kristofer Pierson, showing an animated graphic.

KRISTOFER M. PIERSON

**XXXX Swell Avenue
Bloomington, Minnesota 55437
email: XXXX@XXX.com**

CAREER OBJECTIVE To gain employment in a flight operations position with a company possessing a dynamic concern for the aviation industry.

EDUCATION

- Rocky Mountain College, Billings, Montana
  B.S. in Airway Science, Aircraft Systems Management, 1997
  Minor in Music

- Thomas Jefferson Senior High School, Bloomington, Minnesota
  Graduated, June 1993

PILOT QUALIFICATIONS

- Commercial Pilot/Certified Flight Instructor - Instrument and Multi-Engine

- Multi-Engine Land, Single-Engine Land, and Instrument Ratings

- 600+ hrs. Total Time, 45 hrs. Multi, 220+ hrs. Dual Given

- First Class FAA Medical

WORK EXPERIENCE June 1998–present

**Flight Operations Manager
Academy Flight Operations, Inc.
Crystal, Minnesota**
In this position, I administrate the flight training operations center for the Academy of Aviation, where I also flight instruct and serve as academic faculty (listed separately below). Duties include management of our aircraft fleet.

September 1997–present

Academic Faculty and Flight Instructor

Academy of Aviation
Academy Education Center, Inc.
My position includes full-time flight instruction, as well as ground school for pilot certification and rating courses, and upper-level academic aviation courses at this private, two-year institution. I am also actively involved in curriculum management and development. Vitae on request.

August 1997–December 1997

Lead Dispatcher
Thunderbird Aviation Inc.
Eden Prairie, Minnesota
Duties entailed the smooth operation and coordination of all flights, schedules, office management, and customer services at this full-service FBO.

January 1996–June 1997

Student Assistant, Office of the Registrar
Rocky Mountain College
Billings, Montana
Duties included organizing and handling special research projects and reports as assigned by the College Registrar. Performed general office duties and information management, focusing on student academic data.

May 1996–August 1996 and
May 1995–August 1995

Professional Line Service Technician
Elliott Aviation, Inc., Flying Cloud Airport
Eden Prairie, Minnesota
Performed essential flight line and customer service duties at an executive-class FBO. Aircraft parking, fueling, servicing, cleaning, towing, fuel farm management, and aircraft storing comprised main duties. Also assisted customers with shuttle service to local hotels, other airports, and meeting sites.

May 1994–August 1994

Ground Ops Personnel, UPS/Corporate Air
Billings Logan International Airport
Billings, Montana
Worked on the UPS Billings Gateway Operation. Handled air cargo and ground service equipment in close proximity to several aircraft.

May 1994–May 1995

Resident Assistant
Rocky Mountain College
Responsible as a role model, counselor, teacher, and administrator

(continues)

(continued)

for 150 students in my residence hall. Assisted in coordinating the implementation and use of automated campus security systems.

INTERNSHIPS/ FIELD PRACTICUM

1994 Internship: Big Sky International Airshow
I served on the flight operations committee of this large airshow, helping to coordinate show acts, flights, and operating as a roving liaison between officials and participants.

1995 Field Practicum: NIFA Region I SAFECON Flight Competition Director
In this practicum, I acted as the Director of this annual intercollegiate flight competition. A large part of my role was to coordinate flight operations with airport administrators and other operators.

AVIATION-RELATED ACTIVITIES AND ORGANIZATIONS

Academy of Aviation Precision Flying Team
National Intercollegiate Flying Association (1998–present)
Coach and Advisor

Rocky Mountain College Precision Flying Team,
National Intercollegiate Flying Association (1994–present)
Assistant Coach, 1997
NIFA Council Student Representative, 1996–97
Team Captain, 1996
National Competition Participant, 1995, 1996

Rocky Mountain College Aviation Club (1993–1997)
Vice President, 1996

Alpha Eta Rho Aviation Fraternity, Rho Alpha Chapter (1996–present)
Charter Member and Vice President, 1996 to 1997

Active member of AOPA, NIFA, and NAFI.

SPECIAL AWARDS

- **Presidents Cup** Rocky Mountain College 1997

- **Outstanding Aviation Senior** Rocky Mountain College 1997

- **Eagle Scout Award** Boy Scouts of America 1993

PERSONAL

Marriage Status: Single
Health: Excellent, First Class FAA Medical
Hobbies: Fishing, Hiking, History

References, curriculum vitae, and a complete listing of collegiate activities and awards are available on request.

Return to Kris Pierson's Homepage

Objective

Most classic resumes contain an objective. The objective—also known as a career goal, career focus, or target occupation—lets the employers know why you are contacting them. The objective also provides you with a blueprint to follow in constructing your resume. After you state an objective, everything following it should support it. Thus, if you are writing a resume with the stated objective of being an outside sales representative, including your experience as a janitor will not serve that particular resume. All the information that follows your objective in the resume should confirm the stated objective and reinforce your fitness for the job in question.

Objectives are a statement, not just a word or phrase. Many objectives contain a mini-plan for moving forward with the company. For example, some objectives make mention of a desire for growth opportunity within the company, as in the following example:

> A position in food service, with a career path leading to food-service management.

Some objectives discuss plans for continuing education, as in this example:

> Staff teaching position, where I can continue my doctoral studies in English literature.

Some objectives are merely a straightforward declaration of the job sought, as in the following examples:

> A position as a CAD drafter.

> Sales/Marketing Director in the Retail Trade Industry.

Other objectives are very specific, as follows:

> Staff Accountant/Audit Division, Public Accounting Firm.

In any case, your objective should be broad enough that you merit consideration for related jobs, but specific enough to show the employer that you have a focused goal. An objective that is too specific is limiting. Lastly, your objective should be only one statement long.

Summary

A summary is the hook that entices an employer to read the rest of your resume. The summary—also known as qualifications, profile, or overview—is a brief snapshot of your qualifications. The best summaries contain the most attractive highlights of your career and skills, in order of importance. You should also include some accomplishments, such as the percentage that sales increased after you became sales manager.

Note

The summary discussed in this section should not be confused with keyword summaries. Keyword summaries are used in scannable resumes, which are discussed in chapter 4.

In the interest of brevity and readability, summaries are best written in bulleted form. In the following summary for an advertising executive, bullets are used to briefly spotlight key skills. This summary begins by stating the number of years of experience attained in the desired position, and goes on to provide information about what makes the applicant a professional in the targeted field:

- More than ten years in advertising
- Award-winning television and print campaigns
- Creative market and needs analysis
- Focus groups and customer surveys
- Sales-force training

Remember that the summary paragraph is a brief commercial. It should highlight your best qualifications and present them in a way that raises the employer's interest. In the summary for the advertising executive, for example, the *award-winning* qualifier on the resume invites an employer to read on and discover which award was won and for what purpose. The idea is to get the employer to click on that all-important down-arrow and read on.

As with other areas on your resume, you should use bullets to present the information in your summary for ease of reading. Let's look at another summary that successfully uses bullets:

- Over 15 years in professional sales management
- Designed and implemented competitive marketing strategies
- Boosted sales 102 percent
- Recruited and trained productive sales team
- Generated $1.5 million in new accounts

Again, the use of impressive figures is an incentive for an employer to read on. Putting the proof of the applicant up front ensures a closer look.

Education

Following the summary, you will lead with either your education or experience, depending both on the position desired and your individual qualifications. For example, for a teaching position, where your educational background is of paramount importance, you should obviously start your resume with your education. Likewise, for positions that require an advanced degree in the field of science, you should put your educational background first. If the job in question requires certain vocational certificates, list them first. For recent college graduates, the advice is the same: Put your newly acquired degree and relevant coursework at the top of your resume.

However, if the most valuable asset you offer the employer is your work history, by all means, lead with that. And, of course, if you do not have a college degree, you should begin with your work experience. Let's take a look at how to list your education.

Vocational Certificate

When listing vocational education, you should mention a few specifics contained within the certificate program. Often, the certificate itself is offered as proof of skills. If you have this kind of certificate, you should provide details of the relevant coursework as much as possible. If you distinguished yourself academically, say so. List the name of the school and the city and state where it is located. Then give the name of the certificate program. If you received the certificate recently, add the year that you completed it. The idea behind listing a date is to show the employer that your skills are fresh. Fresh skills are important in vocational education, where training is tied to current labor-market needs. The following examples show different ways of setting up your vocational education information:

ITT Technical Institute, Los Angeles, CA

Medical Office Assistant Certificate, 1996

- 3.8 GPA
- Front and Back Office
- Medical Terminology

Summit Career College, Colton, CA

Business Office Operations, 1997

Class Valedictorian

- Excel
- Basic Accounting and Bookkeeping
- Bookkeeping
- Keyboarding and Computer Operations
- Word Processing
- Electronic Spreadsheets
- Office Machines
- Business Communications

Undergraduate Degree

Regardless of occupation, employers value a college education, whether or not you completed your degree program. It is important, then, to list your education on your resume. Put your information in order, beginning with the name and location of the college or university. When you have attended a state school, and the name of the state is part of the name of the school, as in the University of Mississippi, you should list the city and state where the school is located:

> University of Mississippi, Oxford, MS

It is also acceptable with state universities to list the city only, as in the following examples:

> University of California, Los Angeles

> California State University, Fullerton

Where the name of the college may not be readily recognizable, such as in Central University, or where the name does not contain the location, such as in Purdue University, you should definitely list both the city and state:

> Central University, Central, AL

> Purdue University, West Lafayette, IN

Following the name of the college, you should list the degree you attained. The preferable way to list the degree is to spell out the degree, such as Bachelor of Arts. Do not write *Bachelor's of Arts* or *Bachelor's degree*.

If you choose to use the acronym, do not use periods, as you can see in the following examples:

> BS Degree, Accounting

> AA, Liberal Arts

The exception to this rule is Ph.D., where you do place a period after the *h*.

Next comes the field of study. Spell out these words, such as Liberal Arts, not L.A.; Physical Education, not P.E. or Phys. Ed.; Political Science, not Pol Sci. If you had a particular area of emphasis within your major, list the area. If you took a minor, be sure to indicate the field of study, with the *minor* designation, as in the following example:

> Bachelor of Science, Economics
> Minor: International Business

The following are examples of how you can list your undergraduate degree:

University of Minnesota, Duluth
Bachelor of Arts, Communication
Emphasis: Public Relations
Highest Honors

Bronx Community College, New York, NY
Associate of Arts, Accounting, 1997

Advanced Degree

Advanced degrees appear first in the Education section of your resume. Then you list your other degrees, if applicable, in descending order: Master of Arts, Bachelor of Arts, Associate of Arts.

In general, the graduate degree is listed without further detail, except for honors designations, as in the following example:

Framingham State College, Framingham, MA
Master of Arts, Counseling
cum laude

> **Note**
>
> The designation *cum laude* refers to the degree of educational excellence attained by the candidate. *Magna cum laude* refers to high honors; *summa cum laude* refers to highest honors (a 4.0 G.P.A., usually). These honors are written in lowercase. Applicants typically use only the *cum laude* designation, widely understood to mean that honors were bestowed.

Remember that you do not have to include the year of graduation on your resume. Including the year enables an employer to label your age. Of course, the year of graduation is no longer an accurate way of gauging the age of an applicant because people attend college at many different ages. However, if your degree is recent and constitutes the basis of your qualifications and the reason you are seeking work in your field, it is acceptable, and even wise, to put the year of your diploma on the resume.

Significant Coursework

In the Education area of your resume, you may want to list courses that detail your educational background. This approach is typically used by a recent college graduate who is attempting to demonstrate pertinent knowledge of the desired field, although seasoned career professionals also use the approach. Consider the following Education entry on a resume for a photographer:

Brooks Institute of Photography, Santa Barbara, CA
Bachelor of Fine Arts, Photography, 1997
Relevant coursework:

- Layout and Design
- Lighting Techniques
- Graphic Design
- Digital Images
- Portraiture
- Darkroom Techniques
- Large Format
- Adobe PhotoShop

Look at the following example for a business administration graduate:

University of California, Riverside
Bachelor of Science, Business Administration
Departmental Honors
Significant coursework:

- Business Law
- European Economics
- Human Resource Administration
- Organizational Development

Some College

To list college experiences that did not result in a degree, you can simply put the name and location of the school and the major course of study with no further explanation, as in the next two examples:

University of North Carolina, Charlotte
Sociology and Urban Studies

Pasadena City College, Pasadena, CA
Classes in Drug and Alcohol Counseling

Or you can detail any relevant coursework that you completed, although you did not finish your degree program, as in the following example:

Hanover College, Hanover, IN
BA Degree Program, Business Administration
Courses in:

- Business Law
- Economics
- Accounting
- Finance

You can also project the graduation date if the work is currently in progress with completion likely in the near future, as follows:

San Diego State University
Bachelor of Science, Biology
Projected Graduation: June 2002

If you have college coursework to list on your resume, you do not have to list high school classes. In fact, if you have any work-related classes, whether college-level or not, it is preferable to list them, rather than your high school history. For high school or undergraduate college students, of course, listing the high school data is obligatory. But in general, adults do not list their high school background in the education block unless the employer has specified a high school diploma as a prerequisite for the job.

Specialized Training

If you have had certain work-related courses outside of college, vocational school, or high school, you should list them on your resume. These courses can include in-house training programs set up by former employers or extension courses that you took on your own to bolster your expertise on the job. You can list these courses under a subheading, such as Continuing Education Studies, within the Education block; or you can give them a separate heading altogether, such as Specialized Training.

Work History

The work history is really the heart of the resume. What you choose to include here will determine whether the employer decides to contact you. Remember that the work history you include must be relevant to the objective of the resume. Therefore, remove all data that does not support your stated objective, or realign duties from other jobs so that they reflect relevant experience. Keep in mind that you should include accomplishments here, too. These accomplishments make the resume interesting to read and keep you from simply reciting job duties. The accomplishments also demonstrate your performance in relation to other candidates.

You can use several different headings to name this section, depending on what kind of information you want to impart to the employer. For example, Work History or Experience are descriptive but not too creative. Relevant Experience and Significant Experience, on the other hand, let the reader know that you will be concentrating only on the work history that is significant to the stated job objective. Career Highlights, Career History, and Professional Background are other options.

Bear in mind that a resume should not go back more than 10 years. Job skills more than 10 years old are considered stale by most employers. For high-tech fields, that number is shortened considerably. If, however, you have had sustained employment at the same company for more than 10 years, your resume will necessarily break the

10-year rule. Concentrate on showing the skills and experiences you have had most recently with that company.

To write your work history in a chronological format, begin by putting the dates you were employed at the company (starting with your most recent job) in the left margin of the resume. Use the month and year, writing out the month and using all four digits of the year: August 1991–August 1997. These dates must fit in a rather small column, so you will need to stack them as in the following example:

August 1991–
August 1997

Then, after leaving a fair amount of spacing between the dates and the body of the resume, type the name of the company and the city and state where it was located, all on the same line. Following this information, type your position title.

You may want to put your position title first, followed by the company name and location. After you pick a style, however, make sure that you keep the order consistent throughout the resume. Look at the following examples to see how this information is set up.

SIGNIFICANT EXPERIENCE

June 1992– Atlas Home Sales, Boulder, CO
June 1997 **General Sales Manager**

or

RELEVANT EXPERIENCE

June 1992– **General Sales Manager**
June 1997 Atlas Home Sales, Boulder, CO

If you are writing an HTML resume, you may want to make your job title bold or put it in a different font. Some applicants type the company name in all caps, with the job title in bold. Or they put the company name in italics. All of these options are fine as long as you don't go crazy with different fonts, which junk up a resume. And as you will see in chapter 3, you don't use special font enhancements at all on a scannable resume.

Job Duties and Achievements

After you have indicated where and when you worked and what you did for the company, it's time to list your most significant job duties and achievements.

To write a job description for a resume, start by making notes for each job you held. Make a list of all the duties you handled during the course of a day. Think about the job you are applying for and decide which of your former duties best fit the new job. List the duties from the old job in order of importance to the new job.

Next, list any special achievements for which you were responsible. Consider their worth in painting you as a desirable candidate. Include only those achievements that have some relevance to the job and your fitness for it.

Then write a short summary of how your job fit the organization and helped meet its goals. This step is important in helping you to see yourself as part of the big picture in any company. When you understand your place, you can then communicate it to an employer.

Finally, take all the information that a prospective employer should know and that supports the objective at the top of your resume, and boil it down into a few short sentences that you put in bullet form. When you add each job description to your resume, be sure that the duties are in order of importance.

Building a Sample Job Description

Now, let's build a job description based on the following information about Jessica:

> Jessica is the Human Resource Manager for a medium-sized hotel, which is part of a large, international chain. She handles recruitment for all positions, from the room cleaners to the junior manager. She conducts new-hire orientation and supervises the training programs. She plans the advertising budget for recruitment and hotel events. She administers the employee benefits packages and keeps personnel records for over 100 employees. She directly supervises 8 managers and indirectly oversees 15 department supervisors. Whenever necessary, Jessica travels to other hotels and conducts training for new HR managers. She serves on the task force that plans the redesign of new facilities and the remodeling of existing ones. She was cited as HR Manager of the Year, Western Division, for her innovative ideas in conflict resolution.

> Jessica is applying for a position as regional HR manager for a large hotel chain. Her main responsibilities will be overseeing the HR operations of several hotels in her division. She will train management staff and hire new HR managers at various sites. She will conduct quality-assurance checks to make sure that all branches are conducting HR operations according to hotel policy. Jessica's bulleted job description should look like the following example:

> - Trained and supervised new Human Resource managers at multiple sites.
>
> - Planned recruitment for several hotels within Western Division.
>
> - Designed training plan for desk managers, utilized throughout chain.

- Supervised 8 managers and 15 division supervisors.

- Hired staff at all levels.

- Developed advertising and marketing strategies for events and recruitment.

- Designed and conducted Conflict-Resolution training program, adopted throughout the chain.

- Named Human Resource Manager of the Year, Western Division, for Conflict-Resolution program.

Notice that the job description starts with the most important duty of the new position: overseeing the HR staff at other hotels. She makes reference at different times to her experience with other sites. She also mentions the innovations she made that were adopted throughout the chain, a response to the part of the job that requires assurance of uniform operations. Hiring and training are prominently featured. Jessica has also highlighted her achievements—such as employee of the year and developer of innovative programs that were adopted company wide—not merely reciting her job duties.

Caution

Resume examples in this chapter include bullets, formatted text, underlining, and graphics. These little enhancers will render your resume unreadable to some resume scanners. To facilitate scanning, a resume must be prepared using 10- or 12-point Times New Roman, Courier, or Helvetica typefaces. You should avoid using any special fonts or formatting, such as bold text, underlines, italics, and bullets. Graphics are incomprehensible to a scanner. Think of the scannable resume as basic "vanilla." In the next chapter, you will explore scannable resumes and learn how to construct one.

CHAPTER 3

How Resume Scanning Works

Whether you are searching for work by going online or by perusing newspaper ads, you will increasingly find employers who ask you to send them a *scannable* resume. You will still need a printed, or presentation resume for companies that don't request a scannable resume, but you have to be aware of the problems that lie in wait for the paper resume that will be scanned. Many of the enhancements that make your paper resume attractive—such as special fonts, graphics, and even fancy paper—will not work with resume scanners. You will need to make some changes in your resume to make it scannable. In this chapter, you'll learn how resume scanners work and how you can write a resume that will make it past the scan and all the way to a job.

The process of electronic recruiting through the use of scanners and other software is known as *automated staffing*. The services that provide automated staffing assistance to businesses are generally referred to as *applicant-tracking* or *resume-tracking services*.

Some automated companies refer to the service they provide in other ways. Resumix®, for example calls the service "human asset management." Resumix is a leader in automated staffing. We'll look more closely at Resumix in this chapter, to give you an idea of how an applicant-tracking service works.

Converting Your Paper Resume to a Computer File

When you write a scannable resume, you are actually writing initially for a computer rather than a person. You are making your resume readable to a scanner, so that it can be converted back into computer text. Then, employers use applicant-tracking software to search these online resumes for the qualifications and skills they are looking for.

Applicant-tracking programs are made up of two parts: the scanning process (done with optical character recognition software) and the skills-extraction process. An explanation of how these parts work will help you to understand what is needed to create a scanner-friendly resume.

Scanners

In the simplest terms, a scanner is the device that takes a "picture" of your resume so that it can be put into a computer. A scanner captures an image of your resume by using a moving beam of light. The scanner then digitizes the image so that it can be stored on a computer. Essentially, the scanner puts what you have written on paper into a form that is usable by a computer.

If you enlarge a photograph, page of text, or other image many times, you discover that it is made of thousands of tiny dots. These dots are known as *pixels.* Pixels are actually individual elements of varying shades that, taken altogether, make up a picture. As your resume passes through the scanner, light is bounced from the paper original to photosensitive cells within the scanner. These cells read the image by examining and analyzing each pixel. The cells then translate the light waves into impulses. These impulses are sent to the computer, where software takes the data and converts it to computer-friendly language. So what you end up with is an electronic representation of your resume.

OCR: Optical Character Recognition

After the image is scanned, the next step is for the image to be read by OCR—optical character recognition—software, which often comes with the scanner. OCR takes the data you have written—the printed text in the form of words—and converts it into usable computer language known as *ASCII* (American Standard Code for Information Interchange). Optical character recognition accomplishes this task by taking patterns of dots—again, the pixels—created by your scanner and organizing the dots of the scanned image into characters. This process is known as *segmentation.* Computers can then read those converted characters.

To convert the image, however, the OCR program must first read the document that has been scanned. OCR utilizes a feature known as artificial intelligence to read printed text, such as your resume. It can be part of both the OCR software and the resume-tracking software. Artificial intelligence enables the computer to "think" for itself. It can make assumptions based on information that is available to it. Essentially, it can "reason." This capability to reason allows for some interpretation of what you have written.

In effect, OCR is the process of turning an image, such as a scanned paper document, into computer-editable text so that the recipient does not have to retype the text manually in order to get it into electronic form. After your resume is in ASCII format, it becomes editable text that can be manipulated and revised in a word-processing program, and then plugged into a database.

What can confuse the OCR process is the condition of the document itself. When you prepare a traditional paper resume, you have lots of choices about fonts, color, graphics, formatting, and other features to make the resume look attractive. When you prepare a scannable resume, however, you must think in simplified terms. OCR responds best to a plain-vanilla resume. As we discussed in chapter 2, you need to use simple fonts and avoid underlining and formatting. Using these font-enhancing features can cause characters to become degraded; in other words, they become fuzzy, misshapen, or otherwise difficult to read. When underlining is used, for example, characters can appear to touch, or link together. The OCR software can have difficulties figuring out where one character stops and another starts. Since OCR looks at the shape of the letters themselves to figure out what they are, fancy-shaped fonts, such as are available on word-processing programs, can cause real problems with recognition. Basically, if the shapes of the letters are too fancy, the OCR software can get confused.

There are any number of things that can make characters difficult for OCRs to read. Besides boldfacing, italicizing, and other font enhancements, factors such as poor printer quality and photocopying, making the font too small, or making the space between characters too tight, can all make the process difficult.

To further enhance the readability of your resume, your copy must be very clean, with no smudges, specks, streaks, or lines—elements often caused by poor-quality photocopies or faxed images. If you do fax a resume, set the fax machine to the "fine" setting to ensure that your resume will be scannable when it arrives. If you make a photocopy, clean the platen glass and inspect your copy for any extra marks or streaks. If it is a poor-quality copy, it will not scan properly.

Scannable Resume Tips

To prepare a resume that is most likely to be successfully read by OCR, consider these suggestions:

- Keep layout simple.
- Keep fonts simple.
- Keep your copy clean.
- Use good-quality paper.
- Send originals wherever possible.
- Use a high-quality photocopier for reproductions.

Improved Technology

Over the last few years, new OCR technology has mitigated to a great degree the problem of unusual fonts or degraded text. First came the use of trainable fonts, where letters from various scanned images could be added by hand to the existing images in the OCR program, a laborious, time-consuming task. This led eventually to the concept of omnifont OCRs. Omnifont technologies enable OCR packages to recognize many of the different font styles and sizes available in your word processor. These enhancements also improve the OCR's capability of distinguishing and identifying, with a fairly high degree of certainty, letters and characters that have been boldfaced, underlined, or degraded. The programs are better able to determine where one letter ends and another begins.

So how does this vastly improved OCR technology impact job seekers who want to write a resume that will be successfully scanned? Glenn Whitten, whose company, Recruiters Online, processes thousands of electronic resumes through the use of scanners and OCR, has this to say:

> Several OCR packages advertise a 98 percent or better recognition accuracy rate. As with the federal mileage estimates for your car, the rate is seldom, if ever, so good. In the best case (let's suppose 95 percent accuracy), there will be 5 errors out of every 100 characters. If we assume an average word length of 5 characters, this means that the program will misread your resume at a rate of one word out of every 20. I don't know about you, but that was enough to flunk me in any English class I ever took. Even worse, though, is the fact that the mistakes will not be randomly distributed. If the program misreads the characters *mi* as *ml* once, it is likely to do so throughout the document. If this happens to any of your keywords, your resume will not be found in searches for those words.
>
> The objective is to get your resume into the Human Resources system of the target company. Anything that interferes with this goal—whether typos, OCR-induced inaccuracies, layout problems, and so on—is counterproductive. The *best* system cannot be expected to produce good results with poor-quality resumes. Garbage in; garbage out.

Skills Extraction

Now, let's follow a resume through the process. First, you send your resume to company X via mail, e-mail, or fax. Your resume is then put through a scanner that uses OCR software to make a duplicate image of your resume and turn it into a computer file.

After the resume is in the applicant-tracking system, a technician may edit it to make sure that the computer version matches the paper version you originally sent to the company. Unfortunately, many changes can occur in the resume. Remember that many things can impact the way the OCR reads what you have written. Such processes as faxing and photocopying, as well as the use of font-enhancing features like boldfacing, underlining, and italicizing, can degrade your text and impede the OCR process.

After a technician has cleaned up your resume, it is put in a database program for future retrieval. The employer can search this database for applicants with qualifications that match the job openings they have.

The technology used by resume-management systems to pull information from your resume is known as the *extraction engine*. The nucleus of the extraction engine is its knowledge base, the collection of career-related vocabulary that enables the engine to recognize similar terms in your resume. This collection is known as the *rules*. Rules specify and define the many factors that make up an applicant's career profile. These factors include education, work history, skills, job titles, and even personal traits. The knowledge base of an extraction engine comes from recruiters, technicians at automated staffing services, and the job seekers themselves. When a recruiter interviews a client who describes a new skill or term not yet included in the knowledge base, it is added.

The knowledge base is comprised of millions of job-related terms and phrases, as well as a variety of contexts in which these factors occur. Thus, comparisons can be made between your skills as you have defined them and how the employer has specified those same skills. Applicant tracking software is programmed with hundreds of thousands of job-related terms so that there is the potential for recognition of synonyms.

Resumix is a leading automated staffing company (see the following section). Its knowledge base, for example, contains 25,000 skills that combine into more than 10 million matching combinations of search terms!

Ideally, the core grammar of an extraction engine should be a continually evolving collection. Employers are often able to customize the knowledge base to suit their needs by including in it their own in-house jargon, for example. Knowledge bases also need to keep pace with developing technology.

To begin the extraction process, your resume is first sectioned by the program into such areas as Education, Work History, Skills, and so on. Then each of these sections is perused and the relevant data extracted. The extraction process is very thorough. It searches through every section and gleans all information that can be meaningfully categorized. The resulting data is then put into broad vocational categories, such as Finance, Sales, Marketing, Engineering, and so on. When your resume is perused by the software in an applicant search, these categories provide the first level of matching the employer's criteria.

Following the initial categorization, your resume is next put through a skill extraction. Here the extraction engine seeks out specific skills, not just the broad vocational classification. So under the vocational category of Human Resources, for example, the organization may require the specific skills of Interviewing, Benefits Administration, EEOC, and Grievance Procedures. The knowledge base is key in making these selections. Remember that most extraction engines contain millions of terms within their knowledge bases.

An interesting aspect of the extraction process is that some systems can recognize not only words, but also the context in which the words occur. This context can derive either from the placement of the term within the structure of the resume or from the sentence itself.

Resumix offers the following explanation:

> The resume structure context allows Resumix to differentiate among applicants with a first name of Ada; a person living in Ada, Michigan; and a person with the skill of ADA. The sentence context allows

Resumix to further differentiate between a dentist with membership in ADA (American Dental Association), a programmer having experience with the language ADA, or a Human Resources professional who works with ADA (the Americans with Disabilities Act).

Besides context, extraction systems are often capable of interpreting concepts, not just words or phrases. In concept-based searching, the extraction engine actually makes assumptions by assigning skills based on related terms it encounters. Consider these examples. If a resume stated "researched cases for precedent," the system would assign the skill of Paralegal. A resume listing "graded papers and tests for professor" as a responsibility would yield a skill assignment of Teacher Assistance. And the system would infer the skill of Programming from the notation "wrote in BASIC."

Experienced human resources and recruiting professionals routinely make these conceptual links. It is extraordinary to think that sophisticated extraction engines possess this same capacity. However, this remarkable capability of reasoning with concepts increases your chances for a match.

In addition, extraction engines have the capability to recognize key concepts and terms even when they are misspelled. The engines also look for synonyms and similarities. Consider the following: University of California at Berkeley, UC Berkeley, UCB, Berkeley, and even Cal are all ways of referring to the same school. A sophisticated system recognizes all of them! All these diverse ways of retrieving data work in your favor and increase your chance of getting a hit on your resume.

Some resume-processing systems extract a summary from the scanned resume. These summaries contain the key information about the applicant. They list your name, address, phone number, and other contact information; the pertinent data from your work history, such as companies, job titles, and dates; your educational background, including names of schools and degrees or certificates held; and all job-related skills, including the relevant keywords and phrases that describe your abilities. This summary is also stored in the company's database for searching.

To summarize: Your resume goes through a scanner. It is then looked at by OCR software and converted to usable computer language. It is read by artificial intelligence, from which a summary is extracted. It is cleaned up by a technician and is stored in the applicant-tracking system, where it is ready to be retrieved by employers. Sound simple? Okay, let's look at the automated staffing company, Resumix.

An Example Applicant-Tracking System: Resumix

One of the best-known automated-staffing (resume-tracking) companies—or, as it refers to itself, Human Skills Management Systems—is Resumix, headquartered in Sunnyvale, California (see figure 3-1).

Figure 3-1

The Resumix home page.

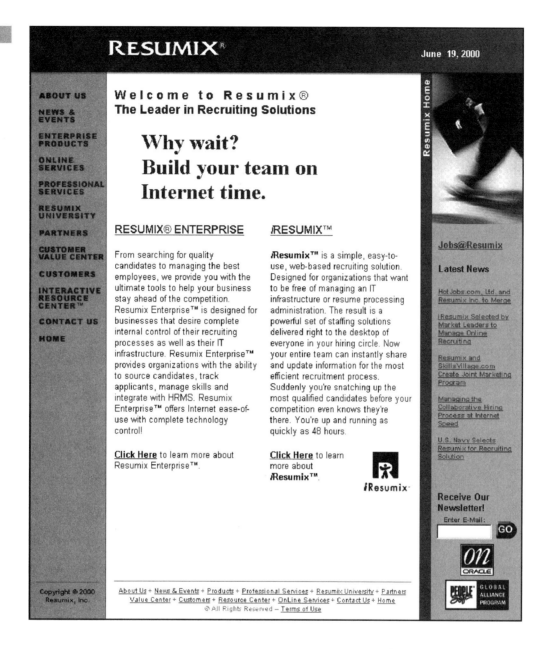

Resumix has been around since 1988, when developers of artificial intelligence software from ESL/TRW Labs decided that the emerging technology could be used to manage the flood of resumes the company received every year. The developers initially marketed their product to two Bay Area companies, and their businesses grew from their original base of high-tech concerns to include a variety of other industries. Today, Resumix has over 400 customer installations and counts many clients among Fortune 1,000 corporations, as well as universities, health-care organizations, and government entities.

Resumix is *not* a resume-posting service, however. You cannot send your resume directly to Resumix, unless you are applying for a job with the company itself.

Instead, Resumix provides an applicant-tracking system to companies that need help managing their staffing process. Simply put, Resumix takes over the cumbersome task of managing the crush of resumes that inundate most companies. It enables a company to identify top candidates—both internal and external—for positions within the company. It is a software company that provides advanced automated staffing and skills management to organizations. The Resumix service enables companies to source and identify the most qualified people to fill their open positions.

Once a company purchases and installs the Resumix system, it can be used for both internal and external hiring needs. It can also monitor college-recruiting efforts, handle both full-time and part-time staffing, and perform other human resource functions.

In addition, the company's Resumix Internet Recruiter™ integrates Resumix with the Internet. Resumix Internet Recruiter is available to employers through a no-cost download and enables them to access the resumes at online job boards, such as JobOptions™ and Monster.com.

Once candidates are entered into a company's Resumix system, they can be considered for any open position for which they are qualified. Moreover, a candidate's resumes and progress through the hiring process can be tracked and documented directly in the Resumix system.

> Once an applicant is hired, the status of her resume becomes unavailable. Should a candidate be interested in other positions/opportunities with the same company in the future, her resume can be made available again for consideration for other opportunities. Resumes are retained in the Resumix database for a minimum of six months to a maximum of two or more years. Applicants can update their resumes and resubmit them to reflect new or additional skills. Of course, how long the resume is retained in general by the company varies by company policy and state regulations.

Scannable Resume Hints from Resumix

Resumix suggests the following tips for creating a resume that will get the maximum number of hits:

- Use enough keywords to define your skills, experience, education, professional affiliations, and so on.

- Describe your experience with concrete words, rather than vague descriptions. For example, it's better to use "managed a team of software engineers" than to use "responsible for managing and training."

- Be concise and truthful.

- Use more than one page if necessary. Additional pages permit you to provide more information than you would for a human reader.

- Use jargon and acronyms specific to your industry (spell out the acronyms for a human reader).

- Increase your list of keywords by including specifics. For example, list the names of software that you use, such as Microsoft Word and Lotus 1-2-3.

- Use common headings, such as Objective, Experience, Employment, Work History, Positions Held, Appointments, Skills, Summary, Summary of Qualifications, Accomplishments, Strengths, Education, Affiliations, Professional Affiliations, Publications, Papers, Licenses, Certifications, Examinations, Honors, Personal, Additional, Miscellaneous, References, and so on.

- If you have extra space, describe your interpersonal traits and attitude. Keywords can include skill in *time management, dependable, high energy, leadership, sense of responsibility,* and *good memory.*

A final word of caution: Remember that your scannable resume will still be read by a human reader at some point. Write a cohesive, organized resume that will succeed whether it is read by a computer or by a human being. After all, a computer will not be saying the words you want to hear: "You're hired!"

CHAPTER 4

PREPARING AND SUBMITTING YOUR SCANNABLE RESUME

After you have prepared your scanner-friendly resume, you have several different choices of how you send it to the employer. Some employers request that you mail your resume the old-fashioned way. Other employers may prefer that you fax your resume. Sometimes, you will simply respond to an online advertisement by sending your resume via e-mail. Other times, you will find the job online and then submit your resume online by pasting it into a resume template or form, where it will be scanned into a database without ever having been seen by human eyes! In this chapter, we will explain the finer points of each of these methods. In any case, you should assume your resume will be scanned and you should prepare your resume for that.

How Many Resumes Do You Need?

Resume scanners are not especially particular about the style of resume you choose: chronological, functional, or a combination of the two. Skill extraction can be accomplished on any resume that is clean and of good quality. Formatting choices like graphics, lines, fancy fonts, and custom papers are what make the process difficult. However, at some point, human eyes will still read your resume, and these special enhancements make a resume more attractive for a human reader. So how do you accommodate both audiences?

There are two schools of thought here. Some companies recommend that applicants send two different resumes, one for the scanner and another for the human resources representative. For the former, you follow all the rules for preparing a scannable resume: use plain paper, simple fonts, and so on, as detailed in chapter 3. For the latter, you prepare an attractive resume that uses more creative choices in paper, graphics, style, formatting, and the like. You then send the scannable resume via fax or e-mail, and you mail the traditional resume under separate cover or take it with you when you are called in for an interview. (You can also fax the traditional resume, but you will sacrifice the overall quality and the impact of your expensive paper.)

The Argument for Having Two Resumes

To understand why some companies see a need for two different resumes, you need to think about how a printed scannable resume looks. Scannable resumes with an abundance of facts and skills for the artificial intelligence program to extract tend to be more data-intensive than the traditional resume, and they often contain a keyword summary.

In the early days of resume scanners, people thought that a separate paragraph of nothing but job-related keywords could facilitate the scanning process. This reasoning was based on a notion of competition: If the scanner hit on you right away, you would have a better chance of getting called in for an interview. Consequently, many job seekers put a grouping of words that they hoped would be picked up in a scan at the beginning of their resumes. This grouping became known as a *keyword summary.*

When a human reader reads these resumes, the keyword summary stands apart from the rest of the resume and looks like a disembodied jumble of nouns. Scannable resumes may also be more than one or two pages in length, a major infraction of the rules governing traditional resumes. Traditional resumes do not contain keyword summaries and are, in general, only one page long.

Although you want to include as many keywords as possible on your resume, you don't want to end up with a disjointed jumble of words on a page. You should write comprehensive job descriptions that contain as many job-related terms as possible; therefore, a keyword summary is not necessary. Remember that a scanner passes the entire length of the document and that the OCR (optical character recognition) software reads the resume in its entirety. The extraction engine will do its job whether the keyword is at the beginning, the end, or buried somewhere in the middle of your resume.

The aim of sending two resumes, then, is to look good in both formats. Glenn Whitten of Recruiters Online recommends preparing two versions of a resume:

> The presentation resume is designed to be viewed by a person. As such, we would all want it to *look* as good as possible. Prudence requires us, however, to acknowledge the possibility that the resume might be scanned for OCR at a later date. The OCR resume is designed from the outset to be scanned. Visual beauty is subordinate to OCR accuracy.
>
> Bring both types to an interview, if you can. Often the interviewer can review the "pretty" one while sending the OCR into the system. In this case, you gain the best of both worlds: You come across as understanding the interviewer's situation, too.

One Resume That Does It All

Even though two different resumes are preferred, you can prepare one resume that accomplishes both objectives by choosing the type size, style, and font carefully. If you limit the type sizes on your presentation resume to between 10 and 14 points, and stick to Times, Arial, or Helvetica fonts, your resume will scan accurately. Using the larger fonts and all-caps for the headings still enables you to give your scannable resume more visual appeal for the human reader.

Even with a dual-purpose resume, however, you should still follow the general advice for all scannable resumes. Avoid boldface and underlined text because this formatting doesn't scan well. We recommend using italics only when it is needed to represent publication titles and the like. Resist using symbols (such as diamonds, checkmarks, and arrows) for bullets because the OCR program will not know how to scan the symbols. Instead, use an asterisk, an "o," or some other character from your keyboard. Use the keyboard test: If you don't see the symbol on the keyboard, don't put it in your resume. All in all, you should use plain text as much as possible to avoid errors in OCR scanning.

Other companies recommend that you prepare only a scannable resume. We learned that many companies simply discard paper resumes that are not scannable. Although many other companies still don't use electronic applicant-tracking systems, eventually these systems will become the norm. As with other technology, the price for these systems is coming down, making them available to a much wider public. Therefore, you need to learn how to prepare an attractive resume that will still pass a scanner by focusing on content and keeping your formatting choices simple.

What many companies are saying now is that you don't have to send several resumes that have different objectives to fit the various jobs you may be qualified for within the company. If you include all your skills in one resume, the scanner will select you for those various positions. After your resume is in the database, your skills will be extracted, regardless of which of them you have emphasized. These companies say that sending one resume that highlights all your skills and experience is sufficient, even if two or more pages are necessary.

The Bottom Line

We recommend that you prepare two resumes: one traditional and one scannable. Send a scannable resume that has been written to maximize hits. But after you have received a hit, follow up with an attractive, well-planned presentation resume. Bring the resume with you to the personal interview. If you send a cover letter with your scannable resume, put a notation in it that you will be following up with a traditional resume. In this way, you accomplish both objectives.

Mailing Your Resume

Although many companies now refrain from accepting paper resumes altogether, some companies still accept resumes only by regular postal mail—"snail mail" in Internet parlance. One advantage to mailing your resume is that you can send both a scannable-type one that is written to pass the OCR and a presentation-type one that is attractive for a human reader.

Another advantage of mailing your resume is that you can send an original resume straight off your printer, or you can send a first-generation photocopy. Remember that scannable resumes must be clean and free of "noise" so that they can be scanned efficiently. Be sure that your photocopy is very clean, with no dark streaks or black flecks. Put the original resume on the platen glass straight. If your photo-copied resume comes out crooked on the page, it could cause problems for the OCR program.

When you mail your resume, you should send it flat in a large envelope to avoid the wrinkles that can bedevil the scanner. Scanners have difficulty reading into a fold. A crease can introduce errors into the OCR process.

Faxing Your Resume

Several companies prefer to accept resumes via fax. Long before applicant-tracking systems existed, employers discovered that receiving resumes by fax was more effi-cient than taking them in person or receiving them by postal mail. Fax machines eliminated long lines in the human resources department and cut down on the labor-intensive task of sorting through, opening, and distributing mail. When applicant-tracking systems came along, some companies continued to accept scannable resumes by fax, but some problems developed.

Think about the faxes you have received. Often, they look dirty, with lots of streaks and lines. Sometimes one sheet has overlapped another, which wipes out several sections of the second sheet. Sometimes the sheet has a wrinkle, which causes the letters to look squashed and misshapen. And sometimes the resolution of the fax machine based on its dpi (dots per inch) doesn't match the dpi of the OCR. The faxed image is composed of millions of tiny dots at different shades. The greater the number of dots per inch, the better the detail in the image; the lower the dpi, the grainier or muddier the image appears to be. Such problems can wreak havoc with the scanning process.

Most OCRs are tuned at 300 dpi, while most standard fax machines are set to a low dpi 100×100. Even fine-mode settings are only 100×200 or 200×200 dpi on most fax machines. Although most OCRs can handle these lower resolutions, the difference can cause some problems and prevent clean scanning. Also, faxing can add a lot of "noise"—lines, specks, and smudges—that makes faxes very difficult to read for humans, let alone OCRs. All of these factors can degrade the results of OCR.

If you must fax your scannable resume, take steps to ensure that your faxed resume is still usable when it arrives at the other end. Set your fax machine to the fine setting. This adjustment increases the dpi and eliminates much of the noise on your faxed copy. Also, be sure to begin with a very clean and unwrinkled copy of your resume.

E-Mailing Your Resume

Many companies ask applicants to e-mail resumes. To ensure that your resume arrives at the employer's screen in a usable and scannable form, it is best to prepare it in ASCII text. ASCII (American Standard Code for Information Interchange) is pure text, the simplest form that allows the exchange of information between computers. The beauty of ASCII is that it enables employers to view your resume, regardless of the computer platform they use.

Glenn Whitten, an expert in OCR with Recruiters Online, says that e-mail resumes are a smart idea. He goes on to say:

> I recommend sending e-mail whenever possible. It totally bypasses the errors, which *will* be introduced into your resume by OCR. The good news is that recruiters are increasingly seeing the value of this medium. In fact, there is a significant percentage of recruiters who no longer solicit paper resumes. Many no longer accept them at all.

Your plain-text resume should be lean and mean, with no special fonts, formatting, graphics, or other pretty effects—exactly the way a scanner likes it! The resume also should be completely left-justified, even the headings. If you want to center a line or indent a sentence, you must perform this action by spacing everything as you type it. Remember, in ASCII you cannot use the centerline feature or tabs. You must use the spacebar.

Before-and-After Examples

Take a look at the following samples to see the differences between a standard resume and a plain-text resume. Sample resume 4-1 is a conventional resume, also known as a presentation resume. This resume is prepared for a human reader. Note all the font enhancements.

Figure 4-1

A conventional
presentation
resume.

Gayle Burnham
222 W. 5th Avenue
Toronto, ON
B3Q 3X8
XXX-XXX-XXXX (W)
XXX-XXX-XXXX (H)
Email: aaa@aaaaa.aaa

HIGHLIGHTS OF QUALIFICATIONS

- Over 10 years progressively responsible administrative/management experience
- Proven ability to manage effectively in complex environments
- Demonstrated ability to supervise in a team environment
- Completed MBA while working full-time
- Effective communicator, motivated problem-solver

WORK EXPERIENCE

19XX–present ADMINISTRATIVE OFFICER, Department of Medicine
 Prestigious University, Toronto, Ontario

The Department of Medicine at Prestigious encompasses an administrative office and 13 divisions, is situated in 6 locations, and employs over 200 faculty, 65 secretarial/support staff, and 50 grant paid/technical employees. This position coordinates the administrative management of the department including teaching and research programs and is responsible to:

- Participate in the development and monitoring of departmental goals and objectives;
- Manage and administer all aspects of financial management;
- Coordinate personnel management of 120 employees in two bargaining units; direct supervision of 15 staff;
- Assist in the screening, selection, and orientation of residents and undergrad medical students;
- Manage the practice plan for a group of 60 physicians;
- Serve on Department and Faculty Committees;
- Liaison between the Director, Dean's Office, Committee Chairpersons, university, and government officials;
- Manage a variety of special projects, conduct research, write reports, implement recommendations.

Recent Accomplishments

- Developed and implemented personnel, financial, and management guidelines that were accepted at the Faculty level;
- Computerized and streamlined financial management system resulting in more effective control and analysis;

GAYLE BURNHAM
Page 2

- Implemented a comprehensive selection process for students and staff in consultation with faculty and human resource development;
- Implemented quality initiatives as a component of regular departmental meetings;
- Developed and monitored project teams within department; drafted a comprehensive report for government on financial needs of the Department, which was approved by the Department Head and Dean of the Faculty of Medicine.

19XX–19XX ADMINISTRATIVE ASSISTANT, Faculty of Medicine
Prestigious University, Toronto, Ontario

- Monitored the finances of 30 departments within the faculty;
- Provided assistance to departmental administrators;
- Managed accounts receivable/salary recovery data information system;
- Administered Dean's Office accounts payables;
- Monitored finances of restricted/endowment accounts for the faculty;
- Processed payroll information at the faculty level;
- Prepared detailed financial reports for government on monthly basis;
- Participated in budget projections and year-end financial operations

EDUCATION

19XX—Master of Business Administration, Prestigious University
19XX—Bachelor of Business Administration, Another University

CURRENT COMMITTEES

Finance Committee, Faculty of Medicine
Employee Relations Committee, Some General Hospital
Employment Equity Advisory Committee, Prestigious University Admin Group
Representative

MEMBERSHIPS

National Board of Trade
Human Resource Association of Nova Scotia

REFERENCES
To be supplied upon request

Sample resume 4-2 shows what happened when the presentation was saved as a text document. Note that the bullets in the bulleted lists were turned into the letter *n*, but the asterisks (*) made the transition unchanged. The asterisk was preserved because it is a letter on the keyboard, not an imported symbol, which is really a picture. Also, notice that the indents were not saved and that words wrapped at unusual places at the ends of the lines.

Figure 4-2

A presentation resume saved as a text document.

```
Gayle Burnham
222 W. 5th Avenue
Toronto, ON
B3Q 3X8
XXX-XXX-XXXX (h)
XXX-XXX-XXXX (w)
Email: aaa@aaaaa.aaa                          .

Highlights of Qualifications

* Over 10 years progressively responsible administrative/management experience
* Proven ability to manage effectively in complex environments
* Demonstrated ability to supervise in a team environment
* Completed MBA while working full-time
* Effective communicator motivated problem-solver

WORK EXPERIENCE

19XX-present  ADMINISTRATIVE OFFICER, Department of Medicine
                    Prestigious University, Toronto, Ontario

The Department of Medicine at Prestigious encompasses an administrative office
and 13 divisions, is situated in 6 locations and employs over 200 faculty, 65
secretarial/support staff and 50 grant paid/technical employees. This position
coordinates the administrative management of the department including teaching
and research programs and is responsible to:

n  Participate in the development and monitoring of departmental goals and
objectives;
n  Manage and administer all aspects of financial management;
n  Coordinate personnel management of 120 employees in two bargaining units;
direct    supervision of 15 staff;
n  Assist in the screening, selection and orientation of residents and undergrad
medical students;
n  Manage the practice plan for a group of 60 physicians;
n  Serve on Department and Faculty Committees;
n  Liaison between the Director, Dean's Office, Committee Chairpersons,
university and government officials;
n  Manage a variety of special projects, conduct research, write reports,
implement recommendations

Recent Accomplishments

n  Developed and implemented personnel, financial and management guidelines that
were accepted at the Faculty level;
n  Computerized and streamlined financial management system resulting in more
effective control and analysis;
```

```
GAYLE BURNHAM
Page 2
------------------------------------------------------------------------

n  Implemented a comprehensive selection process for students and staff in
consultation with faculty and human resource development;
n Implemented quality initiatives as a component of regular departmental
meetings;
n Developed and monitored project teams within Department; drafted a
comprehensive report for government on financial needs of the Department, which
was approved by the Department Head and Dean of the Faculty of Medicine.

19XX-19XX ADMINISTRATIVE ASSISTANT, Faculty of Medicine
          Prestigious University, Toronto, Ontario

n  Monitored the finances of 30 departments within the faculty;
n  Provided assistance to Departmental administrators;
n  Managed accounts receivable/salary recovery data information system;
n  Administered Dean's Office accounts payables;
n  Monitored finances of restricted/endowment accounts for the Faculty;
n  Processed payroll information at the Faculty level;
n  Prepared detailed financial reports for government on monthly basis;
n  Participated in budget projections and year-end financial operations

EDUCATION

19XX - Master of Business Administration, Prestigious University
19XX - Bachelor of Business Administration, Another University


CURRENT COMMITTEES

Finance Committee, Faculty of Medicine
Employee Relations Committee, Some General Hospital
Employment Equity Advisory Committee, Prestigious University Admin Group
Representative

MEMBERSHIPS

National Board of Trade
Human Resource Association of Nova Scotia


REFERENCES
To be supplied upon request
```

Finally, after editing the text copy, sample resume 4-3 is the ASCII version that is suitable for sending to the employer via e-mail.

Figure 4-3

An ASCII resume suitable for e-mailing to an employer.

```
Gayle Burnham
222 W. 5th Avenue
Toronto, ON
B3Q 3X8
XXX-XXX-XXXX (H)
XXX-XXX-XXXX (W)
Email: aaa@aaaaa.aaa

Highlights of Qualifications

* Over 10 years progressively responsible administrative/management experience
* Proven ability to manage effectively in complex environments
* Demonstrated ability to supervise in a team environment
* Completed MBA while working full-time
* Effective communicator, motivated problem-solver

WORK EXPERIENCE

19XX-present  ADMINISTRATIVE OFFICER, Department of Medicine
              Prestigious University, Toronto, ON

The Department of Medicine at Prestigious encompasses an administrative office
and 13 divisions, is situated in 6 locations and employs over 200 faculty, 65
secretarial/support staff and 50 grant paid/technical employees. This position
coordinates the administrative management of the department including teaching
and research programs and is responsible to:

Participate in the development and monitoring of departmental goals and
objectives;

Manage and administer all aspects of financial management;

Coordinate personnel management of 120 employees in two bargaining units; direct
supervision of 15 staff;

Assist in the screening, selection and orientation of residents and undergrad
medical students;

Manage the practice plan for a group of 50 physicians;

Serve on Department and Faculty Committees;

Liaison between the Director, Dean's Office, Committee Chairpersons, university
and government officials;

Manage a variety of special projects, conduct research, write reports, implement
recommendations

Recent Accomplishments

Developed and implemented personnel, financial and management guidelines that
were accepted at the Faculty level;

Computerized and streamlined financial management system resulting in more
effective control and analysis;
```

```
GAYLE BURNHAM
Page 2
-------------------------------------------------------------------------

Implemented a comprehensive selection process for students and staff in
consultation with faculty and human resource development;

Implemented quality initiatives as a component of regular departmental meetings;

Developed and monitored project teams within department; drafted a comprehensive
report for government on financial needs of the Department, which was approved
by the Department Head and Dean of the Faculty of Medicine.

19XX-19XX ADMINISTRATIVE ASSISTANT, Faculty of Medicine
         Prestigious University, Toronto, ON

   Monitored the finances of 30 departments within the faculty;
   Provided assistance to Departmental administrators;
   Managed accounts receivable/salary recovery data information system;
   Administered Dean's Office accounts payables;
   Monitored finances of restricted/endowment accounts for the Faculty;
   Processed payroll information at the Faculty level;
   Prepared detailed financial reports for government on monthly basis;
   Participated in budget projections and year-end financial operations

EDUCATION

19XX - Master of Business Administration, Prestigious University
19XX - Bachelor of Business Administration, Another University


CURRENT COMMITTEES

Finance Committee, Faculty of Medicine
Employee Relations Committee, Victoria General Hospital
Employment Equity Advisory Committee, Prestigious University Admin Group
Representative

MEMBERSHIPS

National Board of Trade
Human Resource Association of Nova Scotia


REFERENCES
To be supplied upon request
```

Prepare your resume in your word processor. Make sure that you keep the lines to no more than 70 characters long. This spacing ensures that your resume will not come out looking haphazard on the receiving end. Then save the resume as ASCII text. (In Microsoft Word, choose File, Save As, Text Only.)

Be sure to spell check and examine your resume carefully for appropriate spacing. We recommend that you e-mail your resume to yourself first to make sure that the look is professional, with even borders and line spacing. Copy and paste your text resume directly from your word processing program into the body of your e-mail message and send it to yourself.

After you have looked at the resume you sent yourself and fixed any glitches, copy your resume once again, paste it directly into the body of a new e-mail message, and send it to the employer. Most online posting services and employers request that you put your name and the word *Resume* in the subject line.

The ASCII resume is also the preferred form for pasting into an online resume template. You'll read more about this in the next section, "Resume Templates and Forms."

Caution

Nearly every resume site we visited and all the employers we interviewed cautioned job seekers *not* to submit their resume as an attachment to an e-mail message.

An attachment is a file that has to be downloaded separately from your e-mail into the recipient's computer. In the case of a resume, an attachment would be a document created in a word-processing program. One problem with attachments is that the word-processing program you use may not be recognizable by a program at the employer's site. Another problem with attachments is that they usually arrive in a compressed form and need to be expanded when they reach their destination in order to be readable. The employer's computer may not be compatible with that program; thus your resume is rendered useless.

Still another problem with sending attachments is that many Internet users believe viruses often ride in on attachments. In 2000, several nasty viruses made their appearance in Microsoft Outlook e-mail programs. The virus arrived as an attachment to an e-mail message and, when opened, corrupted or destroyed millions of documents worldwide.

We have always warned readers about sending their resumes to employers as attachment. Then, in spring 2000, a virus arrived at many companies' desktops as a resume from a fictitious job applicant! The virus, dubbed "killer resume," was a variant of the Melissa virus that hid in an e-mail attachment called "Resume—Janet Simons." The message said

> *To: Director of Sales/Marketing*
>
> *Attached is my resume with a list of references contained within. Please feel free to call or email me if you have any further questions regarding my experience. I am looking forward to hearing from you.*
>
> *Sincerely, Janet Simons*

This virus not only eloquently proved our point about the danger of attachments, it discouraged employers even further from opening them. Many employers simply will not bother with an attachment, and they will skip it entirely.

Resume Templates and Forms

Many companies now use resume templates or forms to help their applicants submit resumes. If you apply for a job at a company's Web site, you will often find a fill-in-the-blank form at the end of the job posting. This easy-to-use template ensures that your resume is in a format that is easily read by the company's scanner. The template helps increase your chances of getting "hit," in retrieval that is, when an employer searches for qualified candidates.

More companies are choosing to use resume templates as they increasingly opt for automated staffing. Through our research, we determined that templates are becoming the preferred means of obtaining resumes in usable form for a number of reasons:

- By designing their own forms, employers are able to specify and control the information they get from applicants.

- Employers can control the length of the resume. The templates we reviewed provided space for only three to six prior jobs in the Work History block, with three being the standard.

- Resumes that are pasted into a template are guaranteed to be scannable. They arrive in text form and go directly into the company's applicant-tracking system.

- With an online template, employers are spared the task of wading through paper.

To submit your resume online, paste your ASCII plain-text resume directly into the template on the Web site. You can also type your resume online, filling in the blanks as you go. Certain resume templates may ask for information that you did not include on your standard resume, so you would simply provide that information separately by typing it directly into the blanks. Remember, however, that your resume should be a text document and must fit the parameters of the employer's template.

Resumix makes its ResumeBuilder™ template available to its client companies for posting at their Web sites or on their Intranets, although it is no longer at the Resumix site.

Resume templates are also available at most of the large online job-posting sites, such as Monster.com and CareerMosaic. The templates enable organizations to get more in-depth information on each candidate and take the uncertainty out of the scanning process. Remember, resumes built on templates are guaranteed to be scannable!

CHAPTER 5

YOUR OWN HTML RESUME

HTML is the language used to create Web pages. An HTML (Hypertext Markup Language) resume enables you to take advantage of all kinds of creative possibilities that the World Wide Web offers. For example, you can add art, sound, links to other Web sites, and video to your resume.

Why Have an HTML Resume?

An HTML resume gives you more control of the content and form of your resume on the World Wide Web than if you simply posted it on a resume data bank. One benefit of an HTML resume is the flexibility you have in the presentation of your resume. In the text itself, you can use bold, italic, underlining, and various font sizes. You can also include tables and graphics, and you can use shading and color.

A second benefit of an HTML resume is that it can potentially increase your exposure. If your resume is in only one resume data bank, potential employers have to be in that site to find you. With an HTML resume that you've indexed in the major Internet search engines, anyone can find your resume by searching on your keywords.

With an HTML resume, you have your own unique Internet address, or URL, which you can include in correspondence and on your business card. The URL directs people to your presence on the Internet. This online presence with your own URL demonstrates to employers your awareness of technology and may be the little extra that puts you ahead of the competition.

What to Avoid on Your HTML Resume

HTML enables you to use many creative, fun, and interesting items on your resume; however, some of these items may not serve you well in the job search process. This section contains several warnings that we have developed.

Skip the Photo!

First of all, don't use photographs. For many years, job seekers have been warned not to include a photo of themselves with a resume. The one exception to this rule has been for people in the arts, such as actors and television personalities. You should omit personal photographs because you don't want to include anything that may prejudice the employer *in any way.* Visual cues are powerful. Decisions may be made about you—rightly or wrongly—based on your facial expression, your mode of dress, or even your hairstyle in the picture. Before the advent of the Internet, conventional recruiting advisors never recommended the gamble of putting a photograph on a resume.

Then along comes the World Wide Web, and job seekers feel duty-bound to take advantage of all its capabilities, including photographs. Photographs of yourself are just not appropriate on a resume. Even in the electronic labor market of today, photographs can be risky. If the photograph is unprofessional or of poor quality, it can actually harm your chances. Some computer-generated images are so muddy that you can end up looking as if you suffer from chronic insomnia. Remember, this online resume is the very first look the employer has of you and your capabilities. You don't want to leave an employer with a bad impression because of a poor photograph.

Craig Bussey, formerly the head of human resources for Hüls America, Inc., a chemical manufacturing company in New Jersey, stated his feelings about photographs on a resume very bluntly:

> *Putting your picture on a resume is stupid. It will tend to disqualify you because it sends the wrong message. I'm not looking for a "pretty face"; I'm looking for a skill. What you look like is not a skill.*

Because human resource professionals don't want to view photographs of potential employees, many of them use a text-only WWW browser, which replaces slow-loading images with a graphics icon.

Don't Overdo the Links

The second warning is don't overuse links to other sites because the links may not be in your best interest. You can add links to the university you attended and to your former employers, but remember that links take the reader *away* from your resume. The employer may get sidetracked and never return! Or you may have included links that the employer may find offensive or that are not in line with the interests of the company. For example, if you are sending a resume to UPS (United Parcel Service) and you plug in a link to the home page of your former employer, which happens to be Federal Express, the link may not sit well with the UPS representative reading your resume.

Don't include a link to your personal home page, particularly if it includes photos of you at last year's New Year's Eve party, trivia about your dog, and your poetry. Your personal home page may not be the side of you that you want a potential employer to see. Most home pages are much more informal than what would be appropriate to show an employer.

Use Colors with Care

The third caution is to use colors with care. When you create an HTML resume, you need to make several choices about headings, fonts, graphics, and background. Be especially careful in choosing a background color and pattern. A background that is too busy or dark may obscure parts of your text. For example, we had to squint to read a link on one resume we saw. The background was a variegated purple and black. The link—her e-mail address, a vital piece of information—was almost impossible to see.

Finally, if you choose to use a graphic on your resume, make sure that it is simple, tasteful, and appropriate. Remember that a graphic takes time to download, so it needs to be important to the resume. You don't want to "lock" an employer on your page, waiting and waiting for your page to finish downloading. Most employers use the Internet during normal business hours, and many use modems instead of a faster T1 line. If a resume takes longer than 10–15 seconds to load over a modem, the employer will stop and go on to the next one.

Keep Graphics Appropriate

Keep graphics tasteful and appropriate. You want everything about your resume to reflect your professionalism. Remember, too, that not all artwork is in the public domain. You don't want to put a cartoon that is protected by copyright on your resume. Software packages for building Web pages usually include clip art that is available for public use.

What to Include in Your HTML Resume

Now that we have warned you about items that should not be on your HTML resume, you need to know about the creative ideas you *can* use to catch an employer's attention. This section offers several pointers for improving your resume.

Include a Counter

You should include a counter. A counter simply records the number of times your resume has been viewed. Keep a record of the number of hits that are your own so that you know how many times potential employers have reviewed your resume.

Use Some Links

Although we have already cautioned you about using too many links or using inappropriate links in a resume, putting one or two links in your resume can improve your resume's chances of being read. The key is to keep the employer interested in your resume. The resume should be the destination, and the link should enhance that destination, not take the employer away from it. Keep the links to a minimum, and use these ideas:

- **E-mail address:** This is one link we highly recommend because it is a fast, no-hassle way for the employer to get to you directly.

- **Publications:** If you've been mentioned favorably on a Web site, consider a link to that site. If you have been published, consider a link to a favorable review of that work. The same advice applies to designs, compositions, and artwork.

- **Notable people and organizations:** If you have worked with someone who is a known public figure, link to an informational site about that person. However, be sure to consider carefully an employer's reactions to politically and religiously affiliated people.

- **Colleges and universities:** Boola-boola and all that network stuff. Remember, however, that some college and university sites may also have other graduates' resumes—do you want to lead the employer to your competition?

- **Scholastic societies:** Phi Beta Kappa, Phi Kappa Phi, and so on.

- **Awards:** If you mention an award you have received, an employer may be interested in learning more about it. Link to a site that gives the details.

- **Multiple languages:** If you are seeking work in another country and you speak the language, prepare a separate resume in that language and then put a link to it within the English-language resume. We noted several resumes in other languages. One resume in German looked appealing. Although Fred has some facility with the language, we couldn't translate the resume fully. It would have been helpful to have found a link to a version in English.

Even though anyone can use sites on the Web to translate documents, you want to avoid having the *employer* make the extra effort to go to these sites. The *job seeker* should provide that link instead. In addition, by putting in a link your-self to a resume you have prepared in another language, you demonstrate your facility with that language. Remember that the WWW is international. Write for that audience.

You may want to consider including two more links in your HTML resume as well. At the top or bottom of your HTML resume, you should put a link to the other versions of your resume, including a scannable version (written in ASCII text) and a printable version (a PDF version that contains the attractive format choices missing from the scannable version). The printable version is always shorter than the HTML version, and you can use it as attractive hard copy to be handed around within the company. The scannable version can be printed and put in a scanner, or it can be cut and pasted into the Web form at the employer's site.

You may also want to put another link at the bottom of the page that brings the reader back to the top of your resume. This link is a timesaving feature that employers will thank you for.

Convert Your Resume to a PDF File

We have seen many more resumes today that are in PDF (Portable Document Format) format. PDF can be used with text, image, or multimedia files. It is designed to publish and distribute electronic documents, so PDF preserves all the fonts, formatting choices, and layout exactly as you created them. This ensures that your document will appear online just as it did when you first built it. If you include a link to a PDF version of your resume at your Web site, and if the employer has Acrobat Reader, you can be assured that the resume will print out exactly as you originally meant it to look.

To convert your resume to a PDF file, you will need to purchase the Adobe Acrobat Distiller program. To read PDF files, you can download Adobe Acrobat Reader for free from http://www.adobe.com/products/acrobat/readermain.html.

Using Forms: A Shortcut to Creating an HTML Resume

You don't need to know any HTML to create your own HTML resume. You can simply use existing forms on the World Wide Web. We'll use the Resumix ResumeBuilder program to show you how a form creates an HTML resume.

You start by filling out the form. Let's look at a sample form completed for fictional job seeker Clark Kent (figure 5-1).

ResumeBuilder™

Sample Form

Form Instructions

Personal Information

Name (as you'd like it to appear on the resume): | Clark Kent |

Address 1: | Home ▼ |

| 1001 Main Street |
| Apt 321 |
| |

City: | Metropolis | State: | MN | Zip: | 43211-000 |

Address 2: | Work ▼ |

| The Daily Planet |
| Journalism Dept. |
| 100 Planet Ave. |

City: | Metropolis | State: | MN | Zip: | 43200-000 |

Phone Numbers

| Home ▼ | 612-555-3221 | (optional)

| Work ▼ | 612-555-3000 | (optional)

| Fax ▼ | 612-555-1000 | (optional)

E-Mail Address: | ckent@dplanet.com | (optional)

Figure 5-1

Clark Kent's resume form.

Objective

Give a brief one or two sentence description of the type of employment or position you desire.

> A fast-paced job in journalism that expands and builds upon my skills as an experienced reporter.

(Please use carriage returns.)

Education

Please fill in your educational background. List at least one school you attended.

School: Metropolis University   Major: Journalism

Degree: B.A. Year of Graduation: 1988 GPA: 3.75

School: Smallville High School   Major: English

Degree: H.S. Year of Graduation: 1984 GPA: 3.8

School: Major:

Degree: Year of Graduation: GPA:

School: Major:

Degree: Year of Graduation: GPA:

Employment History

Please fill in the name of the employer, your job title, the dates you work (MM/YY format), and a brief description of your job responsibilities. Fill in at least one.

Employer: The Daily Planet

Job Title: Reporter

From: Sept. To: Present

Description of Duties: (please use carriage returns)

(continues)

(continued)

Headline reporting for a major metropolitan newspaper. Responsibilities include in-the-field reporting, writing and editing front page stories, and working closely with other reports in covering the daily events of the world.

Employer: Smallville Gazette

Job Title: Editor

From: Oct. To: Sept.

Description of Duties: (please use carriage returns)

Head Editor and Chief for the Smallville Gazette. Managed a team of four reporters, plus oversight of typesetting and delivery of a newspaper with a subscription of over 600 loyal readers. Also managed fundraising and

Employer: Smallville Pizza Plaza

Job Title: Delivery Person

From: June To: Aug.

Description of Duties: (please use carriage returns)

Delivery of hot, fresh, pizza to customers' doorstep. Never delivered a pizz late.

Employer: Smallville Red Cross

Job Title:

From: July 1988 To: June

Description of Duties: (please use carriage returns)

First-aid and CPR instruction, swimming and water-safety instruction. Member of the Smallville National Disaster team.

Employer:

Job Title:

From: [____] To: [____]
Description of Duties: (please use carriage returns)

[text area]

Employer: [_____]

Job Title: [_____]

From: [____] To: [____]
Description of Duties: (please use carriage returns)

[text area]

Additional Information

Use this area to write any additional information you may wish to include on your resume (e.g. - additional skills, strengths, abilities, etc.). (Please use carriage returns.)

In addition to my experience and abilities as a reporter, and background with the Red Cross, I can also leap tall buildings in a single bound, fly faster than a speeding bullet, stronger than a locomotive, have X-ray vision, and super-hearing.

To format your resume, press this button: [Format]

To clear this form, press this button: [Clear Form]

At the end of the form, you simply click the Format button to create a resume for Clark Kent from the information in the form. Figure 5-2 shows how this resume will look.

Figure 5-2

The resume that the form created.

Clark Kent

Home Address:
1001 Main Street
Apt 321
Metropolis MN 43211-0000

Work Address:
The Daily Planet
Journalism Dept.
100 Planet Ave.
Metropolis MN 43200-0000

Home: 612-555-3221
Work: 612-555-3000
Fax: 612-555-1000

E-mail: ckent@dplanet.com

OBJECTIVE:

A fast-paced job in journalism that expands and builds upon my skills as an experienced reporter.

EMPLOYMENT HISTORY:

Sept. 1990 - Present, Reporter at The Daily Planet

Headline reporting for a major metropolitan newspaper. Responsibilities include in-the-field reporting, writing and editing front page stories, and working closely with other reports in covering the daily events of the world.

Oct. 1989 - Sept. 1990, Editor at Smallville Gazette

Head Editor and Chief for the Smallville Gazette. Managed a team of four reporters, plus oversight of typesetting and delivery of a newspaper with a subscription of over 600 loyal readers. Also managed fundraising and finances.

June 1988 - Aug. 1989, Delivery Person at Smallville Pizza Plaza

Delivery of hot, fresh, pizza to customers' doorstep. Never delivered a pizza late.

July 1982 - June 1988, Smallville Red Cross

First-aid and CPR instruction, swimming and water-safety instruction. Member of the Smallville National Disaster team.

EDUCATION:

B.A. in Journalism, Metropolis University, 1988, GPA: 3.75
H.S. in English, Smallville High School, 1984, GPA: 3.8

ADDITIONAL SKILLS:

In addition to my experience and abilities as a reporter, and background with the Red Cross, I can also leap tall buildings in a single bound, fly faster than a speeding bullet, stronger than a locomotive, have X-ray vision, and super-hearing.

Now, let's go one more step so that you can see the HTML coding that created Clark Kent's HTML resume. You will now see this Web page in HTML coding, as shown in sample resume 5-3. Of course, an employer would never actually see these codes onscreen. They are just the directives that tell how things should be formatted and displayed. In regular HTML, you'd have to type these things yourself. But by using the form, the hard work is done for you.

Figure 5-3

The HTML coding behind Clark Kent's resume.

```
<!DOCTYPE HTML PUBLIC "-//W3C//DTD HTML 4.0 Transitional//EN">
<HTML><HEAD><TITLE>Resume of Clark Kent</TITLE>
<META content="text/html; charset=windows-1252" http-equiv=Content-Type>
<META content="MSHTML 5.00.2314.1000" name=GENERATOR></HEAD>
<BODY bgColor=#e4e4ff link=#0000ff vLink=#0000ff>
<CENTER>
<H2>Clark Kent</H2><STRONG>Home Address:</STRONG><BR>1001 Main Street <BR>Apt
321 <BR>Metropolis MN 43211-0000
<P><STRONG>Work Address:</STRONG><BR>The Daily Planet <BR>Journalism Dept.
<BR>100 Planet Ave. <BR>Metropolis MN 43200-0000
<P><STRONG>Home: </STRONG>612-555-3221 <BR><STRONG>Work: </STRONG>612-555-3000
<BR><STRONG>Fax: </STRONG>612-555-1000 <BR>
<P><STRONG>E-mail:</STRONG> ckent@dplanet.com
<P></CENTER>
<H3>OBJECTIVE:</H3>A fast-paced job in journalism that expands and builds upon
my skills as an experienced reporter.
<P>
<H3>EMPLOYMENT HISTORY:</H3>
<DL>
  <DT><STRONG>Sept. 1990 - Present, Reporter at The Daily Planet</STRONG>
  <DD>Headline reporting for a major metropolitan newspaper. Responsibilities
  include in-the-field reporting, writing and editing front page stories, and
  working closely with other reports in covering the daily events of the world.
  </DD></DL>
<DL>
  <DT><STRONG>Oct. 1989 - Sept. 1990, Editor at Smallville Gazette</STRONG>
  <DD>Head Editor and Chief for the Smallville Gazette. Managed a team of four
  reporters, plus oversight of typesetting and delivery of a newspaper with a
  subscription of over 600 loyal readers. Also managed fundraising and
  finances.</DD></DL>
<DL>
  <DT><STRONG>June 1988 - Aug. 1989, Delivery Person at Smallville Pizza
  Plaza</STRONG>
  <DD>Delivery of hot, fresh, pizza to customers' doorstep. Never delivered a
  pizza late. </DD></DL>
<DL>
  <DT><STRONG>July 1982 - June 1988, Smallville Red Cross</STRONG>
  <DD>First-aid and CPR instruction, swimming and water-safety instruction.
  Member of the Smallville National Disaster team. </DD></DL>
<DL>
  <DT><STRONG></STRONG></DT></DL>
<DL>
  <DT><STRONG></STRONG></DT></DL>
<H3>EDUCATION:</H3>B.A. in Journalism, Metropolis University, 1988, GPA:
3.75<BR>H.S. in English, Smallville High School, 1984, GPA: 3.8<BR>
<H3>ADDITIONAL SKILLS:</H3>In addition to my experience and abilities as a
reporter, and background with the Red Cross, I can also leap tall buildings in a
single bound, fly faster than a speeding bullet, stronger than a locomotive,
have X-ray vision, and super-hearing.
<P></P></BODY></HTML>
```

What you see is all that you need to create the resume for Clark Kent. For the most part, this is done right at the employer's site, either by typing the information in or by copying and pasting your text resume from your word processor to the employer's template.

Writing Your HTML Resume in a Word-Processing Program

You can create an HTML resume in your word-processing program. We created a resume using Microsoft Word 97. If you go to Help, Find, type in create Web page, and select it from the list of topics at the bottom of the box, you will get instructions on how to make an HTML document.

Word provides step-by-step instructions (called a *wizard*) that enable you to do the following things to your Web page:

- Add bullets and numbering.
- Add horizontal lines.
- Add a background.
- Add tables.
- Work with graphics.
- Set text colors.
- Create hyperlinks.
- Add a video.
- Add scrolling text.

You can also use Word to insert a hyperlink that goes to another document, file, or Web page. Word makes these functions very easy. In Word 2000, you can accomplish most with a simple click and type.

Word offers two ways for you to create your HTML resume. You can either create a new Web page from scratch, by using a wizard or template, or you can convert your existing Word resume to HTML. Word customizes some toolbars, menu commands, and options to provide the Web page–authoring features you need when creating a Web page.

WordPerfect also enables you to create Web pages. Use the Help feature and follow the directions.

You may want to purchase software—such as Microsoft FrontPage, Dreamweaver, and HoTMetaL—for creating HTML documents. These HTML editors simplify the coding process and greatly reduce the HTML you need to know to create a page.

Posting Your HTML Resume on the Web

The next step is to upload your HTML resume to the server that will store it and make it available for viewing on the World Wide Web. Web sites have instructions and policies regarding the proper uploading and maintenance of Web pages. Contact the system administrator or the Help desk for specific information.

Your URL Address

Although you may relocate to a new residence, your HTML resume can remain your permanent address on the Internet so that employers can find you no matter where you have moved. You can ensure that employers can find you in two ways: You can register your home page with search engines, and you can link your home page with other sites.

One way to register your home page with search engines is through free submission services. These submit your resume to various search engines. You can check out two free services located at the following addresses:

Free Domain
```
http://www.webpage-register.com/popup_freedomain.htm
```

and

The Web Site Garage
```
http://register-it.netscape.com/O=wsg/
```

These submission services register your site with up to two dozen top search engines including AltaVista, Open Text, Webcrawler, and Yahoo!.

A second way to publicize your URL address is to link your home page with other sites. When a search engine robot—such as those used by AltaVista—visits a site, it automatically indexes all linked pages at that site. Note that your HTML resume must be linked from somewhere else in the site; it is not enough to be located at a site that the robot visits. The search engine automatically indexes your resume so that it will come up in keyword searches.

Adding Your HTML Resume to Resume Banks

The following list contains some resume banks that simply list your HTML resumes. Part II of this book fully describes these resume banks.

- **Entry Level Job Seeker Assistant** (http://www.dnaco.net/~dantassi/ jobhome.html): This resume bank is for people who have never held a full-time, permanent job in their field or who have less than a year of nonacademic experience. This bank does not accept resumes; instead, it contains links to your World Wide Web resume. There is no charge for being listed.

- **The Australian Resume Server** (http://www.resume.net.au/): This resume bank provides an optional free HTML resume home page.

- **Your Resume Online** (http://www.southerncross.net/rz/rz12.htm): This resume bank provides resume Web page design, hosting, or promotion for a fee.

Sample HTML Resumes

Let's check out some sample HTML resumes from the World Wide Web.

Links to each section of resume

Link to his ASCII-version resume

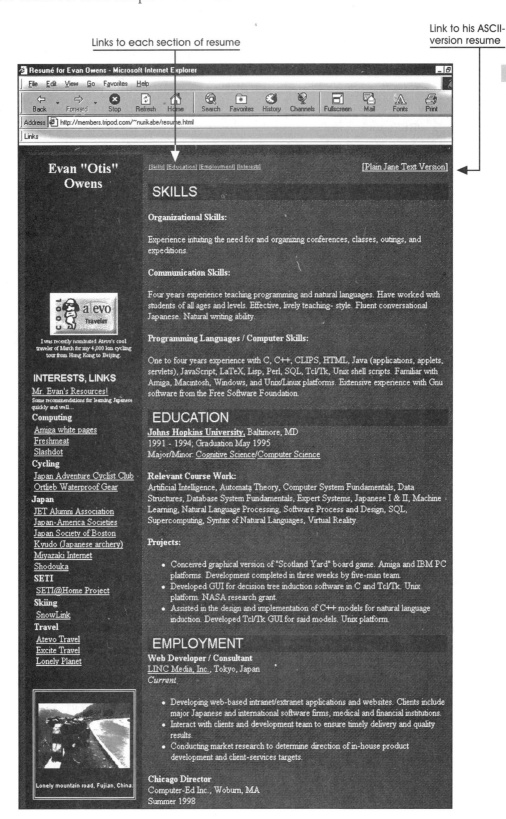

Figure 5-4

An HTML Resume.

Counter

Lonely mountain road, Fujian, China.

Free Speech Online
Blue Ribbon Campaign

This resumé has been visited **51** times since March 1, 1998.

- Developing web-based intranet/extranet applications and websites. Clients include major Japanese and international software firms, medical and financial institutions.
- Interact with clients and development team to ensure timely delivery and quality results.
- Conducting market research to determine direction of in-house product development and client-services targets.

Chicago Director
Computer-Ed Inc., Woburn, MA
Summer 1998

- Organized and directed a new technical training program children in Illinois.
- Responsibilities included staff hiring, procurement of equipment, facilities management, orientation, and curriculum development.
- Success of program rescued over $150,000 in revenue.

Graphics Specialist
Colgate Pharmaceuticals, Canton, MA
Winter 1998

- Responsible for design and layout of customized logos using Adobe Illustrator and Photoshop.
- Maintained SAP customer database.
- Prioritized orders to adhere to tight production schedule.
- Coordinated efforts of sales, graphics, and production departments to ensure high quality and timely delivery of products.

Educator in Japan
Japan Exchange and Teaching Programme, Sadowara, Miyazaki, Japan
Summer, 1995 - Summer, 1997

- Hired by Japan's Ministry of Education to work with the Sadowara Board of Education.
- Developed course material.
- Conducted classes in elementary school, middle school, and adult education curricula.
- Periodically served as translator/interpreter.
- Editor of prefecture-wide English-language newsletter.
- Conceived of and organized weekly, prefecture-wide round-table discussions to improve the quality of English education in Miyazaki.

Score Report from the Japanese-Language Proficiency Test

NASA / HST Research Team Member
Medium Deep Survey, Johns Hopkins University, Baltimore, MD
Spring Semester, 1995

- Investigated methods for the classification of galactic morphology in Hubble Space Telescope data. Designed and customized software written in C with supporting Perl scripts.
- Results published as "Using Oblique Decision Trees for the Morphological Classification of Galaxies," Monthly Notices of the Royal Astronomical Society, 281, 153.

Teaching Assistant
Dept. of Computer Science, Johns Hopkins University, Baltimore, MD
Spring Semester, 1993; Spring Semester, 1993; Fall Semester, 1994
Prepared and graded material for multiple courses, including

- Intermediate Programming in C++.
- Organized and conducted additional lectures in all courses.

Educator
Computer-Ed, High-Tech Camp, Newton, MA
Summer, 1993; Summer 1994

- Taught a variety of classes, including Advanced Programming in C++ and Artificial Intelligence Programming in CLIPS.
- Organized extracurricular activities for groups of over 150.
- Director of Counselor Training, 1994.

Link to HTML version

It's a good idea to put all contact information in one place

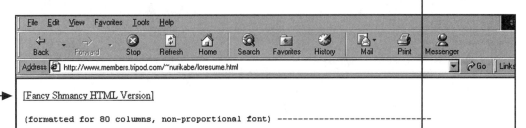

```
File  Edit  View  Favorites  Tools  Help

 ←       →       ⊗       ⟳       ⌂       ⊕       📁        🕐       📧      🖨️      👤
Back   Forward   Stop   Refresh  Home   Search  Favorites  History   Mail   Print  Messenger

Address  http://www.members.tripod.com/~nurikabe/loresume.html                    Go   Links
```

```
[Fancy Shmancy HTML Version]

(formatted for 80 columns, non-proportional font) -----------------------

Evan A. Owens
6-50 Nishi-Shinjuku                         http://listen.to/mr.evan
Shinjuku-ku, Tokyo                          evan@XXXXXXXXX.co.jp
Japan 160-6023                              nurikabe@XXXXX.com


SKILLS

Managerial/Organizational Skills:
  Experience intuiting the need for and organizing conferences, classes,
  outings, expeditions, and educational programs.

Communication Skills:
  Four years experience teaching programming and natural languages.  Have
  worked with students of all ages and levels.  Effective, lively teaching-
  style.  Natural writing ability.

Programming Languages / Computer Skills:
  One to four years experience with C, C++, CGI, CLIPS, FSF (GNU) Software,
  HTML, Java (applications, applets, servlets), JavaScript, LaTeX, Lisp, Perl,
  SQL, Tcl/Tk, Unix shell scripts.  Familiar with Amiga, Macintosh, Windows,
  and Unix/Linux platforms.


EDUCATION

Johns Hopkins University, Baltimore, MD  (Bachelor of Arts, May 1995)
  Cognitive Science / Computer Science
  Concentration in Natural Language Processing

Relevant Course Work:
  Artificial Intelligence, Automata Theory, Computer System Fundamentals, Data
  Structures, Database System Fundamentals, Expert Systems, Japanese I & II,
  Machine Learning, Natural Language Processing, Software Process and Design,
  Supercomputing, Syntax of Natural Languages, Virtual Reality.

Projects:
  o Conceived graphical version of "Scotland Yard" board game.  Amiga and IBM PC
    platforms.  Development completed in three weeks by five-man team.
  o Developed GUI for decision tree induction software in C and Tcl/Tk.  Unix
    platform.  NASA research grant.
  o Assisted in the design and implementation of C++ models for natural
    language induction.  Developed Tcl/Tk GUI for said models.  Unix platform.


EXPERIENCE

Currently     Web Developer / Consulant
              LINC Media, Inc., Tokyo, Japan
                  o Developing web-based intranet/extranet applications and
                    websites.  Clients include major Japanese and international
                    software firms, medical and financial institutions.
                  o Interact with clients and development team to ensure timely
                    delivery and quality results.
                  o Conducting market research to determine direction of in-house
                    product development and client-services targets.
```

Figure 5-5

The plain-text version of figure 5-4.

```
Summer 1998      Director, Computer-Ed Lake Forest
                 Computer-Ed Inc., Woburn, MA
                     o Organized and directed a new technical training program for
                       children in Illinois.
                     o Responsibilities included staff hiring, procurement of
                       equipment, facilities management, orientation, and curric-
                       ulum development.
                     * Success of program rescued over $150,000 in revenue.

Winter 1998      Graphics Specialist, Brush Imprinting Plant
                 Colgate Pharmaceuticals, Canton, MA
                     o Responsible for design and layout of customized client
                       logos using Adobe Illustrator and Photoshop.
                     o Maintained SAP customer database.
                     o Prioritized orders to adhere to tight production schedule.
                     o Coordinated efforts of sales, graphics, and production dep-
                       artments to ensure high quality and timely delivery of
                       products.

1995 - 1997      Educator, Japan Exchange and Teaching Programme (JET)
                 Sadowara, Miyazaki, Japan
                     o Hired by Japan's Ministry of Education to work with the
                       Sadowara Board of Education.
                     o Developed course material.
                     o Conducted classes in elementary school, middle school, and
                       adult education curricula.
                     o Periodically served as translator/interpreter.
                     o Editor of prefecture-wide English-language newsletter.
                     o Conceived of and organized weekly, prefecture-wide round-
                       table discussions to improve the quality of English education
                       in Miyazaki.

Spring 1995      NASA / MDS Research Team Member, Department of Physics & Astronomy
                 Johns Hopkins University, Baltimore, MD
                     o Investigated methods for the classification of galactic morph-
                       ology in Hubble Space Telescope data.  Design and augmentation
                       of software written in C with supporting Perl scripts.
                     o Completed software used to aid in the automatic classification
                       of HST data thereby freeing researchers from this task.
                     * Results published in Monthly Notices of the Royal Astronomical
                       Society, 281, 153.

1992 - 1994      Teaching Assistant, Computer Science Department
                 Johns Hopkins University, Baltimore, MD
                     o Prepared and graded material for multiple courses, including
                       Intermediate Programming in C++.
                     o Organized and conducted additional lectures in all courses.

1993, 1994       Educator, Computer-Ed
                 Lasell College, Newton, MA
                     o Taught a variety of classes, including Advanced Programming
                       in C++ and Artificial Intelligence Programming in CLIPS.
                     o Organized extracurricular activities for groups of over 150.
                     o Director of Counselor Training, 1994.


INTERESTS

Long distance cycling, skiing/snowboarding, film, travel, languages.



References furnished upon request
```

Nice artwork because
resume is for design

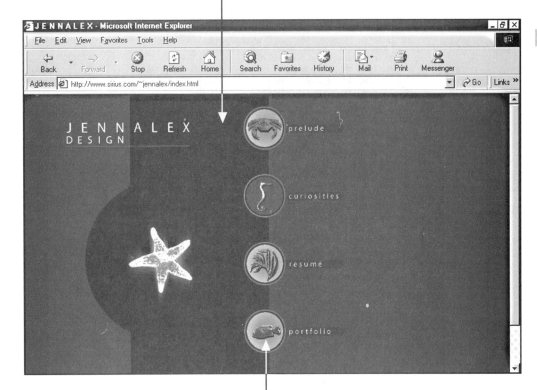

Figure 5-6

An animated
Web resume.

Nice buttons for links

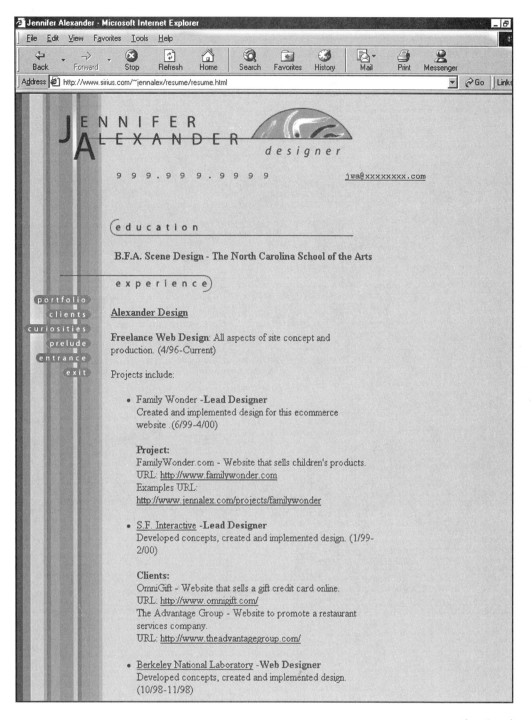

(continues)

(continued)

Project:
Science Beat - Research news magazine, focusing on new discoveries made at the lab.
URL: http://enews.lbl.gov/

- Highway One -**Lead Designer**
Developed concepts, created and implemented design. (5/98-9/98)

Client:
Visa - Private website for exclusive clientele.
URL: http://www.visainfinite.com/

- Modem Media -**Lead Designer**
Developed concepts with writers, created and implemented banner designs. (3/98-5/98)

Clients:
3com - Created a banner promotion for a computer conference.
Women's Wire - Created a series of banner promotions.
Looksmart - Created banner art.

- Organic Online -**Designer**
Developed concepts, created and implemented designs for proposals, banners, and active websites. (8/97-12/97)

Clients include:
Feld Entertainment (aka. Ringling Bros and Barnum and Bailey) - Proposal
Hyundai - Proposal
eBay - Banners
Palm Pilot - Proposal
Netgrocer - Production

- eMergingmedia -**Designer**
Created template designs, as well as new elements for pre-existing designs (11/97-2/99).

Cybernautics

Lead Designer/Project Director : Project direction, graphic design, interface design, site architecture, animation, and HTML. (9/96-4/97)

Projects include:

- <u>Turner Interactive</u> -**Project Director**- *Space Ghost*
  Directed project from concept through completion. Guided the overall artistic vision, managed a team of artists, designers, and writers, and created most of the design work.
  URL: http://www.jennalex.com/sgfinals
- <u>Netiva</u> -**Project Director**
  Developed overall design concept, led a team of designers, supervised the web commerce area of the site as well as the BBS implementation.
  URL: http://www.jennalex.com/projects/netiva
- <u>NetChannel</u> -**Interface Designer**
- <u>Microprose</u> -**Production Graphics and HTML**
- <u>Diamond Multimedia</u> -**Production Graphics and HTML**

Links to examples of work

Mt. Lake Software

Designer: Created original content and design for a young web-savvy crowd. (7/95-5/96)

Projects include:

- <u>Cyberteens</u> -**Designer**
  Created several award winning Shockwave animations and developed the design interface for the main body of this website geared for teenagers.
  URL:
  http://www.jennalex.com/projects/cyberteens/cyberteens.html
  URL:
  http://www.cyberteens.com/multimedia/shockwave/index.html
- <u>Cyberkids Launchpad</u> -**Designer and Content Developer**
  Compiled links for this vast kid safe resource, wrote commentary and designed banners.
  URL: http://www.cyberkids.com/Launchpad/Launchpad.html

CMP Media/Woodwind Internet Services

Designer and Illustrator: Basic Web development for a wide range of clients (7/95-3/96)

Projects include:

- <u>NetGuide</u> -**Designer**
  Designed prototypes for an online web service
- <u>Bank of America</u> -**Designer**
  Basic HTML and graphics manipulation
- <u>Ketchum Kitchen</u> -**Designer**
  Basic HTML and graphics manipulation
- <u>Weblust</u> -**Designer**
  Created a few graphics, but wrote commentary for much of the site.
  URL: http://www.weblust.com/links/women.html
- <u>Woodwind Internet Services</u> -**Designer**
- <u>George Coates Performance Works</u> -**Designer**

Cartoon is better than photo because it adds interest

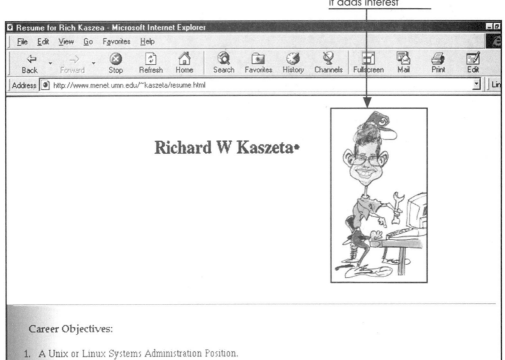

Figure 5-7

An HTML resume with a graphic.

Richard W Kaszeta•

Career Objectives:

1. A Unix or Linux Systems Administration Position.
2. A Mechanical Engineering research position focusing on heat transfer and turbomachinery.
3. A combination of the above.

Available: 1 July 1999

Education:

PhD. in Mechanical Engineering
University of Minnesota, Minneapolis, MN. In Progress.

M.S. in Mechanical Engineering GPA: 4.0
University of Minnesota, Minneapolis, MN. January 1998

B.S. Mechanical Engineering *High Honors*,
Michigan State University, East Lansing, MI. May 1995

Work Experience:

Mechanical Engineering Dept., Univ. of Minn., Minneapolis, MN. 8/95 - present.
Systems Administrator: Assisted in system and network administration of a heterogeneous computer network. Systems include Sun, SGI, Linux, and Windows 95/NT. Responsible for maintaining 25+ Linux Workstations. Other responsibilities include setting up and configuring Unix workstations for all three platforms, configuring NFS and NIS, and providing experimental laboratory support by maintaining IEEE-488 software and hardware. Also responsible for maintaining system security, building and installing software, and providing software and hardware support.

Mechanical Engineering Dept., Univ. of Minn., Minneapolis, MN. 7/96 - Present.
National Science Foundation (NSF) Fellowship: Conducting research on turbulent fluid flow and heat transfer in gas turbine flows (Wake-Induced Turbulent Boundary Layer Transition in Low-Pressure Turbine Blades).

Mechanical Engineering Dept., Univ. of Minn., Minneapolis, MN. 3/96 - 6/96.
Teaching Assistant: Assisted in the teaching of the graduate level course ME 8332: Radiation

Mechanical Engineering Dept., Univ. of Minn., Minneapolis, MN. 8/95 - 7/96.
Graduate Research Assistant: Conducting research on turbulent fluid flow and heat transfer in gas turbine flows (film cooling).

Oak Ridge National Laboratory, High Flux Isotope Reactor, Oak Ridge, TN. 5-8/95, and 5-8/94.
Assistant Systems Administrator and Engineering Intern: Responsibilities included Unix systems administration for Linux and AIX machines, engineering software development, and conducting mechanical analyses of spent fuel storage arrays.

Oak Ridge National Laboratory, High Flux Isotope Reactor, Oak Ridge, TN. 9-12/93.
Engineering Intern: Developed and implemented a x-ray based technique for verifying the thickness of cadmium sheeting in spent-fuel storage shrouds.

Michigan State University, Thermal Engineering Research Laboratory, East Lansing, MI. 9/91-5/95.
Research Assistant: Assisted primary researchers in a variety of thermal engineering projects, including thermal property measurements of live tree tissue, electro-rheological (ER) fluids, R134a refrigerant, and silver-tin solder. Also developed software for interpretation of Mach-Zender interferometry images.

Computer Related Experience:

Operating Systems: Various flavors of Unix including Solaris, SunOS, IRIX, and Linux; and MS-DOS/Windows;

Computer Hardware: Sun, SGI, IBM PC, IEEE-448 devices.

Networks: Ethernet, ATM, TCP/IP, Internet, and Appletalk.

Computer Languages: Perl, C, C++, FORTRAN, [c]sh, HTML, Java, and Pascal.

Personal: Own and administrate a private Unix system in my home. Also a software developer for the Debian Linux Project.

Miscellaneous: TeX/LaTeX, Internet News, Anonymous ftp, WWW, GPIB, Process Control, ssh, PGP/GPG, and other assorted topics.

Heat Transfer Related Experience:

Experimental Methods: Hot Wire Anemometry, Various Flow Visualization Techniques, Thermocouples, and Computer Controlled Data Acquistion.

Graduate Course Work: Courses have focused on heat transfer (conduction, convection, and radation), thermal design, experimental methods, turbulence, fluid dynamics, and computational modelling of fluid flow and heat transfer.

(continues)

(continued)

Notable Web Publications and Tools:

X Window System Terminals: A New Use for Old and Outdated PCs, published in the April 1998 Linux Gazette.

The Crappy Divesite Home Page, a guide to inexpensive diving in lakes, quarries, and rivers. Listed as one of the top 50 scuba-related web sites by Rodale's Scuba Diving Magazine, and featured in the Aqua magazine's series "Diving Across America" (April/May 1998).

VR Chia Head, a Java applet which allows you to interactively "spin" our department's Chia Head. Selected for inclusion on Bonus.Com, the web site for kids.

CoffeeCam, a web page showing the real-time status of our office's coffee maker. Winner of the Editors' Choice Award from Goto.Com.

The ME/AEM Pressure Server, a page which shows both the real-time atmospheric pressure and the last week's pressure history, which is used to support departmental research activities, with interfaces via C, http, telnet, and the unix command line.

Recent Technical Publications:

Kaszeta, R.W., Oke, R.A., Burd, S.W., and Simon, T.W., "Flow Measurements in Film Cooling Flows with Lateral Injection(draft)," ASME Paper 98-GT-54, presented at the 1998 Turbo Expo, Stockholm, Sweden. (also available as postscript).

Burd, S.W., Kaszeta, R.W., and Simon, T.W. "Measurements in Film Cooling Flows: Hole L/D and Turbulence Intensity Effects." ASME Paper 96-WA/HT-7, presented at the 1996 IMECE.

References: Available upon request.

Richard Kaszeta kaszeta@me.umn.edu

Figure 5-8

An HTML resume with each section on a different page.

Animated arrows

Each section title is a link to the section itself

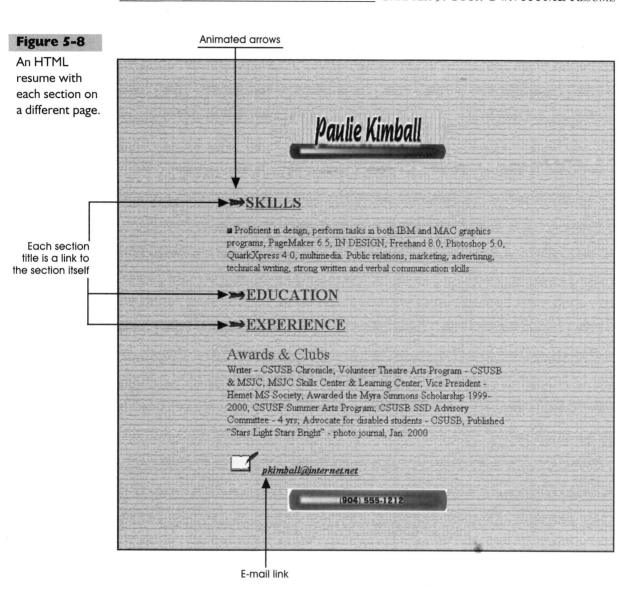

E-mail link

(continues)

(continued)

Skills

- Proficient in design, layout and paste-up, perform tasks in both IBM and MAC graphics programs, PageMaker 6.5, IN DESIGN, Freehand 8.0, Photoshop 5.0, QuarkXpress 4.0, web page authoring, multimedia.

- Public relations, marketing, advertising, technical writing, sales, training, customer service, strong written and verbal communication skills, preparing bids and quotations, safety training.

- Publish newsletters, newspapers, magazines, write training manuals, write news spots for TV and radio.

- Proficient in making negatives, plates and PMT's, folder operation, padding, bindery, stripping, velox, color separations, Challenger cutter, Proficient in the operation of small offset presses, AB Dick 9410, Multi 1250, Multi 1560

Home ■ Education■ Experience ■

pkimball@internet.net ■

(904) 555-1212

Buttons to take readers to other areas

Education

- **Georgia State University ~ Atlanta, Georgia**
Marketing and Management Communications

- **National Staff College ~ Maxwell AFB, Alabama**
Marketing, public relations, verbal and written communications, media relations

- **Palomar College ~ San Marcos, California**
Electronic desktop publishing, advanced desktop publishing and printing

- **ROP ~ San Diego County, California**
Printing and graphics I & II electronic desktop publishing, graphic and commercial art

- **Mt. San Jacinto College**
San Jacinto, California
Computer Science Major ~ Graduate May 1996

- **Calfornia State University San Bernardino**
San Bernardino, California
Major: Communications with a specialty in Graphic Communications

Graduate with a BA June 2000

Home ■ Skills ■ Experience■

pkimball@internet.net ■

(904) 555-1212

Experience

■ 1994-Present ~ Owner PK Publications
685 N. DeAnza Dr. #7A
San Jacinto, CA 92583
Graphic Design, Publishing and Consulting

■ 1990-1994 ~ Oceanside Baptist Church
3208 S. Clementine St.
Oceanside CA 92054
Production Manager- ~ Provide all aspects of design, layout and printing for West Coast Independent Churches. Computer and hand generated design, all pre-press and post press work, all bindery, necessary camera work,pricing, budget, ordering supplies and equipment and supervise others. Marketing and public relations.
Volunteer Position (40+ hr. week)

■ 1966-1992 ~ American Red Cross
various locations
Instructor, trainer, marketing, public relations, advertising, manager of safety services, budgets, newsletters, manuals, books, sales developing courses, purchasing, scheduling.

■Home ■ Skills ■ Education■

■pkimball@internet.net ■

(904) 555-1212

E-mail link   Resume URL

Figure 5-9

An HTML
resume
including links.

jim·ospenson

tel: (300) 602-2000   email: ospoo@loog.com

fax: (300) 604-0005   resume: http://www.termite.org/members/ospo/resume.html

Top | Experience | Education

experience

1999 - present   **Manager, Community Development**, How2.com, Santa Monica, CA / San Jose, CA / Dallas, TX.
Internet startup: business model has evolved from B2C content/ commerce to a B2B application service
provider specializing in Post-Purchase Customer Care.

Manage all aspects of community and user-supplied content. Responsibilities include:

- Design and develop user interface and experience. Refine Community strategy relative to
  How2.com's rapidly evolving business model.
- Work with cross-functional team of managers in Marketing, Art, Editorial, and Networks to guide
  overall site development, consistency, and coordinated programs.
- Plan and implement site administration tools for content management and reporting.
- Program entire Web Crossing Message Board area using WCTL, with extensive look-and-feel
  customization.
- Formulate user policies and terms of service.
- Manage off-site consultants for board moderation.

Examples of work

Message Boards: http://msgbrd.how2hq.com:9876. Consumer Message Boards will transition to
password-protected Business Partner Center, April 2000.

1995 - 1999   **Producer**, 2-Lane Media, Inc., Los Angeles, CA. Interactive communications agency specializing in
entertainment and corporate clients. Wholly acquired by How2.com in March 1999. Website:
http://www.2LM.com (now dark).

Produced a variety of websites and cdroms with responsibilities including:

- Conceptualized projects: translated client business practice, strategic and marketing vision into
  functionality, content, and branding requirements that fit project scope and schedule.
- Synthesized my artistic and technical strengths for successful client interaction and leadership of
  technical and creative teams.
- Effectively managed projects, budgets, schedules. Established systems and methods for on-time
  completion of key project deliverables. Experienced in locating, contracting, and managing off-
  site consultants and free-lancers.
- Conducted Competitive Analyses of websites for functionality, usability, branding, and creative;
  wrote reports for client pitches and presentations.
- Developed documentation and style guides for client site maintenance and expansion, including
  asset specification, process description. Clearly and precisely framed tasks, processes, issues,
  and general concepts. Developed clear and comprehensive Requests For Information and
  Requests For Proposal.
- Code: Expert: Web Crossing Template Language (WCTL). Intermediate knowledge of HTML,
  Javascript, browser compatibilities, Lingo. Familiarity with Unix; TCP/IP and SMTP protocols.

Selected Project Highlights:

Links to projects

- **Pacsun.com**. E-commerce website for teen-oriented clothing retailer. Developed site metaphor of "clothing rack" frame to display merchandise. Drafted clear and usable user flow for checkout, taking into account wish-list, gift certificates, and multiple ship-to functionality. Website: http://www.pacsun.com.
- **Goldenbooks.com.** Website promoting Golden Book's catalog of classic children's books. Specified and documented production processes for client to produce assets for Kid's Club area with daily joke, story, coloring image. Website: http://www.goldenbooks.com (redesigned 1999).
- **VeriFone, Inc.** CD-rom promoting new suite of e-commerce payment services for Hewlett-Packard subsidiary. Programmed Lingo, directed digital video preparation. Website: http://www.verifone.com.
- **Advanced Medical Ventures, Ltd.** Medical cdrom series on Gastrointestinal Motility (seven cdroms in all). Developed information design and production processes for rapid segment completion using client-supplied assets and digital video. Website: http://www.amv.com.

Links to work

1992 - present   **Founding Artist**, Termite Television Collective. Conceptualized unique collage format for this alternative TV series. Structure emphasizes genre-bending, multi-vocal approach to subjects sacred and banal. To date 33 shows have been produced, cablecast and exhibited nationwide, including the Philadelphia Museum of Art and New York's Museum of Modern Art, and through the programming service Free Speech TV. Website: http://www.termite.org.

1992 - 1993   **Video Producer**, CoreStates Financial Corporation (now First Union National Bank), Philadelphia, PA. Staff producer for Corporate Communications Department. Projects included Video CoreStates Review, a quarterly employee newsmagazine; and diverse training projects for internal use by regional superbank. Served variously as producer, director, scriptwriter, editor, director of photography.

1990 - 1992   **Staff Producer**, Temple University Television Services, Philadelphia, PA. Directed and edited monthly half-hour medical talk show *TempleCARE*. Producer/Director for series based on Martin Bernal's book *Black Athena*.

1986 - 1994   **Independent Filmmaker:** creative and technical work on dozens of independent features and documentaries, videos, dance and performance pieces. Roles included Assistant Editor, Assistant Director, Director of Photography, Director and Producer. See detailed resume for selected Filmography.

education

Links to schools

1995   American Film Institute, Los Angeles, CA. Advanced Technology Program. Internship and immersive training in technical and aesthetic aspects of multimedia and digital video.

1990 - 1994   Temple University, Philadelphia, PA. Master of Fine Arts in Film and Media Arts. Specialized in experimental video, documentary filmmaking, and interactive installation.

1981 - 1985   University of Pennsylvania, Philadelphia, PA. Bachelor of Arts in Philosophy of Science and Computer Mathematics.

Figure 5-10

Eric Martin's
HTML resume.

Eric Martin

1414 Armacost Ave #6
Los Angeles, CA 90025
310.479.7147
E-mail: emartin@ix.netcom.com
Personal site: http://www.ericmartinonline.com
View and Print in PDF format

Objectives:
To utilize my experience as a Developer/Programmer/Innovator of web related projects.

Profile:
Extremely strong background in web technology with an emphasis in front-end programming.
Proven skills in a wide range of Internet programming with over 3 years experience at award-winning Internet companies. A strong desire to learn, train, and educate myself on the use of new and established technologies.

Employment History:
April 2000 - Present
Sapient Corp.
Currently working as a Site Developer to build and implement front-end solutions.
http://www.sapient.com

January 1999 - April 2000
How2.com, Inc.
Built and maintained dynamic and evolving web site utilizing HTML, Javascript, CSS, and SSIs.
Assisted backend technical team with e-commerce solutions.
Developed production process specifications and guidelines.
Coordinated with partners/affiliates to meet business needs.
Managed, trained and oversaw production staff to meet tight production deadlines.
Responsible for hiring additional staff.
Worked with Netscape Communications, Inc. programming team to integrate Java-based e-commerce application.
Worked with Screaming Media, Inc. to implement real-time news streaming.
http://www.how2.com

April 1997 - January 1999
2-Lane Media, Inc.
Developed website solutions for clients such as Nestle, Golden Books, Transamerica, and Disney.
Contributed to projects ranging from websites, CD-ROMs, Intranets and Extranets.
Actively involved in brainstorming sessions and project proposals for RFPs.
Developed and implemented QA for CD-ROMs and dynamically built web sites.
Research and documentation for browser compatibility issues, advanced HTML coding techniques, and analyzing information flow and navigation structure.
Maintained assets of company marketing portfolio.
http://www.2-lanemedia.com

Clients list:
http://www.wonka.com WONKA Website (a division of Nestle)
http://www.ta-retirement.com Transamerica Retirement Services
http://www.goldenbooks.com Golden Books
http://www.youngeagles.com EAA Young Eagles

http://www.jumpstart.com Jumpstart Website (Knowledge Adventure)
http://www.microprose.com Microprose
http://www.pacsun.com Pacific Sunwear

1996-1997
Communications Department, CSUSB
Designed and maintained website for use by 300 student department with three person web team. Worked independently to meet production goals delegated by site director including content acquisition, HTML coding and weekly maintenance of time sensitive content. Coordinated page development from multiple sources including faculty, student clubs, and department staff. Note: Site version has changed.

The Getty Information Institute, LA Culture Net
Web Raising Facilitator (June 1998)
Led discussions on HTML programming and web site design.
Worked with participants of all skill levels in such areas as FTP, e-mail, web browser capabilities, HTML and web page design.

Education:
B.A. Communications
California State University San Bernardino

Skills and Abilities:
Hand-code all HTML using Homesite or BBEdit.
Knowledge of basic UNIX commands and server administration.
Use of CGIs and Javascript to process and validate forms.
Use and embedding of Real Player/Media files.
Quicktime Video compression for the web.
Build and maintain client Extranets and company Intranet.
Knowledge and use of Ad server products such as Net Gravity and Doubleclick.
Thorough understanding of website development, design, and navigation structure.

References:
How2.com
Paula Gibb pgibb@ix.netcom.com - Senior Internet Programmer
Kerry Hagan kerry@bluedevil.com - Technical Manager

2-Lane Media
David Lane david@davidslane.com - President, 2-Lane Media

SPECIALTY RESUMES

As electronic resumes have increasingly become the norm for business and industry, the government has also begun to utilize this new approach. When you consider the numbers of applicants for government jobs and the thousands of military personnel who separate or retire from the service and enter the labor market every year, you can see the need to automate some of the process. The same is true for the large numbers of college students who join the workforce annually. In this chapter, we profile the procedure for filing a resume with one branch of the federal government and introduce you to very successful online job services for separating and retiring military personnel and college students. We also discuss the ins and outs of another new concept in specialty resumes: the video resume.

Federal Department of Defense Resumes: The STAIRS Program

In response to the droves of federal applications it receives every year, the Federal Department of Defense (DoD) decided to try to automate the applicant-tracking procedure. The DoD went to Resumix, the company that designs resume-tracking software for private industry (described in chapter 3). The people at Resumix developed Resumix Federal™, a customized version of its image-processing software, just for federal applicants. The DoD integrated the Resumix Federal program into its application procedures, and the result was STAIRS, the Standard Automated Inventory and Referral System now used by the DoD.

Working with Resumix, the DoD developed a system in which applicants could file for jobs online via e-mail, conventional mail, or a Web site resume template that utilizes a scannable-resume format. However, given the reporting responsibilities of the federal government, the system also needed to track other governmental information. Resumix complied and developed a sophisticated system that was responsive to federal agency needs.

In 1995, the first Resumix system was installed at Bangor Naval Submarine Base. The pilot program was so successful that STAIRS has now become the standard throughout the DoD.

Resumix Federal incorporated a program called FormReader™ that "reads" federal forms, including OF-612, the federal job-application form that was in use at the time STAIRS was developed. The same patented artificial intelligence feature that Resumix uses for skills extraction on its commercial software is utilized to pull information from federal forms. A summary containing skills and qualifications is then prepared and put into a searchable database. When a job opening occurs, a list of qualified candidates—consisting of applicants for new hire, promotion, or reassignment—is compiled.

FormReader can also generate reports and handle information that is typically needed by federal agencies. Government applications require certain applicant information not usually requested on private-industry applications, such as veteran preference eligibility, U.S. citizenship status, and the highest civil-service grade held. Applications also include the job announcement number. FormReader can capture all this information.

Because STAIRS has come into wide use throughout the DoD, the old OF-612 and SF-171 forms have been discontinued. What the DoD now uses is a scannable resume. You prepare these resumes using the same rules as we have discussed in previous chapters: typed, with black ink on white paper; no special fonts or enhancements such as boldfacing, underlining, or column formatting; clean copies or original laser prints; and so on. The skills extraction is accomplished in the same way, with a summary in a searchable database from which qualified candidates can be selected in response to a job requisition.

When the federal government generates a job announcement, Resumix Federal enables the government to build a requisition that contains all the requirements. The requisition includes the position description as well as the knowledge, skill, and ability—KSAs in federal parlance—that are needed for the job. When the requisition is entered into the Resumix Federal system, a list of qualified applicants is generated. These applicants match the criteria as specified by the requisition.

Resumix Federal also uses the folder concept. This feature enables users to attach to the resume certain other documents that often accompany a federal job application. For example, veterans are required to furnish a copy of their DD-214, the document that defines their veteran status. Some other appended documents include college transcripts and personnel action forms, which document a federal employee's career progress. With the folder concept, a case record can be built without a bulging paper file.

Human Resource Services Center (HRSC)

The Washington Headquarters Services (WHS) National Capital Region (NCR) Human Resource Services Center (HRSC) is the federal agency that accepts scannable resumes under the STAIRS program (see figure 6-1).

Figure 6-1

The HRSC
home page.

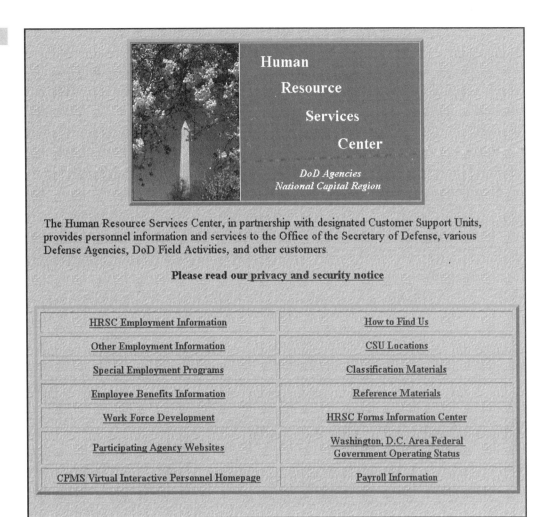

HRSC advises that under this new system, a major difference for federal job applicants is that only one resume is now required for positions at several different locations. Prior to STAIRS, applicants had to file separately for *every* new position in which they were interested. The old SF-171 was a bulky, complicated application form that, when unfolded, was almost three feet long! The automated process is a major time-saver for federal employees and applicants. Another positive outcome of converting to STAIRS is that the process of applicant selection has greater objectivity because the method of skills extraction is uniform and consistent.

HRSC enables applicants to update their resumes when necessary. When STAIRS first became available, this capability was not usable unless candidates had a change in education or skills. Now HRSC permits changes to be made but will process them only on the first working day of each month. HRSC further requires that you submit a cover memorandum explaining your desire to *replace* your current resume on file in STAIRS with your revised resume. Timing is important here. For example, if you filed for a job that closes in the middle of the month and you revised your resume to qualify for the position, the updated resume would not display until the first of the following month; therefore, the new resume would not be used.

Just as with other automated staffing programs, STAIRS is skills based. The scanner reads from top to bottom and extracts up to 80 different skills. HRSC recommends that you list your most important skills first and that you make them as specific and relevant as possible.

For entering your work experience in STAIRS, HRSC suggests that you list only the jobs that pertain to your career goals. However, with recent governmental downsizing, current federal employees may want to enter previous KSAs, too, as space allows. Remember, the old SF-171 is gone and your old work history with it. The Office of Personnel Management (OPM) won't be able to refer to your old SF-171 to determine your prior skills. Entering your prior skills on the new resume may keep you in the mix for reassignment to other jobs in the event of a reduction in force. Remember, however, that you can list only 80 skills, so make every one of them count!

For each job listed, you must include dates, hours, titles, pay (series and grade, if federal employment), the full name and address of the employer, and the supervisor's name and phone number. Besides duties and KSAs, HRSC recommends that you list your accomplishments and specify the programs in which you worked. HRSC also advises that you list the tools and equipment you used, if relevant.

In STAIRS, you should use nouns and verbs to excerpt the most relevant information. When training current federal employees in scannable resume preparation, HRSC suggests that they go over the federal position description (PD) and line out all words *except* nouns and verbs to get the flavor of what to include in their scannable resumes.

STAIRS resumes are limited to three pages. In fact, only the first three pages of longer resumes will be scanned.

On a federal resume, you are required to include your Social Security number (SSN) at the top of the first page along with your contact information. This information ensures that you will be distinguishable from other applicants who may share your name and birth date. The federal government has been using the Social Security number to order records since 1943, under Executive Order 9397. Although providing your Social Security number is voluntary, the NCR HRSC cautions that it cannot process your application without it. You should also put your name at the top of each subsequent page of your resume.

If you are not currently employed by a defense agency served by the HSRC, you are required to submit a supplemental sheet with your resume. On this sheet, you include the vacancy announcement number, your name and SSN, any specialized training and licenses, and awards and other information pertaining to your career goals (language skills, professional affiliations, and so on). If you are a current or former Civil Service employee, you must also include your highest grade held and length of service for each position and your employment status. This information is to be submitted on a separate 8½-×-11–inch sheet of paper. For veterans, you include your preference-points standing and also provide a photocopy of your DD-214.

Submitting Your Federal Resume

You can submit your federal resume in any of the following three ways:

- E-mail it to resume@hrsc.osd.mil.

> **Note**
>
> The word **resume** must be in the subject line; include a string of ten @ symbols immediately before the start of your text; type your resume in the body of your e-mail message or paste in an ASCII version; do *not* send the resume as an attachment. Make sure you have a hard return at the end of each line.

- Upload it at the Web site:

  http://hrsc.psd.whs.pentagon.mil/

- Mail it to:

  Resume
  Washington Headquarters Services
  NCR Human Resource Services Center
  5001 Eisenhower Avenue, Room 2E22
  Alexandria, VA 22333-0001

As of April 1998, HSRC no longer accepts faxed resumes because they are often of poor quality. Before this change in policy, applicants had to be notified individually to resubmit their resumes via conventional mail if the faxed version was of poor quality. In addition, the fax number is no longer viable because it had a tremendous volume of traffic, with some applicants faxing multiple copies of their resumes. (See chapter 4 for a discussion about faxing scannable resumes.)

Online Resume Writer

To simplify the process of preparing a scannable resume, HRSC provides an On-line Resume Writer at its Web site. From the HRSC homepage, click on "submit resume" and you will be taken to the Online Resume Writer. The URL for this page is http://storm.psd.whs.pentagon.mil/cgi-bin/apply.pl?action=PrepRes.

The Online Resume Writer looks similar to other online forms, but it contains some notable exceptions, such as a place for your Social Security number, federal grade, military service information, and merit promotion procedures—all information limited to the federal job-application process. The work-history area has room for six former jobs, and the education area contains blocks for six former schools, more room than you generally find on private-sector resume templates.

Applying for Federal Civilian Jobs

The HRSC also provides detailed instructions for applying for federal civilian jobs: The Civilian Job Kit. Besides resume-preparation instructions, the HRSC Civilian Job Kit also contains a list of do's and don'ts and explains who can apply, how they can apply, and when they can apply. The Job Kit is located at http://www.hrsc.osd.mil/instruct.htm.

Sample Format and Resumes

Let's look at a suggested resume format from the HRSC (see the sample HRSC format on the next page). It shows all the information you need to include on a federal resume.

We'll also examine some sample resumes from the HRSC site (see figures 6-3 through 6-6). You will notice some key differences between these resumes and resumes for private-sector jobs. Each of the federal resumes contains a Social Security number at the top, per HRSC instructions. The job titles contain the pay plan, series, and grade of the positions held. Former supervisors' names and phone numbers are listed. The resumes also specify the lowest grade acceptable to the applicant and the highest grade attained and career status in the federal civil service. Military preference is listed as well. None of this information would ever appear on a resume for a private-sector job. Notice that the federal resumes are text-intensive, containing many keywords and KSAs.

Figure 6-2

Sample HRSC format.

RESUME FORMAT

View sample resumes

NAME: FIRST MIDDLE INITIAL LAST (NOTE: Use <u>all</u> capital letters)
SSN: XXX-XX-XXXX
MAILING ADDRESS: (NOTE: Use <u>all</u> capital letters in address with <u>no</u> punctuation)
STREET, APT NO.:
CITY, STATE ZIP CODE:
HOME TELEPHONE NUMBER:
WORK TELEPHONE NUMBER:
E-MAIL ADDRESS:
VACANCY ANNOUNCEMENT NUMBER:
SUMMARY OF YOUR SKILLS: Include in this portion of your resume a summary of the skills you possess. Describe these skills in one or two words. It is not necessary to list all of your skills. Be sure to emphasize those skills in occupations where you are most interested in employment and those that are relevant to your career.
EXPERIENCE (When Describing Duties Be Sure To Include):
Start and end dates (month and year, be sure to include all four digits in the year, e.g. 2000)
Hours worked per week
Position Title
Pay Plan, Series, Grade (if Federal civilian position) List highest grade held and number of months held at that grade level. If experience describes Federal civilian positions at different grade levels, include month and year promoted.
Employer's name (agency or company name) and mailing address
Supervisor's name and telephone number
All major tasks Be sure to include any systems which you have worked on; software programs or special tools and equipment you have used; and any special programs you have managed.
Any other job related information you wish to include, e.g., licenses/certificates (including date(s) certified and state), awards, language proficiencies, professional associations, etc.
TRAINING/EDUCATION: Give your highest level of education. If degree completed (e.g., AA, BA, MA), list your major field of study, name of college or university, year degree awarded and GPA. If your highest level of education was high school, list either the highest grade you completed; year you graduated; or the date you were awarded your GED. List specialized training pertinent to your career goals.

LIMIT THE ABOVE RESUME INFORMATION TO THREE (3) PAGES
USE 8.5" x 11" WHITE BOND PAPER, PRINTED ON ONE SIDE
****

SUPPLEMENTAL INFORMATION: To Be Submitted by Applicants not Serviced by the HRSC Along with Your Resume

NOTE: Submit the following supplemental information on a separate sheet of 8.5" x 11" white bond paper, printed on one side. **If the information does <u>not</u> apply to you, please respond with "N/A"**. At the top of the page, repeat your <u>Name</u> and <u>Social Security Number</u> for identification purposes.

1. **CURRENT/FORMER FEDERAL CIVILIAN EMPLOYEES:**

(A)   List highest grade held and number of months held at that grade level.

(continues)

(continued)

(B)   Provide employment status (i.e., career, career-conditional, temporary, indefinite).

(C)   Position occupied: Competitive Service; Excepted Service

2. **MILITARY SERVICE AND VETERANS' PREFERENCE:**

Provide photocopies of all DD-214(s) (Member–4 Copy). In addition, if claiming a compensable disability or other 10 point veteran's preference you must provide an "Application for 10 point Veterans' Preference (SF-15)" and supporting documentation listed on the reverse of the SF-15. Answer **all** of the following questions:

(A)   Discharged from the military service under honorable conditions: No _____ Yes _____ (List dates and branch for all active duty military service.)

(B)   If all your active military duty was after October 14, 1976, list the full names and dates of all campaign badges or expeditionary medals you received or were entitled to receive.

(C)   Retired Military: No _____ Yes _____, Rank at which Retired _____, Date of Retirement _____

(D)   If claiming Veterans' Preference, indicate eligibility: 5 Point; 10 Point/Compensable; 10 Point/Other; 10 Point/Disability; or 10 Point/Compensably Disabled, 30% or more.

If you are claiming 10 Point Preference, you are required to provide documentation at the time of application to verify eligibility. If you are sending your resume or self-nomination via electronic means, you must mail in required documentation separately. Be sure to include the vacancy announcement number you are applying for. REMEMBER MAIL COPIES – NOT ORIGINALS.

Figure 6-3

Sample resume for a maintenance worker.

RICHARD P. JONES
SSN: XXX-XX-XXXX
3456 GENERIC STREET
POTOMAC MD 88888
Home Telephone No: (301) 000-0000
Work Telephone No: (301) 123-4567
E-Mail address: none
Vacancy Announcement Number: XXXX
SUMMARY OF SKILLS:
Rigger, Maintenance Mechanic (carpentry, electrical, plumbing, painting). Work leader. Read schematic diagrams. Flooring: wood, linoleum, carpet. Electrical: switches and plugs, basic wiring. Plumbing: faucets, pipes, fixtures and fire sprinklers. Operate cranes and forklifts. Work planner and inspector.
EXPERIENCE:
Nine years experience in the trades - apprentice to work leader.
July 1996 to March 1997; 40 hours per week; Maintenance Mechanic Leader WL-4749-10; Smithsonian Institute, 1111 Mall Ave., Washington DC, 12345; Supervisor: J. McGuire (202) 123-4567
Lead 9 employees working in all trades including: plumbing, painting, electrical (facilities), carpentry. Prioritize work, make assignments through oral instruction and sketches and assigning tools. Inspect and approve work or direct re-work. Tracked hours spent on each job and input into DBASE tracking system. In supervisor's absence, approve leave, maintain overtime log, counsel and take disciplinary action. Ensure all work done in accordance with Museum and OSHA safety requirements.
May 1992 to June 1996; 40 hours per week; Rigger/Maintenance Mechanic, WG-5210-10 (promoted 9/94); Smithsonian Institute, 1111 Mall Ave., Washington DC 12345; Supervisor: L. S. Walker, (202) 123-0987
Used forklifts, cranes, skids and rollers to safely move priceless museum exhibits. Assisted other trades in carpentry, plumbing, painting, and electrical work. Installed door alarms. Prepared all kinds of surfaces for work. Laid linoleum and carpet. Repaired wood floors, carpet and furniture. Installed door alarms. Wired switches and repaired plugs. Replaced piping, faucets and fixtures in plumbing.
March 1988-April 1992; 40 hours per week; Rigger Apprentice, WT-5210-8; Portsmouth Naval Shipyard, Portsmouth, NH 98765; Supervisor: S. Barnett, (207) 456-7890
Lifted, moved and positioned heavy objects and loads (machines and large structural parts.) Selected equipment. Estimated sizes, weights and equipment capacities. Ensured safety. Used cranes, chainfalls, skids, rollers, jacks, forklifts to move all types of ship equipment. Qualified signalman for cranes.
TRAINING/EDUCATION:
HS graduate - 1987; Residential Electricity, Drywall, Refrigeration and A/C, Regulated Waste Disposal, Certificate; Certificate in Industrial Blueprints

---

RICHARD P. JONES
SSN: XXX-XX-XXXX
1. Highest Grade Held: WL-10; 8 months
   Federal Employment Status: Career
   Position Occupied: Competitive Service
2. Military Service/Veterans' Preference: N/A

Figure 6-4

Sample resume
for an engineer.

JANE E. SMITH
SSN: XXX-XX-XXXX
11712 MAIN STREET
ANYTOWN VA 88888
Home Telephone No.: (703) 111-1111
Work Telephone No.: (703) 123-4567
E-mail Address: xxxx@xxxx.xxx.xx
Vacancy Announcement Number: XXXX
SUMMARY OF SKILLS:
Mechanical Engineering; aerospace engineering; Spacecraft; AHIP Helicopter; Symbolic
Manipulation Program; IBM 3090; VAX; FORTRAN; NASTRAN; UNIX; DOS; Department of
Defense Top Secret clearance. Extensive experience in the disciplines of structural and simulation
dynamics, structures, aerospace engineering, mechanical engineering, and software application
and development. Demonstrated ability to apply these methodologies to analyze, evaluate, and
incorporate design changes to fixed and mobile structures, vehicles, and other environments.
EXPERIENCE:
May 1991 to present; 40 hours per week; Staff Engineer, GS-0801-14; promoted to GS-14 July
1994; Imaginary Agency, 123 West Image Dr., Arlington, VA 88888; Supervisor: John Doe,
(703) 123-4567.
Developed detailed comprehensive element structural models for dynamic and stress analysis
with particular expertise to model and evaluate integrated spacecraft and mechanical systems.
Designed theoretical model and software for dynamic and aeroelastic response of coupled, rotor-
airframe helicopters in high speed forward flight. Participated in vibration test requirements and
data reduction for AHIP and YAH-64 helicopters.
September 1989 to April 1991; 40 hours per week; Staff Engineer; $XX,XXX per year; Any
Aircraft Corporation, Anytown, MD 22222; Supervisor: Amy Jones, (410) 111-2222.
Project leader for major projects under the Symbolic Manipulation Program (SMP). Conducted
time simulation studies of complex multibody systems. Applied SMP for developing dynamic
equations of motion of multibody systems. Programming and computer experience includes
developing software on IBM 3090 mainframe, VAX, and PC computers using FORTRAN,
NASTRAN DMAP, BASIC, and C languages under DOS and UNIX operating systems.
Membership in the Society of Women Engineers: Chair, Annual Meeting, 1994. American
Society of Mechanical Engineers: Chair, membership Committee, 1991-92.
EDUCATION:
Doctorate in Aeronautical Engineering, University of California at Los Angeles, 1989.
Master of Science in Mechanical Engineering, University of Virginia, 1986, GPA 3.5.
Bachelor of Science in Mechanical Engineering, Summa Cum Laude, University of Maryland,
1984, GPA 3.5.

JANE E. SMITH
SSN: XXX-XX-XXXX
   1. High Grade Held: GS-14, 3 years
       Federal Employment Status: Career
       Position Occupied: Competitive Service
   2. Military Service/Veterans' Preference: N/A

SHERRI M. LEVAN
SSN: XXX-XX-XXXX

7890 LAWFUL AVE Apt 123
WASHINGTON DC 99999
Home Telephone No: (202) 111-1111
Work Telephone No: (202) 222-2222
E-Mail address: levans@personal.access.com
Vacancy Announcement Number: XXXX
SUMMARY OF SKILLS:
US Air Force and Defense Protective Services; keep law and order; arrest and interviewing
techniques; experience in high crime areas; foot and vehicular control; weapons and munitions
qualified; SWAT qualified; undercover experience; report writing; training officer; weapons
supply officer; access control; Excel, WordPerfect and Dbase proficiency.
EXPERIENCE:
May 1993 to present; 50 hours per week; Police Officer, GS-083-6; Defense Protective Services,
Washington Headquarters Services, 1234 Defense, Washington DC, 11119; Supervisor: Joan
Doe, (703) 111-2222
Preserved law and order by enforcing laws and regulations on a daily basis. Maintained security
by foot and vehicular patrol. Controlled potentially violent and disruptive situations with tact and
professionalism. Controlled access to highly sensitive areas. Trained and drilled in counter
terrorism practices. Maintained qualifications and proficiency in weapons use. Investigated
crimes. Performed undercover assignments. Wrote reports and testified in court as necessary.
Supply Officer for weapons, ammunition and munitions.
October 1989 to April 1993; 60 hours per week; Police Officer, Gustine Police Department, 3456
Main Street, Gustine, WI 09876; Supervisor: Lt. D. Goode, (555) 555-5555
Enforced felony and misdemeanor laws of Wisconsin. Apprehended, detained, arrested and
interviewed suspects and witnesses; prepared and processed reports; maintained fitness and
weapons qualifications.
July 1985-February 1989; 45 hours/week; Training Sergeant, E-6; promoted August 1985;
Aviano Security Unit, PO Box 111, FPO NY 22222; Supervisor: 1st Lt. J. Guy, DSN 111-2222.
Scheduled training and maintained training records for all law enforcement personnel assigned to
the Unit. Scheduled and operated weapons ranges and fitness tests. Trained incoming personnel,
react teams, perimeter guards on security and protection procedures and techniques.
TRAINING/EDUCATION:
AA Criminal Justice, Central Illinois University, May 1988, GPA 3.0
Certified in Biological and Chemical Anti-Terrorism Techniques

SHERRI M. LEVAN
SSN: XXX-XX-XXXX
1. Highest Grade Held: GS-06; 2 years, 3 months
   Federal Employment Status: Career status
   Position Occupied: Excepted Service (VRA)
2. Military Service/Veterans' Preference:
   Honorable Discharge (July 1985-Feb 1989, USA)
   Campaign badges/expeditionary medals: N/A
   Retired military: No
   Veterans' Preference: N/A

Figure 6-6

Sample resume
for an external
secretarial
applicant.

JOHN Q. DOE
SSN: XXX-XX-XXXX

555 WEST CAPITAL STREET
WASHINGTON D.C. 99999
Home Telephone No.: (111) 111-1111
Work Telephone No.: (111) 111-1112
E-Mail Address: xxxx@xxxx.xxx.xx
Vacancy Announcement Number: XXXX
SUMMARY OF SKILLS:
Secretary, receptionist, typing (40 WPM), stenography (80 WPM), word-processing,
file management, records management, editing, proofreading, office management,
PowerPoint software, customer service.
EXPERIENCE:
Three years, progressively responsible work in office management.
January 1995 to present; 40 hours per week; Secretary (OA), GS-0318-07, promoted to
GS-07 August 1995; Imaginary Agency, 123 West Image Dr., Arlington, VA 88888;
Supervisor: Fred Smith, (703) 123-4567.
Perform various secretarial duties to manage the administrative functions of the office.
Type correspondence, take and transcribe dictation, answer telephone calls and greet
visitors, create and maintain office filing system, coordinate conferences and meetings,
make travel arrangements. Read all incoming correspondence, determine proper action,
and occasionally prepare response before referring to supervisor. Explain non-technical
policies and procedures promulgated by the supervisor. Make recommendations on
administrative matters. Use suite of business software (OfficePRO, WordPRO, and
PointPRO) to prepare briefing charts, graphs, and text documents. Maintain supervisor's
calendar and schedule meetings.
February 1993 to December 1994; 40 hours per week; Receptionist; $22,000 per year;
Jay's Lumber Company, 123 East Tree Dr., Bethesda, MD 77777; Jay Smith, (301) 123-
4567.
Answered the telephone and greeted customers at the receptionist desk. Directed
customers to the appropriate office. Heard, resolved, or referred customer complaints.
Received all incoming and outgoing mail and routed items directly to the appropriate
office for actions. Made travel arrangements for supervisor and staff. Provided advice to
clerical personnel in subordinate branches concerning such matters as time and leave
procedures, travel vouchers, and reporting and correspondence procedures. Organized
and maintained files and records, manuals, handbooks, and other related materials.
Typed correspondence and other items.
EDUCATION:
AA, Business Management, Texas State University, 1993, Austin, Texas; GPA 3.2

JOHN Q. DOE
SSN: XXX-XX-XXXX
1. GS-07; 2 years, 11 months
   Federal Employment Status: Temporary Appointment
   Position Occupied: Excepted Service
2. Military Service/Veterans' Preference: N/A

Before sending your resume, verify that you have prepared it in accordance with HRSC instructions. You will be notified of receipt within two weeks.

Caution

HRSC warns that unscannable resumes will be destroyed!

Military Resumes: Transition Assistance Online (TAOnline)

Military personnel who separate or retire from the service face a host of problems in their transition back to civilian employment. Many of these people haven't experienced life outside the military environment for a long time, and many have never experienced civilian employment at all. They will discover quickly that the two worlds are vastly different. Behavior, etiquette, structure, and even language differ sharply between the two cultures: In private industry, a leader *manages;* in military service, a leader *commands.* And subordinates in a bank are not likely to salute a passing executive! These illustrations point up some of the challenges facing former military personnel as they re-enter private life. They often need special help in making this daunting transition.

Among the resume sites we explored, we came across an online service called Transition Assistance Online, or TAOnline (www.taonline.com), which is just for transitioning military job seekers, although it makes clear that veterans, retirees, reservists, and family members of all are welcome also. In fact, because of its unique resources for those with security clearances and government contracting experience, it has become very popular with individuals leaving the federal government for civilian careers as well.

TAOnline, which was launched in January 1997, was founded jointly by a company called Digital interWorks, Inc. (DI-USA, Inc.), and the Army Times Publishing Company. Digital interWorks, Inc., is a successful software publishing company that was started by military veterans Richard Scott Rodriguez and Rocky Gillette along with Bob Lindsey, a non-veteran. Bob Lindsey, vice president and CFO of Digital interWorks, explains the unusual history of the company:

> Digital interWorks is primarily a software Internet company. It was founded in Florida by three partners, two of whom are reserve military officers. It began as Divers International-USA, Inc., with a subsidiary division in Cozumel, Mexico called Divers International-Mexico, S.A. The president is Scott Rodriguez; the vice president is G. Roderick (Rocky) Gillette. The company was originally formed to provide scuba and snorkeling tours to cruise-ship passengers visiting the Mexican island of Cozumel.

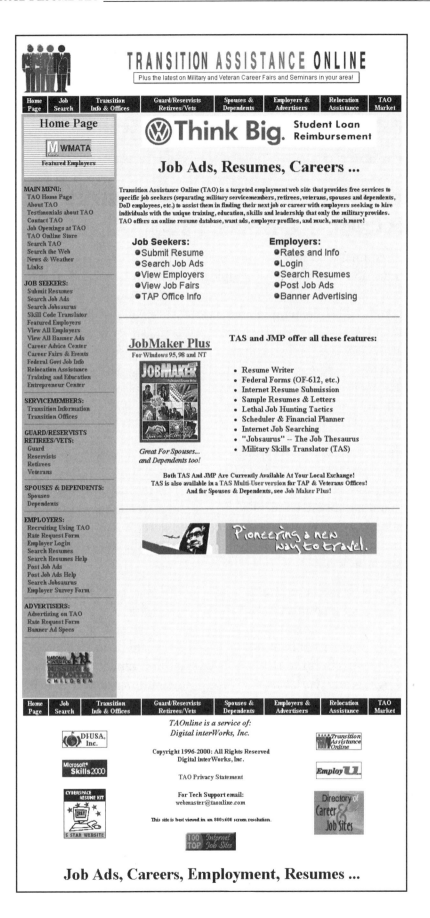

Figure 6-7

The Transition
Assistance
Online home
page.

The company received many resumes from veterans seeking employment because times were tougher economically then. The resumes were not of the highest quality, nor did they portray the finest qualities of the "best of the best"—men and women who were disciplined, dependable, educated, and well trained. These individuals were quite accomplished but never had the need to write a resume in the military. The idea of a resume writer designed for transitioning military took shape, and so an idea was born—Transition Assistance Software (TAS)—to help these fellow veterans seeking employment in the civilian job market. Subsequently, an Internet resume bank for the military was conceived from these resumes.

In early 1996, Digital interWorks set up its first Web site at **www. di-usa.com** to promote its TAS software. In late 1996, Rocky Gillette, recognizing the growing importance of the Internet and the World Wide Web as a job seeking and hiring tool, developed a partnership with the Army Times Publishing Company (ATPCO) to produce Transition Assistance Online (TAO). TAOnline, at **www.taonline.com**, was launched in January 1997 and has been growing ever since. As of June, 2000, the number of hits logged at TAOnline has regularly exceeded one million per month, with close to 20,000 unique visitors in a one-month period.

TAO offers separating service members, veterans, spouses, dependents, and DoD federal civilian employees advice on their second careers in the Transition Information Center (www.taonline.com/ticpages/ticindex.asp). Users can submit their resumes to a password-protected resume database, which means that only employers who have registered with TAOnline can view their resumes. Separating military can also seek relocation assistance, career-fair information, continuing education advice, and so on. Chris Gillette, VP for Marketing and Business Development at Digital interWorks adds:

> Servicemembers, veterans, reservists, retirees, and their family members can search thousands of jobs posted by hundreds of employers that have signed up with TAO. Employers, including Airborne Express, ACS Defense, Boeing, ENRON, General Dynamics, General Motors, Litton PRC, MCI WorldCom, Manpower, Raytheon, Wang, and so on, have signed up to post nationwide job openings, search the resume database, and advertise. Many also offer special recruiting and/or training programs designed specifically for transitioning military personnel and individuals with military experience and backgrounds.

TAS Software

TAS 3.5 software is sold at military exchanges worldwide and is available online at http://www.di-usa.com/.

Figure 6-8

The TAS
software site.

DI-USA.com Transition Assistance Softw

| HOME | PRODUCTS | UPDATES | JOB TIPS |
| JOB LINKS | SUPPORT | CEO Message | CONTACT US |

Transition Assistance Software Version 3.5

**TAS Version 3.5!! (32 Bit)
"Designed by Veterans for Veterans"**

**This comprehensive software package guides
you step - by - step in translating your military
skills and experience into a resume that will get
you the job you want.**

Customer Reviews

- A Resume Writer plus a whole lot more!
- Information database "creates" your Resume for you.
- Chronological, Functional & Federal Resume Formats.
- Federal Forms: OF-612, OF-306, SF-15.
- Military to Civilian Skills Translator.
- Sample Military Resumes, Cover and Post-Interview Letters.
- Online access to Internet job banks and employers
- Ability to post your Resume to *Taonline* and other Internet resume databases.
- Includes an Organizer, Scheduler, Address Book, and Financial Planner.
- Lethal Job Hunting Tactics guide!
- Year 2000 capable.

System Requirements:
- Intel-based PC or compatible
- Microsoft Windows 95, NT or 98.
- Hard Disk with 8-10 MB's of space available
- 1 MB of RAM memory
- High Density 3.5" drive or 2x CD-ROM drive

CD Price ($US)	Download Price ($US)
$31.75	$25.50

ORDER NOW !

Multi-User Version Available

| Home | Products | Updates | Job Tips | Job Links | Support | CEO Message | Contact Us |

© 2000 DI-USA, Inc. All Rights Reserved

The software's name originated with the Transition Assistance Program (TAP) offices that were springing up on bases around the country as a result of the massive "drawdowns" taking place in the U.S. military at that time.

We reviewed the software and found TAS to be an excellent resource, not only for transitioning military personnel, but for any job seeker. TAS is easy to use and logically organized. It contains sample resume and cover-letter formats and a Job Search Organizer to help keep the whole process on track. A financial planner is included in the package to assist with the economic aspects of looking for work. The "Lethal Job Hunting Guide" provides tips and advice for tackling the sometimes-overwhelming task of finding and keeping a job.

In addition, the software can print federal application forms, such as SF-171 and OF-612, as well as the Veterans' Preference form, SF-15, to assist separating U.S. military servicemembers and veterans seeking civilian and federal employment.

You can purchase TAS 3.5 on CD-ROM in all U.S. military base exchanges around the world or from the Digital interWorks Web site, at the following address:

> www.di-usa.com

In addition to TAS software, Chris Gillette told us about a new resume writer software they are producing called JobMakerPlus (JMP).

> JMP is a "civilianized" version of our TAS resume writer software and is especially useful to the spouses and family members of military personnel who are in need of a professional resume-writing package that still addresses the unique needs and backgrounds of the wives, husbands, and new-to-the-job-hunt children of servicemembers.

MOS/Military Skills Translator

Of tremendous help to veterans is the MOS/Military Skills Translator included in the TAS software package. MOS stands for Military Occupation Series. MOS is the job title given to jobs in the armed forces. When veterans leave the service and enter the civilian labor market, they need to know what their military jobs are called in civilian terms. Sometimes the translation is fairly obvious. For example, MOS titles often contain the word *specialist,* a term not often used in civilian parlance; therefore, an administrative support specialist in MOS terms becomes an administrative clerk, a clerk typist, or a clerk general when translated into civilian terms.

Your DD-214 automatically converts your MOS to an occupational code—which is taken from the federal *Dictionary of Occupational Titles (DOT)*—that translates into a civilian job title. The *DOT* is available online in sections that go through the alphabet, as shown in the following three addresses:

http://www.immigration-usa.com/dot_a1.html

http://www.immigration-usa.com/dot_b1.html

http://www.immigration-usa.com/dot_c1.html

The letter of the alphabet preceding the *1* in the address is the letter that starts your section. For example, **a1.html** brings up the section containing codes for the titles Abalone Diver to Acupuncturist and more; **b1.html** brings up the section containing codes for Boat Builder, Budget Clerk, and Bricklayer; at **c1.html**, you may find codes for CPA, Carpenter, and so on.

Help from an LVER

You can also contact any State Employment Service office for help in translating your MOS. In each of these offices nationwide, you will find a Local Veteran's Employment Representative (LVER), whose job is to assist veterans with employment. Al Harris is an LVER in the San Bernardino office of the State of California Employment Development Department. He does job development and placement with area veterans and assists them with other veterans' services. Harris says:

> Your Local Veteran's Employment Representative will help you find training, benefit information, and local job market information. The representative can also assist you in translating your military occupational specialty into civilian terms. Military job titles can be confusing to people in the private sector, so the representative helps vets with this first step in transitioning into the civilian labor market.

Resumes on TAOnline

According to TAOnline, some 200,000 armed-forces personnel will transition out of military service each year, so it's no wonder they receive so much attention. The site is a comprehensive resource that contains not only job postings, but also company profiles and tips on resume writing and job hunting. TAOnline also accepts resumes from the dependents and spouses of military veterans.

Job seekers are not charged for posting resumes. You follow the guidelines for creating a scannable resume (see chapter 3) and then save it in ASCII text, the required format for resumes at TAOnline. You can transmit your resume by sending it via e-mail or conventional mail, by completing the template form at the Web site, or by using the TAS software found at practically all base exchanges worldwide.

Your resume is put in a database that is searchable by more than 200 employers who subscribe to TAOnline. Chris Gillette, VP for Marketing and Business Development at Digital interWorks explains:

> Employers are able, for a minimal fee, to search the TAO resume bank. TAO has developed the most extensive and current transitioning military resume database available on the Internet due to several factors. We have become an online employment resource of choice for many of the Transition Assistance Program offices throughout the Department of Defense system. We have also developed relationships with the largest military-affiliated organizations and associations in the country, paramount among them the Non-Commissioned Officers Association (NCOA). The NCOA has made us their official national resume database for the resumes they collect at their Nationwide Military Job Fairs. In addition, our TAS resume writer is the best-selling software of its kind sold in the Military Exchange System worldwide, which results in a large number of effectively formatted resumes being regularly received into our system.

To search for resumes, employers enter their login ID and password and then select whether to search the TAOnline resume database, the partial Defense Outplacement Referral System (DORS) resume database, the NCOA resumes, or all databases. Employers then choose whether to conduct a "simple" keyword or "advanced" multi-field search. The employers enter the word(s) and/or field(s) of their query and start the search.

The results of the search are displayed in groups of 15 or less. The employer then clicks on the Displayed Contact Information option for each responsive resume to view it or print it.

Resumes are retained in the TAOnline system for 90 days. If you want to renew your resume posting after 90 days, simply resubmit the resume.

Sample Resumes Created with TAS

Now let's look at some sample resumes taken from the Transition Assistance Software.

Figure 6-9

A sample TAS resume for Roy Taylor, an applicant with a Top Secret clearance.

ROY TAYLOR
2111 HIGHTOWER STREET #2B
HUNTSVILLE, ALABAMA 35801
(205) 456-2578
e-mail: sam@abcom.net

OBJECTIVE:
A career position in systems analysis and design.

PROFESSIONAL PROFILE:
Eight years of specialized experience in operations research, systems analysis and nuclear logistics. Proven experience in systems management and concept design. TOP SECRET CLEARANCE.

EDUCATION:
Master of Quantitative Analysis, 1994
Massachusetts Institute of Technology.

Bachelor of Science, Operations Research, 1984
United States Military Academy.

PROFESSIONAL EXPERIENCE:
September 1992 - Present Operations Research Analyst, Dept. of Defense
Responsible for quantitative analysis and simulation modeling of missile logistics systems. Manager of an automation program within the directorate. Developed courses in new missile distribution concept that resulted in a savings of $700,000.

July 1989 - June 1992 Evaluation Team Chief, US Army
Supervised a 7-man nuclear inspection team. Evaluated all nuclear units in three European countries. Developed and administered a budget of $430,000. Published a quarterly evaluation newsletter. Successfully presented community (politically sensitive) deficiencies to senior NATO officers.

January 1986 - June 1989 Emergency Operations Officer, US Army
Directed a four-man team responsible for executing presidential orders for nuclear weapons in central Europe. Commanded and controlled nuclear weapons during emergency situations. Initiated communication procedures that greatly increased security of unit.

11/01/84 - 12/31/86 Executive Officer, US Army
Second-in-command of a 170-man Ordnance Company. Responsible for maintenance and security of several nuclear storage sites. Supervised 5 officers and 30 soldiers. Received "No Deficiency" inspection ratings (highest) from Defense Nuclear Agency.

July 1983 - October 1984 Platoon Leader, US Army
Directly supervised 34 soldiers. Maintained and accounted for 36 vehicles and $300,000 of equipment. Designed a cross-training program which tripled the manpower available for a sensitive communication project.

Availability Date: 08/01/97

References available upon request.

Figure 6-10

A sample TAS resume for Barry Abshire, a retired military applicant.

BARRY W. ABSHIRE
1711 THIRD AVENUE
NEW YORK, NEW YORK 10128
(212)761-1123

OBJECTIVE: A career in international sales and marketing.

EDUCATION:
Candidate for M.B.A. in Marketing, 1998,
Harvard Business School, Cambridge, Massachusetts.

B.S. in Aerospace Engineering, 1991,
U.S. Military Academy, West Point, New York.

Additional Military Schooling:
- US Army Parachute School - US Army Pathfinder School
- US Army Basic Infantry Officer - US Army Ranger School

PROFESSIONAL EXPERIENCE:

July 1996 - August 1996 MARKETING REPRESENTATIVE, DACOR.
Summer Internship. Traveled throughout Caribbean, set-up three new dealerships, established 10 joint marketing and advertising projects, trained dealers and sold $150,000 worth of SCUBA equipment. Won 1996 Summer Internship Achievement Award.

January 1985 - June 1996 LOGISTICS OFFICER, U.S. ARMY
Manager of supplies, ammunition, and maintenance for a 400 man unit. Controlled a budget of $1.5 million.

July 1993 - December 1995 COMPANY EXECUTIVE OFFICER, U.S. ARMY. Second-in-command of an Infantry Company. Responsible for logistics and administration. Passed all Inspector General inspections. Accounted for $2 million of government equipment.

January 1992 - June 1993 RIFLE PLATOON LEADER, U.S. ARMY. Leader of a 41-man light-infantry platoon. Managed training and welfare of the unit. Platoon was ranked number one out of 16 platoons. Accounted for $300,000 in equipment.

ACTIVITIES:
American Marketing Society, President, Harvard Business School
Cambridge SCUBA Diving Club, Officer
U.S. Army Reserves, Captain

Secret Clearance

Figure 6-11

A sample TAS resume for Steven K. Higgins, an active military applicant.

STEVEN K. HIGGINS
487 Cypress Drive
Rialto, California 52576
(714) 971-9773

CAREER OBJECTIVE:
A leadership and managerial position in the communications field, focusing on the areas of public, media and community relations. Especially interested in environmental affairs and issues.

EXPERIENCE: Major, United States Army.

01/01/93 - Present
Public Affairs Officer, U.S. Army
Handled public affairs maters for 7th Infantry Division of 14,000 men. Planned and coordinated the military and civilian -news media coverage, including Operation Desert Storm. Supervised and coordinated public relations for exercises and operations in the Philippines, Turkey and Honduras. Drafted news releases and stories, conducted press briefing and interviews, and supervised military photojournalists. Developed and implemented a new media training program. Worked with all major national and international print and telecommunication news agencies.

06/16/86 - 05/31/88
Company Commander, U.S. Army
Responsible for 160 soldiers assigned to a headquarters company. Established a training and evaluation program for the company's men and women working in more than a dozen different-job specialties. The program resulted in a 100% pass rate in occupational skills testing. Controlled and accounted for equipment worth more than $3 million.

05/16/84 - 06/15/86
Executive Officer, U.S. Army
Supervised 25 personnel charged with the supply storage and security of weapons, ammunition, vehicles, fuel equipment at an Army training center. Accountable for $6.3 million in supplies.

02/01/83 - 05/15/84
Training Officer, U.S. Army
Directed the training of 460 basic training personnel. Planned and executed all instructional activities during a rigorous 8 week course. Successfully graduated over 5,000 trainees.

10/01/78 - 11/31/80 Platoon Leader, U.S. Army
Gained extensive leadership and management experience. Supervised 41 personnel and managed nearly $1 million in equipment and assets.

EDUCATION:
Master of Public Administration, 1982, University of Colorado.
Bachelor of Science, Civil Engineering, 1978, University of Texas.
Public Affairs Officer Course, 1988, Defense Information School.

References available upon request.

Figure 6-12

A sample TAS resume for Ravi Mullens, a recently separated applicant.

RAVI L. MULLENS
3251 RHINO DRIVE
KINGPORT, TENNESSEE 37663
(615) 727-1998

OBJECTIVE:
A technical career position in the electronics industry.

PROFESSIONAL PROFILE:
3/93-7/96 PETTY OFFICER FIRST CLASS, US NAVY
Missile Technician Nuclear Submarine, Kings Bay, Georgia
Supervised, operated and performed maintenance on submarine weapon systems
Responsible for maintaining electrical circuitry of system, performed complex repairs
and tests of circuitry. Maintained a 93% operational rate of all electronic weapon systems
during three 6 month deployments.

6/94-1/93 PETTY OFFICER SECOND CLASS, US NAVY
Missile Maintenance Technician, Groton, Connecticut
Performed intermediate level maintenance on electric/hydraulic powered missile
launching systems and equipment. Conducted firing and tests of missile system weekly.
Installed explosive components in missiles and operated handling equipment to transport
missiles. Tested and repaired electric circuitry and magnetic amplifier.

3/82-6/84 PETTY OFFICER THIRD CLASS, US NAVY
Torpedoman's Mate, Nuclear Submarine, Kings Bay, Georgia
Conducted maintenance on torpedoes and anti-submarine rockets. Operated and
maintained firing systems, electrical system and test equipment. Qualified as shipboard
safety inspector and cruise -missile technician.

EDUCATION:
Graduated Naval Torpedo, Electrician and various Electronic Technical Schools.

Graduated Hollywood High School, 1982, Hollywood, California.

INTERESTS:
Computers, swimming and golf.

Top Secret Clearance

References available upon request.

EDDIE MORTON
2131 KING GEORGE DRIVE
DALLAS, TEXAS 23452
(214) 871-5732

OBJECTIVE:
A position as a Law Enforcement Officer.

PROFESSIONAL PROFILE:
- Armed Forces Police Training Instructor
- Traffic Accident Investigator
- Small Arms Instructor
- Game Warden

RELATED EXPERIENCE:
- Six years of military police experience.
- Performed criminal investigations for one year.
- Conducted physical security assessments of Naval ports.
- Instructed security forces in small arms training for two years.
- Auto theft investigator for one year

EMPLOYMENT HISTORY:
January 1993 - Present Master at Arms Norfolk Navy Base, Norfolk, Virginia
October 1991 - January 1993 Police Officer Naval Air Station, Key West, Florida

EDUCATION:
Military Police and Shore Patrol Training Courses and Schools.
Graduated Fort Hunt High School, 3.4 GPA, 1984, Fairfax, Virginia

INTERESTS:
Computers, auto repair and karate (black belt).

References available upon request.

CURRENTLY AVAILABLE FOR EMPLOYMENT

Figure 6-13

A sample TAS resume for Eddie Morton, an active military applicant.

Figure 6-14

A sample TAS resume for Gus Ortiz, showing all qualifying experience as military experience.

GUS S. ORTIZ
8266 49th STREET #765
MIAMI, FLORIDA 33166
305-598-1864

OBJECTIVE: An aircraft-mechanic position in the civil aviation industry.

LICENSE:
Airframe and Powerplant License Number A&P 598-68-3454.

EDUCATION:
USAF Basic Jet Aircraft Mechanic Course.
USAF Aircraft Technician Course.
USAF C- 1 30 Airplane General Course.
USAF Flight Control Rigging Course.
USAF Canopy Rigging Course.
Graduated Groveton High School, Alexandria, Virginia.

PROFESSIONAL EXPERIENCE:
- Maintenance and Shop Work on Powerplants.
- Engine Shop Services Q.E.C.
- Trouble Shooting.
- Mounting and Dismounting of Engines.
- Reversers.
- Removal and Installation of Flight Controls & Major Components.
- Rigging Canopies.
- Wheels and Brakes.
- Structural Repairs.
- Sheet Metal Work.
- Interior Conversion.
- Line Maintenance.
- C Checks and D Checks.

EXPERIENCED WITH: C-130, Boeing 707s and 737s; Douglas DC8s, DC9s and DC10s

EMPLOYMENT HISTORY:
04/10/90-03/14/92 AIRCRAFT MECHANIC, IAL, Miami, Florida.
07/24/81-02/28/89 AIRCRAFT MECHANIC, USAF, Homestead AFB, Florida.

PERSONAL:
Fluent Spanish and English.

Top Secret clearance
Available for employment immediately

College Graduates and Recent Alumni: College Grad Job Hunter and JobDirect.com

Many sites on the Internet contain information of interest to college students. You can find advice on careers, college majors, schools, universities, and financial aid;

you can locate alumni associations; you can even take virtual tours of college campuses. However, many people access college Internet sites simply to use their placement services. We looked at two college sites in particular: College Grad Job Hunter and JobDirect.com.

College Grad Job Hunter

`http://www.collegegrad.com`

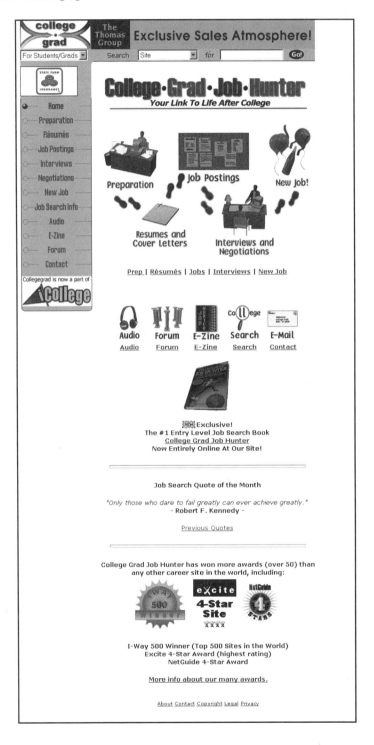

Figure 6-15

College Grad Job Hunter's home page.

Brian Krueger is President of College Grad Job Hunter. He has a BBA from Notre Dame and has 18 years of professional experience working in the technical, human resources, recruiting, sales, and management areas for companies such as IBM and Keane. Brian is also currently Director of Staffing and Employee Development for Keane, Inc.

Brian says that College Grad's mission is to increase employment opportunities for college students, recent graduates, and new alumni. Ninety-six percent of its visitors have a college degree or one in progress, and 84 percent of their job seekers are in the 18–25 age range. The primary population that College Grad serves is college students and recent grads (within five years of graduation). Brian says that College Grad is linked to by more than 2,800 different sites, including more than 1,000 colleges and universities.

> We are an open-access site and work with all colleges and universities. Students at all schools have equal access to all positions at our site—versus restricted access by other sites that require students to be currently enrolled at that college.

College Grad has a realistic view of the labor market for recent college graduates. It focuses on entry-level jobs. "We are the largest open-access entry-level career site in the world," says Brian. "We are exclusively entry-level, so job seekers don't have to pick and sort through the 'Entry-Level Need Not Apply' job postings. We have more than 10,000 job postings at our site, and our entry-level employer database has more than 6,500 contacts throughout the U.S. and Canada."

Besides referrals to jobs, College Grad focuses on the whole range of student pre-employment needs.

> We have more entry-level job search material than any other career site, with more than 1,000 pages of in-depth material. We don't just provide the one or two pages of info—we cover all subjects related to job search in full detail. We offer students and grads full job search life-cycle assistance, from career exploration to resume development to interview prep to job postings to offer negotiation. Visitors can literally manage their entire job search process from beginning to end at our site.

In addition, College Grad features a syndicated college newspaper column for job search, with distribution to more than 300 college newspapers through UWire. Articles are written by a hiring manager who works on the inside of the hiring process. *Ask the Hiring Manager* is an online career forum designed specifically for college students and recent grads. In this forum, Brian Krueger provides answers to many common job search questions.

College Grad helps passive job seekers, those people who are not inclined or don't have the time to go through the process of actively sending out resumes and filling out applications and then searching through many databases to find jobs. These people are often employed and don't want their current employers to know they are looking elsewhere. "We provide our free 'Notify Me!' service, which informs job seekers if a job matching their criteria is posted at our site," says Brian.

College Grad takes steps to protect the privacy of its customers. "We have a very strict privacy policy at our site, whereby no information is used or disclosed without consent of the user," Brian says. "The user decides on the level of privacy and disclosure they provide to prospective employers (including partial resumes and blind resumes), although we certainly encourage full disclosure, especially at the entry level."

College Grad uses Quickstart resume templates to assist students in building their resumes online. But the site can also help you with writing your resume for general submission. Brian says there are more than 100 pages at the College Grad site devoted specifically to resume creation and submission. This information is tailored specifically for entry-level college grads. You will find advice and tips for creating a professional resume and learn some of the pitfalls as well. Brian warns against making the classic mistakes that many job seekers make when preparing an electronic resume:

> Some people make the mistake of being action-verb oriented (which is what most resume books tell you to do) versus being noun oriented (which is what hiring managers keyword search for). The resume must be "findable." Don't leave off the objective. There are plenty of opportunities out there, but you have to narrow the field to the ones that you are truly qualified for. Also, you need to be specific, not general. Don't try to be everything to everybody or you will be nothing to everyone.

Finally, Brian offers this advice for posting a resume at the College Grad Job Hunter site:

> Start with a good format, such as our Quickstart resume templates, but make sure you own the content. Don't create a "cookie-cutter" resume with content that sounds good but isn't you. And don't use a resume service—take the time to do it right and do it personally.

JobDirect.com

http://www.jobdirect.com

Figure 6-16

The JobDirect home page.

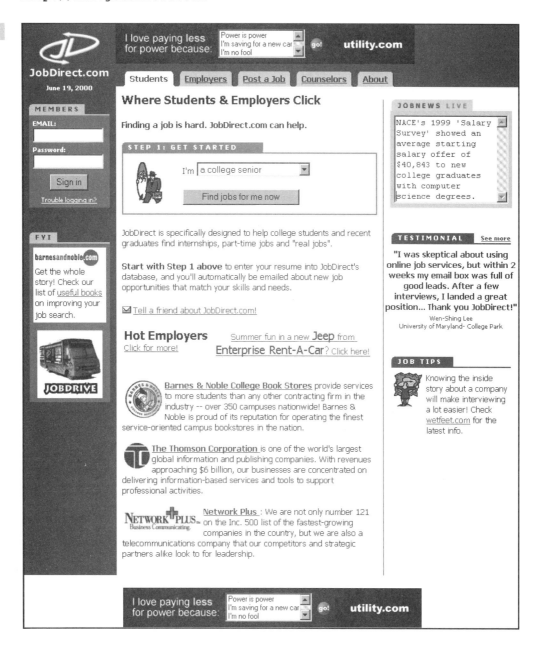

JobDirect.com is an Internet site dedicated to helping college students and recent graduates find jobs and internships that match their interests and qualifications. JobDirect.com focuses on entry-level job seekers, especially those seeking jobs upon graduation from college. Graduates can be from two-year, four-year, or graduate programs. JobDirect.com also assists people transitioning into a new career who are looking for an entry-level experience.

JobDirect.com was founded by two college students for college students. JobDirect, Inc., located in Stamford, Connecticut, was founded by Rachel Bell and Sara Sutton in August 1995. Rachel and Sara were college students contemplating what to with their degrees and facing the stressful process of searching for jobs after graduation. They hit upon using the emerging Internet as an information-exchange tool for young job seekers.

It is the vision of its founders, the company says, that gives JobDirect.com a unique perspective on the needs of the college-level job seeker. That perspective drives the company's marketing strategy. JobDirect.com partners with Internet sites such as Snowball.com and Wetfeet.com—both sites that cater to young Internet users—and Lycos.com to provide the job search function to their college users. In this way, they hope to attract students who will find them by logging on to many of their favorite sites.

Jennifer Brydges is a Manager of Campus Relations for JobDirect.com, working with colleges and universities to implement the company's Resume Exchange software. Prior to joining the company, she coordinated and delivered career services in nonprofit community college and university settings, consulted with several organizations regarding career issues, and developed and instructed college courses in life skills and career preparation.

Like Jennifer, Kristin Volpe is also a Manager of Campus Relations with JobDirect.com. For several years before joining JobDirect.com, Kristin was a college recruiter/program coordinator for a computer-technology company, recruiting thousands of students from over 50 colleges nationwide. Both Kristin and Jennifer were college students who took somewhat circuitous paths to get to their present careers. They call on those experiences in working with students and career centers.

Mary spoke to Jennifer and Kristin about JobDirect.com:

Mary: How does JobDirect.com partner with colleges?

Jennifer/Kristin: JobDirect.com works with colleges and universities in various ways. Over 250 schools nationwide use our Resume Exchange software to manage their job-posting and campus-recruitment needs. Students from over 4,000 different schools have entered their resumes into our site and found great opportunities. JobDirect.com also works with schools by attending job fairs, providing campuses with complimentary magazine subscriptions to giants such as *Fast Company* and *Black Enterprise,* and presenting workshops on topics such as job searching on the Internet. Best of all, our services are offered at absolutely no cost!

Mary: How do you reach students?

Jennifer/Kristin: One of our most successful initiatives is our JobDrive. JobDirect has several buses painted with the JobDirect logo and loaded with laptops that have attended concerts, spring breaks, and campus events to register students right on the spot. In addition, we have hundreds of campus representatives all over the country who spread the word to their fellow students about JobDirect.com.

Mary: What is Resume Exchange?

Jennifer/Kristin: Resume Exchange provides students a one-stop shop to search for jobs, sign up for on-campus interviews, view and register for career-related events, and learn more about the resources and services available on their campus. In addition, students can elect to receive e-mails about job matches from our JobDirect.com database.

Mary: What services do you offer students?

Jennifer/Kristin: As our name implies, JobDirect.com's focus is simple: We find jobs for college students. JobDirect.com makes searching for interesting jobs easy and hassle-free. Students let us know their interests and qualifications and we e-mail them the jobs that are appropriate. Our users can also log on to our site and search for jobs themselves.

One of the primary reasons that students, employers, and college campuses alike choose JobDirect.com is our matching technology. More effective than a general online posting board, JobDirect.com "pre-screens" every resume to ensure that applicants are qualified for positions. This means students understand which positions are a good match for their skills and interests and employers receive resumes from great candidates who are exactly matched to fulfill their needs. Additionally, our site is so easy to use and is available to every college student. Students are able to indicate their job preferences and have new jobs matching those preferences e-mailed directly to them. For the passive job seeker, there is no need to continuously search, because we e-mail the jobs directly to them.

Mary: What protection do you offer students in terms of privacy?

Jennifer/Kristin: Our privacy-protection clause is outlined on our site. The information we collect is for the specific purpose of matching students with employers and jobs. We do not sell their data and we respect their right to privacy. Our users can elect to hide their contact information from employers if they are interested in anonymity.

Mary: How does JobDirect.com keep competitive with other sites?

Jennifer/Kristin: As a company, JobDirect.com is committed to providing the best products and services to all of our constituencies—students, employers, and college campuses. We value feedback and incorporate suggestions from our users to build the best possible tools for their specific needs. Our connection to and continual assessment of user feedback has resulted in expanded features over the course of our existence and will continue to drive our success.

Mary: What advice can you offer job seekers for resume completion and submission?

Jennifer/Kristin: First, we definitely recommend that students take advantage of their college's career centers. This should be the first step in preparing for the job search and drafting a final

(continues)

(continued)

resume. Once students have a complete resume(s), they can use our site to find opportunities of interest.

JobDirect.com offers students two options with regard to resume submission. The first allows the student to build a resume from scratch with the use of our resume template. This is a great option for students who are inexperienced in resume writing. Students benefit from our suggestions along the way, as each field offers guidance for building appropriate text. More experienced job seekers may want to utilize our second option—simply upload their current resume. Our system will maintain the integrity of any resume built with a word-processing application. Students even have the option of saving multiple versions!

Mary: What are come common mistakes seen in resumes?

Jennifer/Kristin: Perhaps the biggest mistake made by job seekers is that they do not take full advantage of the campus resources offered to both students and alumni. Regardless of resume type, a resume is a very important piece of your overall marketing campaign. The best resumes are written for a specific purpose, so the more you know about your interests and skills and the more you know about different industries, the better your resume. Career counselors and industry professionals can offer key insights that will help you to markedly improve your resume's effectiveness. Oftentimes we don't see our true worth (or all of our typos!), whereas others can see these transgressions more easily. Our biggest piece of advice is for students to have their resumes critiqued at their campus career centers or even by a respected professional or friend.

Video Resumes: The New Frontier

Having mentioned in chapter 5 the various reasons not to put photographs on your electronic resume, we must now make you aware of a new trend in online job search: the video resume. Several sites on the WWW now provide a videotape of you presenting your qualifications. Other sites allow you to format a "virtual resume"—an animated version of your background and skills, where sections of your resume are featured in various settings and themes. Here, employers may view your qualifications by clicking on different buttons, which take them via "clever" screens to the desired information.

We looked at two of these sites: CareerShop.com and Cyberview CVs.

CareerShop.com
http://www.careershop.com

Figure 6-17

The CareerShop home page.

Career Toolbox
Jobs
Resumes
Personal Job Shopper
Virtual Job Fairs
Training
Ask Career Dr.
IT Careers
Health Careers
Legal Careers

Employer Toolbox
Employer Login
Recruiting Services
Employer Reviews

CareerTV
Home Page
Program Schedule

Site Resources
Project Marketplace
Video Conferencing
Virtual Resume
HR Consulting
Related Links
Site Map
About Us
Headliners

Virtual Job Fairs

Alabama
Go!▶

Relocation Toolbox
Salary Calculator
Go!▶

This icon indicates the use of streaming video. Click an icon to view the associated video.

To view any video on this site, you must have RealPlayer.

Our site is best viewed using Internet Explorer 4+ or Netscape 4+.

Career Enhancement For The Computer Generation

Search Jobs ▶
Post Resume ▶
Personal Job Shopper ▶

NEWS&FEATURES

TODAY'S NEWS

CAREERSHOP.COM ACQUIRED
As part of a major e-commerce and repositioning initiative, Personnel Group of America (NYSE:PGA) has acquired CareerShop.com (CareerShop).

POLL QUESTION ▼
How would you rate your workload? Go to the CareerShop Poll and let us know what you think.

FORBES BEST OF THE WEB
Once again CareerShop.com has been honored with a Best of the Web award by Forbes Magazine in it's Summer 2000 Issue.

EMPLAWYERNET ▼
EmplawyerNet is the leading provider of legal job information on the Internet. The site includes a database of over 5,000 legal jobs plus tools for employers to find the right candidates.

FREE SEMINARS! ▼
Join us for what promises to be the most innovative recruiting seminar you'll attend this year. Click here to locate a **FREE** seminar near you!

Monday, June 19, 2000

Daily CareerNews Brief

Coke Re-Organizes And Re-Hires
After cutting about 5200 jobs earlier this year, Coca-Cola is re-hiring.

Check out our current show on-line at http://www.careertv.net for tips, advice, interviews and reviews on some of the hottest companies around.

HEALTH CAREERS ▼
We've built a community just for Health Care Professionals. Find news and articles related to your area of expertise and search only Health Care specific job sites!

TRAINING & STUDY MATERIALS ▼
We provide individuals with the hottest training materials and study courses on the market today!

Featured Employer
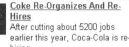

Unprecedented Access to the Best Business Minds!
[Jobs | Events | Video]

Questions or comments? Send mail to webmaster@careershop.com
© 2000 CareerShop.com, Inc. All rights reserved.

CareerShop is a fully multimedia site that features virtual resumes, videoconference interviews, and virtual interviews, and even has its own television program for job seekers.

Virtual Resume is a multimedia presentation that can be prepared either as a link hosted on CareerShop.com's server or an executable file that can be sent to employers by e-mail. CareerShop.com streams your presentation over the Internet for people to view through a Web browser. Your virtual resume can be seen by PC users that have a current browser or get the Macromedia Flash plug-in, or Mac users with the plug-in provided by Macromedia for Flash. Hosting your virtual resume on CareerShop's site costs $14.95 for one month. CareerShop offers several different preset "formats" from which to choose. Examples of these are seen in figs. 6-18 and 6-19.

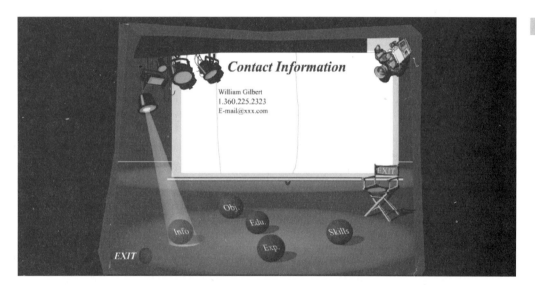

Figure 6-18

A virtual resume format.

Figure 6-19

Another virtual resume format.

After you select a format, you complete a fill-in-the-blanks order form. Twenty-four hours after payment is received, your virtual resume is available.

CareerShop.com also utilizes Candidate Quality Management, CQM, to create 30-minute videotaped interviews of candidates. These interviews address the prescreening portion of the hiring process. Through this initial virtual interview, hiring managers can get a look at a candidate's communication, interpersonal, and presentation skills. Interviews are conducted by a "neutral third party" at over 240 interview locations throughout the United States. Candidates answer the same set of questions for certain positions. CareerShop.com asserts that this process provides employers greater objectivity when evaluating candidates during the prescreening stage.

Employers can also conduct interviews with candidates via desktop conferencing. In addition, at CareerShop, you can access "CareerTV," an Internet television program about jobs and careers. All of these features fully utilize the multimedia capability of the World Wide Web to market your qualifications.

Cyberview CVs
http://www.cyberviewcv.com

Figure 6-20

Cyberview CVs home page.

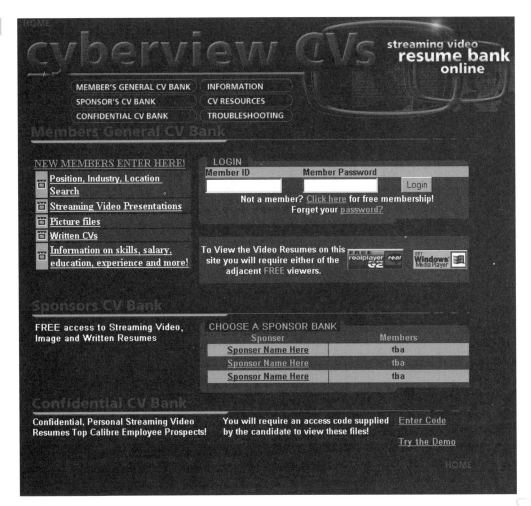

Cyberview CVs is a company in Markham, Ontario, Canada that has taken the electronic resume to the next logical step. Phil Dubois, founder of the company Pride in Personnel Inc., first launched Career Internetworking, an Internet job site that allowed the company's employers to use the Internet to advertise and attract candidates, in 1996. Since then, the company has introduced RecruitersCafe.com (http://www.recruiterscafe.com), a site especially for personnel agencies in North America; Virtual Interview Resumes (http://www.videoyourresume.com), for placing short or long-term video resumes professionally on CD or diskette; and most recently, CyberviewCv.com, a video streaming and hosting site for video resume presentations over the Internet.

Video resumes at the site feature a close-up of the candidate talking about her or his qualifications (see fig. 6-21).

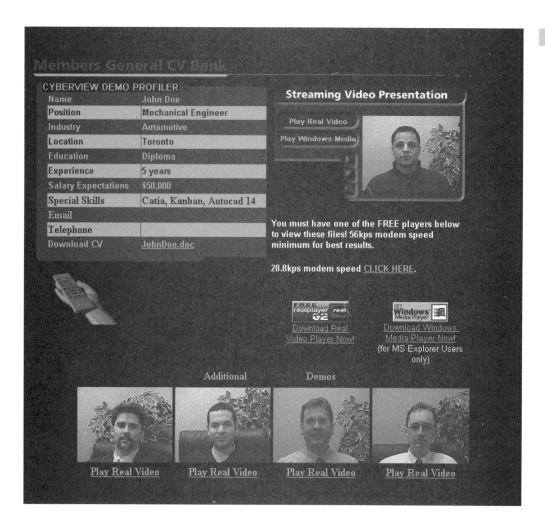

Figure 6-21

A video resume.

You can preview a video resume at the site if you have Real Player™ or Windows Media Player™. Simply select the player and click on the photo of the candidate you want to preview.

We talked to Phil about his service.

Mary: How does the applicant get a video on your site?

Phil: Individuals who wish to supplement their written resume with a video presentation on the net may either send in a VHS tape containing a 30- to 60-second clip profiling their career and interests, or come to our offices in Markham, Ontario for a filming session (usually 10 minutes in duration). The job seeker simply makes an appointment, yet we do request that the candidate first review our recommendations and strategies for videotaping (on our Web page).

Many new computers these days come with free webcams and an individual may just record directly into their computer from the privacy of their own home. Otherwise, we can convert any form of VHS recording (PAL, SECAM, NTSC) if they are mailed to our office.

Mary: Is there a cost to the candidate?

Phil: The cost is listed at our site as $100 Canadian for a one-year hosting.

Mary: What has been the response from employers to the video resume?

Phil: We have just finished our test market and the feedback has been overwhelmingly positive. Employers and recruiters are quite pleased to be able to view an individual's presentation skills prior to meeting with them.

Mary: Have you encountered any reluctance or objections from the applicants?

Phil: Well, there are a lot of camera-shy people out there. Preparation and seeing others on the site tend to make things easier.

Mary: Have there been any problems on the employer side?

Phil: Some employers wish to view the files confidentially so as to avoid any accusations of visual discrimination. We have also had some feedback about the fact that there is a five-minute setup time for first-time users who don't have Real Player or Windows Media Player active on their computers. As our site is geared toward employer viewing, we have structured the minimum download speed as 56kps for clean viewing.

Mary: Let's talk about the discrimination issue. How does viewing a video resume potentially impact an employer?

Phil: As you know, an employer is not allowed to use race, religion, etc. as a basis for hiring or interviewing. Our question was "would the use of a video presentation break any existing statutes regarding human rights or labor practices?" I spoke with the (Canadian) Labour Relations Board and the Human Rights Commission and both assured me there was nothing wrong with the practice itself. However, if an individual can prove an employer refused them an interview strictly because of the way they look, that is grounds for a lawsuit. (The same could be said for a paper resume too!)

Mary: What about privacy? How is the job seeker protected?

Phil: On the site, there is a Confidential Bank where each candidate has a "lock code." Employers or recruiters wishing to see these presentations must possess that code. Cyberview will also direct interview requests through our system for complete confidentiality in the cases where an individual may choose to remove their address, telephone, and e-mail from the resume.

Mary: Do you give advice to applicants about how to prepare and present on video?

Phil: Absolutely, from sample scripts to presentation tips.

For creating a video resume, Phil also offered the following tips from the Cyberview CVs site:

- Sit up straight.

- Look into the camera, but do not stare.

- Show active enthusiasm and be positive.

- Never discuss your dislikes or demands.

- Speak clearly and confidently.

- Fidgeting and hesitating make you look ill-at-ease. Relax and be yourself!

- Pay attention to your voice, diction, and grammar.

- Maintain a pattern or logical flow. Limit yourself to brief and concise presentations.

- Do not read from a script. Use visual aids if appropriate.

- Smile at least once.

- Close, or at least say "thank you" at the end.

Summing It Up

Whether you are a veteran, a college student, or a federal employee, many sites on the Internet can help you with your job search. You can also find services that target other specific groups, such as older workers, youth workers, and certain ethnic groups. If you want to push the envelope a little with your resume, you can even find places to create videos of you, giving your qualifications. The fact is, there is a niche for just about any kind of job seeker on the Internet. Explore. Find your place. A special site is waiting for you.

PART II

RESUME BANKS

In this part, we focus on resume banks—what are they and how do they compare to one another? Chapter 7 presents an overview of resume banks to help you choose the best place to post your resume. We then list detailed descriptions of 80 resume banks—Web sites that collect and make resumes accessible to employers. We rated these sites using the following system:

- **Outstanding site (★ ★ ★ ★ ★):** Meets all the criteria established in chapter 7, with some outstanding features.

- **Good site (★ ★ ★ ★):** Meets all the criteria established in chapter 7.

- **Average site (★ ★ ★):** Satisfactorily meets most of the criteria established in chapter 7.

- **Fair site (★ ★):** Satisfactorily meets some of the criteria established in chapter 7.

- **Poor site (★):** Not recommended.

OVERVIEW OF THE RESUME BANKS

The main way to get your resume on the Internet is to post it in one or more resume banks. Resume banks collect and make resume information accessible to employers.

Internet resume postings are from a variety of job seekers at all levels. Some are from professionals in high-tech and engineering fields as well as in health-care, financial, sales, and marketing fields. Some resume postings are from recent college graduates, and some are from people separating from the military. Some are entry level, and some are from experienced executives. The resume banks we describe in this book contain a total of more than an amazing 13.5 million resumes. If you want your resume to be among them, you'll need the information in this chapter, where you'll read about the various types of resume banks available. Following this chapter, you'll find a detailed description of nearly 80 resume banks to help you decide where you want to post your resume.

Submitting Your Resume

Each resume bank Web page explains how to submit your resume. Some banks ask you to submit your resume via e-mail; however, the overwhelming majority ask you to complete an online form with information about yourself, and then cut and paste your resume into the Web form.

Some resume banks require the job seeker and the employer to fill out similar forms that ask questions about languages spoken, highest degree obtained, and the like. This information results in better matches between what the job seeker has to offer and what the employer is looking for.

If you don't want to use a computer to submit your resume online, you can find resume banks that will enter your faxed and postal-mailed resume for you. For example, the Transition Assistance Online resume bank accepts paper resumes from separating U.S. military personnel; JOBNET.com will enter your paper resume for a $5 fee; and JobExchange will enter it for a $15 fee. You'll find a few others in the following section who accept resumes by fax but did not specify a fee. Also, some will accept paper resumes at job fairs.

Passive Posting

Some resume banks are similar to the Usenet newsgroups because they simply provide an online presence. These data banks store and make your resume available for employers to search. Unfortunately, as on resume newsgroups (see chapter 1), you will never know whether anyone reads your resume. You are passively waiting for employers to contact you.

After your resume has been successfully posted at this type of resume bank, you are dependent on the employer for the next step. The employer must go to that resume bank and select your resume. A few of these resume banks organize resumes only by category, so the employer has to look at each resume under a category heading. Most data banks, however, enable employers to search the text of your resume by keywords. The sophistication of the search program varies from data bank to data bank. For example, CareerPath.com has a sophisticated search engine—developed by I-Search—that presents the employer with a list that ranks the most appropriate candidate first.

CareerPath.com also offers its Resume Scout, which makes it possible to search virtually every resume on the Web. In a single search, the employer can access up to 45 databases simultaneously, rate and sort resumes by keywords, and save or e-mail resumes.

Interactive Data Banks

Unlike passive data banks, some resume banks can interact with you in important ways. Some give you feedback about the number of times your resume was reviewed. Contract Employment Weekly, for example, notifies job seekers by e-mail about who viewed and/or downloaded their resumes and when they did so.

Some data banks have software that monitors job and resume postings and automatically notifies the employer and the job seeker when a match occurs. American Preferred Jobs, CareerShop.com, Contract Employment Weekly, HealthCareerWeb, Jobsite.com, and Transition Assistance Online all notify employers on a regular basis of any resumes that match the skills they requested.

employMAX.com, JobOptions, and Monster.com notify both employers and job seekers. These resume banks e-mail resumes that match a list of criteria to employers, and they notify job seekers of job openings that match their skills.

Public or Confidential?

Some resume banks are open to the world to read; therefore, anyone can find your current address, phone number, e-mail address, and even your employment history. This means that anyone can find you, record your address, and try to sell you something in the future. This free access also means that your current employer may discover that you're looking for a new job.

By having free access to resumes, some employers and resume data banks may also copy your resume and add it to their data banks. For example, such resume banks as CareerShop.com, employMAX.com, and JobBank USA use spiders or robots to search out resumes to add to their data banks. Because of programs and data banks such as these, duplicate resume postings account for an estimated 20–30 percent— or more—of Internet resumes.

Although these resume banks promote this free exchange of information as an advantage to employers, other resume banks promote just the opposite: not adding resumes to their data banks from newsgroups and other resume banks. This viewpoint reflects an ongoing discussion among human resource professionals about the aging of resumes. Some of these professionals believe that new resumes represent people who are actively on the job market and older resumes represent people who are likely to have already found employment. Other human resource professionals accept all resumes regardless of age under the principle that everyone is always looking for a better job.

Nonetheless, even if the resume bank accepts only new resumes, only a few of these resume banks, such as MedZilla and SIRC, contact the poster or verify any information.

Many of the resume banks do offer some degree of confidentiality. Some guarantee that access to resumes is limited to their subscribers, who can access the resumes only with a password; however, your current employer may be one of the subscribers! Other resume banks offer other kinds of confidentiality. American Preferred Jobs, Japanese Jobs, and PursuitNet Online, for example, enable job seekers to indicate any employer to which they don't want to send a resume.

Some resume banks offer a confidential listing. For example, job seekers can request confidentiality on CalJOBS, Canadian Resume Centre, CareerShop.com, Casino Careers Online, Headhunter.net, JobOptions, Minorities' Job Bank, Monster.com, National Diversity Newspaper Job Bank, Resume Network, Science Careers, and VirtualResume. Typically, a confidential listing means that your resume has no contact information; therefore, you are limited to using your resume only for applying for posted positions, not for advertising your availability for positions.

If confidentiality is important to you, you may want to use the resume banks that limit their data banks to anonymous profiles. The data bank secures your permission before your resume and identifying information is released to an employer. At CareerSite, for example, employers can see only the job seeker's profile when they search the data bank. If the employer indicates an interest, CareerSite sends the job seeker a message that requests permission to release the job seeker's identity and resume.

CareerPath.com places priority on job-seeker privacy as well. Employers never see personal information until the job seeker reviews the job description and authorizes CareerPath.com to forward the complete resume for consideration. This feature is available only to registered users. And CareerMagazine does not send resumes to employers; instead, it notifies job seekers by e-mail of job openings that match their skills and requirements.

Another way to conceal your identity is to use one of the recruiter or headhunter resume banks. JobLynx is a resume bank that is limited to headhunters.

Resume Mailing Services

Some people do mass mailings of their printed resumes to companies they believe may be hiring. This process is expensive: Think about how much it costs in time and money to print and mail 200 resumes! Job search professionals try to discourage this strategy, largely because it's rarely effective and always expensive.

Now there's an electronic equivalent that is simple, quick, and much less expensive. Internet resume mailing services use the power of the Internet to distribute your resume to hundreds of employers and recruiters who have indicated that they want to receive resumes from the service. There is no charge to the employers.

Resume Blaster.com can send your resume to 3,000 recruiters nationwide for $49–$89. ResumeXPRESS! can send your resume to thousands of employers, recruiters, and online resume data banks for $39.95–$199.95. ResumeXPRESS! also maintains your resume in its resume data bank for one year. And ResumeZapper.com can send your resume to 5,000 search firms for a price starting at $49.99.

Other resume banks offer this service as an option to their other services. EngineeringJobs.com offers an optional resume e-mailing service to 600 headhunters who specialize in engineering and IT jobs, for a $35 fee.

Resume mailing services distribute your resume for much less than you would have spent in postage alone. However, you shouldn't rely only on this strategy.

Evaluating Resume Banks

Even if posting your resume is free, you are still investing your time. You want your resume to be seen by potential employers; therefore, you need to evaluate the resume banks carefully and decide which ones are most appropriate for you.

In the following pages, you'll find our descriptions of 80 of the most popular resume banks. We first collected the information about resume banks in April 1998 by an e-mail questionnaire. We redid that questionnaire in April 2000 for this new edition. Many resume banks we listed in the 1998 edition are closed or have merged with others.

In our descriptions, we tried to maintain as much of the original language of the person who completed our questionnaire as possible so that you can tell what the resume bank thinks is important. For example, is confidentiality a priority? Does the bank provide job-search tips? You can also determine how helpful the resume bank will be if you encounter a problem. Questions that were not answered by the bank are followed by "n/a," for "not available."

Under the name of each resume bank, we have listed a description of its primary geographical area, the employment fields or job classifications of the majority of the resumes it holds, and our rating of the site from one star to five stars. In making our assessment, we considered the following factors:

- Stability of the sponsorship or ownership

- Cost to the job seeker

- Cost to employers

- Ratio of the number of resumes held to the number of employers who use the database

- Ratio of the number of resumes held to the number of daily hits on the resumes

- Confidentiality available to the job seeker

- Sophistication of the search options

- Technology to notify the job seeker and employer of matches

- Overall ease of entering the resume and using the site

- Other aspects that help the job seeker, such as career information

- Unique, special features

- Geographic specialization of the site

- Demographic specialization of the site

As you review the resume bank descriptions, keep in mind the guidelines that are discussed in the next sections. These guidelines will help you evaluate which resume banks will best serve your interests. The following sections elaborate on some of the more important of these guidelines.

Stability

Resume banks are a new service. As early as 1984, the search firm Lee Johnson International was receiving resumes via FidoNet, which linked bulletin board systems (BBSs). In 1989, Gonyea & Associates created the first career-guidance agency to operate 100 percent online. In 1990, dice.com started accepting Announce Availability forms on a BBS, and then in 1995 on the Web. JobOptions, formerly E.span, began its online recruitment service in 1991 but didn't start accepting resumes until 1995. In 1992, JOBNET.com and Online Career Center (OCC) started accepting resumes. Among the resume banks we review, about eight of them were established in 1994, and about 15 each in 1995, 1996, and 1997. About 10 new resume banks were established in 1998, and five in 1999.

Only a few resume banks have been offering their services for more than a few years. Look to see whether a resume bank with a longer history has kept up to date with technology and services. You can also check to see whether a newer resume bank is starting to be competitive and has gotten employer interest.

Ratio of Resumes to Corporate Subscribers

Compare the number of resumes that a resume bank has online to the number of corporate subscribers and employers it has. The lower the ratio, the better your chances of an employer seeing your resume. Keep in mind, however, that some resume banks are open without registration to any employer, so the ratio can't be calculated for them. In our survey, some resume banks did not provide the information to calculate this ratio. Table 7-1 lists some resume banks that have the most favorable ratio of employers to resumes.

TABLE 7-1: RATIO OF RESUMES TO EMPLOYERS.		
Resume Bank	**Resumes/Employers**	**Ratio**
Engineering Jobs	3,400/3,500	1
Contract Engineering	609/485	1.3
Teachers@Work	2,500/1,200	2.1
Saludos.com	6,500/3,000	2.2
HealthMedjobs.com	1,000/400	2.5
The Job Exchange	60,000/20,000	3
Jobsite.com	1,400/450	3.1
SIRC	3,500/1,000	3.5
National Diversity Newspaper Job Bank	1,000/250	4
The Employment Guide's CareerWeb	26,500/6,000	4.4
JOBTRAK	500,000/100,000	5
MedZilla	3,000/600	5
Bankjobs.com	8,000/1,500	5.3
Future Access Employment Guide	7,000/1,200	5.8
MarketingJobs.com	7,000/1,200	5.8

Ratio of Resumes to Daily Page Hits

Another factor to consider when choosing a resume bank is the ratio of resumes to daily page hits. The higher the ratio, the better chance your resume has of being viewed. In our survey, some resume banks did not provide the information to calculate the ratio of resumes to daily page hits. Table 7-2 lists some of the resume banks that have the most favorable ratios of daily page hits to resumes.

TABLE 7-2: RATIO OF RESUMES TO DAILY PAGE HITS.		
Resume Bank	**Resumes/Daily Page Hits**	**Ratio**
CalJOBS	600,000/10,000,000	.1
Saludos.com	6,500/21,495	.3
AmericanJobs.com	25,000/71,428	.4
Teachers@Work	2,500/6,849	.4
ORASEARCH	4,000/10,000	.4
Minorities' Job Bank	11,500/11,000	1
Contract Employment Weekly	8–10,000/5–7,500	1.6/1.3

Fees

Consider what fees the resume bank charges. Are corporate subscribers and employers charged? Is the job seeker charged?

Many of the resume banks with the highest ratio of employers to resumes and of page hits to resumes are free or inexpensive to employers. CalJOBS, a California state service, is free to both employers and job seekers. The cost to the employer varies widely beginning with the JobExchange, which charges employers only $40 per resume download online and has no charge for the job seeker.

The overwhelming majority of resume banks are free to the job seeker. A small number do charge: JobLynx charges $99.99 to post a resume for 90 days; but if you are not presented with employment opportunities during two consecutive 90-day periods, JobLynx will refund 50 percent of the fee. LatPro and Lawmatch.com charge membership fees ranging from $35 to $150.

In general, we found that job seekers are reluctant to use resume banks that charge a fee—particularly a very expensive one—unless the resume bank is highly specialized. If users go to a general job bank, they don't want to pay anything. A basic rule of thumb: The more expensive a resume bank, the less attractive it is to employers and job seekers.

Length of Time Resumes Remain Online

Review the length of time resumes remain online before the job seekers have to update or renew them. The shorter the period of time that resumes remain online, the more recent—and more desirable—the resumes. Most data banks retain resumes for six months before renewal is required; however, many data banks retain their resumes indefinitely, although some of these banks offer searches based on the length of time the resume has been in the data bank. Table 7-3 lists some of the data banks that have short time periods before renewal is required.

TABLE 7-3: RESUME BANKS WITH SHORT RENEWAL PERIODS.	
Resume Bank	**Renewal Period**
dice.com (Announce Availability)	30 days
CalJOBS	60 days
Net-Temps	60 days
SIRC	60 days
Science Careers	7 weeks
American Preferred Jobs	90 days
JobLynx	90 days
Jobsite.com	90 days
MarketingJobs.com	90 days
Contract Engineering	3 months
EngineeringJobs.com	3 months
JOBTRAK	3 months
National Diversity Newspaper Job Bank	3 months
MedZilla	16–20 weeks

Online Help

What help is available if you have problems submitting your resume? Many of the resume banks offer an FAQ (frequently asked questions) page or e-mail assistance. Some offer more complete help in the entire job search process, as shown in table 7-4.

TABLE 7-4: ONLINE HELP OFFERED BY VARIOUS RESUME BANKS.	
Resume Bank	**Online Help**
CareerMagazine	Comprehensive articles section
CareerShop	CareerTV, presenting topics of interest to job seekers
HealthCareerWeb	Articles and career inventory test
The JobExchange	Online advice and references from the site's participating newspapers
JOBTRAK	Award-winning resume guide
SEEK	Resources to assist job seekers in all aspects of the job-search process
Transition Assistance Online (TAO)	Job-hunting and resume-writing resources

Special Features

Look for any special features that may be helpful to you. Watch for new trends—like video resumes. Watch for new ideas that may become popular with employers. You've read in this book that video resumes are a new idea. As that idea becomes more popular with employers, the job banks that offer it will have an advantage. You'll want your resume to be in those banks.

Geographic Coverage Area

Consider the resume bank's geographic coverage area: global, specific countries, or regions. Although the Internet is global in nature, few resume banks have a global presence. Monster.com is an exception. The majority of banks serve the United States and Canada. Within the United States, some resume banks have a defined geographic focus. This focus offers a definite plus if you want to work in that area.

Demographic Specialization

Are the resumes in the data bank specialized and in the field in which you are seeking employment? Does the resume bank accept resumes from all career fields? General data banks are used by employers seeking employees with a wider range of experience. Specialized data banks are used by employers with clearly defined, specific needs.

Trends in Resume Banks

Since the previous edition of this book in 1998, we have noted two trends: One trend is toward "megabanks," that is, resume banks that include literally millions of resumes. These megabanks have grown through aggressive advertising, mergers, and the use of spiders to bring in resumes from other areas of the Web. The second trend is the development of an increasing number of specialty resume banks that include resumes only in a limited employment area or resumes only from a limited demographic group.

The "Megabanks"

Table 7-5 lists the largest resume banks profiled in this edition. We show the number of resumes they reported in April 2000 and April 1998, the length of time resumes remain on the sites, and the banks' focus at the time of our survey. Read these numbers carefully. A resume bank may have 100,000 resumes, but only 20,000 of them may have been received in the past 90 days.

Resume Bank	Number of Resumes		Length of Time Posted	Specialty
	1998	**2000**		
JobBank USA	60,000	3,100,000	1 year	All fields
Monster.com	340,000	3,000,000	1 year	All fields
America's Job Bank	700,000	2,163,301	n/a	All fields
CareerPath	130,000	1,000,000	n/a	All fields
CalJOBS	n/a	600,000	60 days*	All fields
PassportAccess	151,989	550,000	2 years	Technology
JOBTRAK.com	150,000	500,000	3 months	College graduates
Headhunter.net	35,000	470,000	1 year	All fields
CareerShop.com	12,000	350,000	120 days	Technology, management, sales
employMAX.com	330,000		1 year	Technology

TABLE 7-5: THE TEN LARGEST RESUME BANKS PROFILED IN THIS BOOK.

*Resumes remain for display to employers for 60 days and are stored on the system after that.

Specialty Resume Banks

A major trend we have seen is resume banks specializing by geographic area or by some demographic characteristic. Table 7-6 lists several resume banks by their geographic areas.

TABLE 7-6: GEOGRAPHIC SPECIALIZATIONS OF RESUME BANKS.

Global:

employMAX.com—U.S., Canada, France, United Kingdom

Hospitality Net Job Exchange—global

JobServe—U.K. and global

Monster.com—U.S., Canada, U.K., the Netherlands, Belgium, Australia, France, New Zealand, Singapore, and Hong Kong

Countries:

The Australian Resume Server

Canadian Resume Center

Japanese Jobs

LatPro (U.S., Canada, Latin America, Caribbean, Spain, and Portugal)

Resume Network (Australia and New Zealand)

SEEK (Australia and New Zealand)

Areas in the United States:

CalJOBS

Internet Job Source (largest U.S. cities)

Colorado Online Job Connection

JOBNET.com (Philadelphia area)

JobsNorthwest (Washington, Idaho, Western Montana, and Oregon)

Another major trend we have seen is the development of resume banks with a limited demographic grouping—career specialty or personal identification. Table 7-7 gives examples of specialized resume banks.

TABLE 7-7: SPECIALIZED RESUME BANKS.

Specialty	Resume Bank
Casino/gaming	Casino Careers Online
Education	Teachers@Work
Ethnicity	Minorities' Job Bank, National Association of Broadcasters Career Center, National Diversity Newspaper Job Bank, Saludos.com

(continues)

(continued)

TABLE 7-7: SPECIALIZED RESUME BANKS.	
Specialty	**Resume Bank**
Feminism	The Feminist Majority Foundation
Financial	bankjobs.com
Health	HealthCareerWeb, HealthMedjobs.com, MedZilla
Hospitality	Hospitality Net Job Exchange
Human Resources	TCM's HR Careers, Training Magazine's SuperSite
Law	Lawmatch.com
Media	TVJobs.com
Military, separating	Transition Assistance Online
Real estate/construction	JobSite.com
Recent college graduates	CollegeGrad.com, JOBTRAK.com
Religion	Christian Jobs Online
Scientists	Science Careers
Sexual orientation	GAYWORK.com
Sports and recreation	Online Sports Career Center
Students	CollegeGrad, JobDirect, JOBTRAK.com

The Role of Resume Banks in Your Total Job Search

Resume banks offer an exciting new way to match the job with the job seeker. Always remember, however, that submitting your resume to a resume bank is only part of your overall job search process. Applying directly to employers via online resume forms and e-mail is another part. Following up on e-mail correspondence from employers is one more. And, as we showed you in part I of this book, crafting a winning resume is key to the entire process of online job search.

RESUME BANKS

American Preferred Jobs

USA

All career fields, with emphasis on technical, finance, sales, clerical, and engineering

Rating: ★ ★ ★ ★ ★

Preferred jobs is a network of 83 regional job banks all tied into the national master site, American Preferred Jobs. Job seekers can visit the regional sites of choice and submit resumes for jobs in their areas and locations of choice for free. Regional Preferred Jobs sites are linked to from Yahoo!, about.com, Excite, Go.com, Lycos, Netscape, and others.

- **URL:** http://www.preferredjobs.com

- **Ownership/sponsorship:** Private—Ascent Technology Inc.

- **Started accepting resumes:** 1997.

- **Approximate number of resumes online April 2000:** 86,000 total for all regions.

- **Resume career fields:** Resumes are in all career fields in 180 career categories, with 78 percent in the technical disciplines, financial, administration, and sales.

- **Total number of corporate subscribers/ employers:** 11,456 registered employers.

- **Distribution of corporate subscribers/ employers**

  Direct-hire employers: 55 percent

  Staffing firms: 25 percent

  Contract/consulting firms: 20 percent

- **Fee structure for corporate subscribers/ employers**

Basic: Free. 40-job limit per year. No resume database searching. Jobs are displayed on the regional and master sites. Includes links to employer's Web site, plus resume and e-mail links.

Bronze: $150 for three months. Resume database searching. Basic company profile. Inclusion in the employer's directory. Jobs displayed on regional and master site directory. Unlimited job posting.

Silver: $290 for six months. Unlimited job posting. Batch uploads. Full resume searching. First-look resume searching. Inclusion in job fair with a virtual online brochure. Free "E-mail Resumes" that match job posts. Deluxe company profile. Employer directory listing. Full-page billboard called a "jump page." 20,000 free banner impressions. Jobs displayed on regional and master sites. Priority placement in search results (the order in which jobs appear is Gold, Silver, Bronze, and then Basic).

Gold: $550 per year. Unlimited job searching. Full resume searching. First-look resume searching. Inclusion in job fair with a virtual online brochure. Free "e-mail resumes" that match job posts. Two deluxe company profiles. Employer directory listing. Full-page billboard called a "Jump Page." 30,000 free banner impressions. Mini-Web site on Preferred with four pages of content. Company-branded search page. Jobs displayed on regional and master site. Priority placement in search results (the order in which jobs appear is Gold, Silver, Bronze, and then Basic).

Silver and Gold members receive a first look at resumes prior to their release to the general membership population. Resumes are reserved for three days so that Silver and Gold members can review them before they are available to all recruiters.

- **Methods and rules for submitting resumes:** Can be submitted using a "60-Second Quick Post" form or the "Long Form" for greater detail. Privacy options are available directly on the resume-submission form or within the "resume workstation," a logged-into editing section for their resumes.

- **Percent of resumes submitted by Web form:** 100.

- **Percent of resumes received from individuals:** 100.

- **Limits on length:** None.

- **Format:** Web form with HTML accepted.

- **Fees for person submitting resume:** None.

- **Length of time resumes remain online:** 90 days, but job seekers can elect to keep them active beyond 90 days by selecting "activate" as the resume status or "deactivate" to save the resume online until they are searching for employment again. If job seekers do not elect to "deactivate" the resume, it is purged after 90 days.

- **Procedures for updating/renewing:** All job seekers are given a resume ID number and password. They can access and update their resumes at any time and as often as they want.

- **Privacy/confidentiality:** It is not possible to limit who can see the resume, but job seekers can hide their name, phone numbers, and address on the form. Job seekers are encouraged to use Web-based e-mails. It is possible to shield a resume from being

viewed by a current employer. Job seekers can select from a menu of current job-posting employers and select that employer to not be allowed to see their resume.

- **Assistance provided to the person submitting a resume:** Free e-mail or phone technical support is provided through a toll-free number and moderated onsite; online forums with daily content updates that offer advice on resume creation and tips. Staffed and administered daily.

- **Search options available to employers viewing resumes:** Keyword, years of experience, desired-position entries, degree/ education, current job title, previous job title, skills search (these are ranked by the job seeker on a scale of 1 to 10), special skills search, and salary-desired search.

- **Technology to match jobs to resumes and e-mail results to clients:** Job Notifications^{SM} matches jobs nightly against posted resumes, skills, relocation areas, and desired positions. They are mailed to the employers in scannable format with resume information included and e-mail address and name and address unless the privacy option was selected by the resume poster.

- **Average number of daily hits on resumes:** On average, 300 employers actively search resumes daily, conducting an average of six searches. On average, 20,000 resumes are hit daily in searches.

- **Special features:** Job seeker workstation, My Preferred Jobs^{SM}, allows the job seeker to save the job titles of interest to view again later.

- **Other distinguishing factors:** The site has an interactive Question and Answer section where resume creation, editing, and submission advice is given. Also interviewing and general career advice is responded to daily. The site has three separate original content areas: Financial advice, Resume advice, and Career Advocate sections. It also has free biweekly Career Guide newsletters that offer advice and tips, and highlight the current job fairs running on the site.

AmericanJobs.com

USA
IT, engineering, and sales
Rating: ★ ★ ★

Located in Bloomfield Hills, Michigan, AmericanJobs.com is a relatively new site that has already received some recognition.

- **URL:** http://www.AmericanJobs.com

- **Ownership/sponsorship:** Privately held.

- **Started accepting resumes:** 1999.

- **Approximate number of resumes online April 2000:** 25,000

- **Resume career fields:** Resumes are primarily in IT, engineering, and sales. It accepts all career fields.

- **Total number of corporate subscribers/ employers:** More than 400.

- **Distribution of corporate subscribers/ employers**

   Direct-hire employers: 75 percent

   Staffing firms: 25 percent

- **Fee structure for corporate subscribers/ employers:**

   Employers can search the Resume Database free.

   Unlimited job posting for 3-, 6- or 12-month durations.

   3 months unlimited: $150

6 months unlimited: $240

12 months unlimited: $365

- **Methods and rules for submitting resumes:** Online at http://www.americanjobs.com/search/resume.asp.

- **Percent of resumes submitted by Web form:** 100.

- **Percent of resumes received from individuals:** 100.

- **Limits on length:** None.

- **Format:** Text only. No HTML.

- **Fees for person submitting resume:** None.

- **Length of time resumes remain online:** n/a.

- **Procedures for updating/renewing:** Job seekers can post, edit, and delete their own resumes with a username and password.

- **Privacy/confidentiality:** It is not possible to limit who can see a resume. It is not possible to shield a resume from being viewed by a current employer.

- **Assistance provided to the person submitting a resume:** Yes.

- **Search options available to employers viewing resumes:** Boolean, by state, and by categories.

- **Technology to match jobs to resumes and e-mail results to clients:** Active Search Agents.

- **Average number of daily hits on resumes:** Over 500,000 hits a week.

- **Special features:** AmericanJobs has over 20,000 human resource representatives and recruiters signed up to search resumes.

America's Job Bank

USA
All career fields
Rating: ★ ★ ★
URL: http://www.ajb.dni.us

Note: America's Job Bank is described in detail in chapter 1 (see page 9).

The Australian Resume Server

Australia
All career fields
Rating: ★ ★ ★

The Australian Resume Server was established in August 1995 as a resource for job seekers wanting to work in Australia. The site enables job seekers to upload their resumes into the Australian Resume Server's database and enables employers and agencies to search the database.

- **URL:** http://www.resume.net.au/

- **Ownership/sponsorship:** Owned by HR software developers Herenow Solutions.

- **Started accepting resumes:** 1995.

- **Approximate number of resumes online in April 2000:** 8,000.

- **Resume career fields:** Resumes are in all high-technology career fields.

- **Total number of corporate subscribers/ employers:** 500.

- **Distribution of corporate subscribers/ employers**

  Direct-hire employers: 30 percent

  Staffing firms: 30 percent

  Contract/consulting firms: 30 percent

  Other: 10 percent

- **Fee structure for corporate subscribers/ employers:** Annual subscription fee.

- **Methods and rules for submitting resumes:** You can submit resume text or a URL for a Web resume on another server. Uploading and linking are free for job seekers.

- **Percent of resumes submitted by Web form:** 100.

- **Percent of resumes received from**

  Individuals: 70

  Colleges or universities: 20

  Outplacement firms: 10

- **Limits on length:** None.

- **Format:** Open.

- **Fees for person submitting resume:** None.

- **Length of time resumes remain online:** As long as the job seeker wants.

- **Procedures for updating/renewing:** Job seeker is issued a password for updates, renewal, and deletion.

- **Privacy/confidentiality:** It is possible to limit who can see your resume. Details are kept in a secure area and are available only to subscribers. It is not possible to shield a resume from being viewed by a current employer.

- **Assistance provided to the person submitting a resume:** Pointers for resume-writing on the Web.

- **Search options available to employers viewing resumes:** Free-form text, areas of Australia where you want to work, languages spoken, and citizenship/residency status.

- **Technology to match jobs to resumes and e-mail resumes to clients:** None.

- **Average number of daily hits on resumes:** 100–200.

- **Special features:** Service available to Australian job seekers or job seekers from overseas wanting to work in Australia.

- **Other distinguishing factors:** One of Australia's longest-running Internet employment sites. Highly regarded by industry and industry groups.

bankjobs.com

USA

Financial industry

Rating: ★ ★ ★ ★

bankjobs.com is a career site for banking and financial services.

- **URL:** www.bankjobs.com

- **Ownership/sponsorship:** bankjobs.com, inc., a subsidiary of Careers, Inc., Harrison Dean, President/COO.

- **Started accepting resumes:** 1998.

- **Approximate number of resumes online April 2000:** 8,000.

- **Resume career fields:** Resumes are exclusively in the banking financial services industry.

- **Total number of corporate subscribers/ employers:** 1,500.

- **Distribution of corporate subscribers/ employers**

  Direct-hire employers: 60 percent

  Staffing firms: 20 percent

  Contract/consulting firms: 20 percent

- **Fee structure for corporate subscribers/ employers:** $895 for one year of unlimited resume searches.

- **Methods and rules for submitting resumes:** Must have minimum two years of experience in the banking and financial services industry or education directly related.

- **Percent of resumes submitted by**

  Web form: 95

  E-mail: 3

  Fax: 2

- **Percent of resumes received from individuals:** 100.

- **Limits on length:** None.

- **Format:** Use online form.

- **Fees for person submitting resume:** None.

- **Length of time resumes remain online:** One year. Site contacts each candidate once a quarter to request any updates or changes to the resume within the database. If the job seeker is no longer active, they ask that the job seeker inform them.

- **Procedures for updating/renewing:** Contact site or resubmit resume.

- **Privacy/confidentiality:** It is not possible to shield a resume from being viewed by a current employer. Only those who purchase a resume password may access the contact information within the resume.

- **Assistance provided to the person submitting a resume:** Yes, through 800-999-6497.

- **Search options available to employers viewing resumes:** Available.

- **Technology to match jobs to resumes and e-mail results to clients:** None at this time; however, this is expected to be available in the next scheduled release.

- **Average number of daily hits on resumes:** 2,500.

- **Other distinguishing factors:** Focused exclusively on specific industry—not diluted with resumes and/or candidates who do not qualify.

BestJobsUSA.com

USA
IT, sales, medical, and engineering
Rating: ★ ★ ★ ★

BestJobsUSA.com is a part of Recourse Communications, the publisher of *Employment Review* magazine.

- **URL:** http://www.BestJobsUSA.com
  Also see local sites at
  http://www.BestJobsFlorida.com
  http://www.BestJobsMassachusetts.com
  http://www.BestJobsOklahoma.com
  http://www.BestJobsTexas.com

- **Ownership/sponsorship:** Recourse Communications Inc.

- **Started accepting resumes:** 1995.

- **Approximate number of resumes online April 2000:** 60,000.

- **Resume career fields:** Resumes are in IT, sales, medical, and engineering career fields.

- **Total number of corporate subscribers/ employers:** 360.

- **Distribution of corporate subscribers/ employers**

  Direct-hire employers: 70 percent

  Staffing firms: 10 percent

  Contract/consulting firms: 20 percent

- **Fee structure for corporate subscribers/ employers:** $250 per month or $2,500 per year.

- **Methods and rules for submitting resumes:** Must fill out online form or submit through ResumeMaker software.

- **Percent of resumes submitted by Web form:** 100.

- **Percent of resumes received from**

  Individuals: 50

  Colleges and universities: 20

  Outplacement firms: 20

  Recruitment events: 10

- **Limits on length:** None.

- **Format:** Use online form.

- **Fees for person submitting resume:** None.

- **Length of time resumes remain online:** n/a.

- **Procedures for updating/renewing:** Total control through use of password access.

- **Privacy/confidentiality:** It is not possible to limit who can see a resume, but personal information can be masked. It is not possible to shield a resume from being viewed by a current employer, but personal information can be masked.

- **Assistance provided to the person submitting a resume:** None.

- **Search options available to employers viewing resumes:** Keyword and advanced searches available.

- **Technology to match jobs to resumes and e-mail results to clients:** Yes—category, state, and keyword field matches.

- **Average number of daily hits on resumes:** n/a.

- **Special features:** HTML possible. Resumes can be constantly updated.

- **Other distinguishing factors:** The Resume Gateway service offered by BestJobsUSA.com allows candidates the ability to always maintain control of their resume document. Consequently, these resumes are always fresh and regularly updated.

CalJOBS.ca.gov

United States, primarily California
All career fields
Rating: ★ ★ ★

CalJOBS is an Internet-based job opening and resume listing system that increases the public's access to employment services. CalJOBS is provided by the California Employment Development Department's Job Service to serve both employers who want to fill job openings and individuals seeking employment. The system is designed to be simple and convenient to use, with over 1.4 million job openings listed annually. There are no fees to either employers or job seekers to use this service.

- **URL:** http://www.caljobs.ca.gov

- **Ownership/sponsorship:** State of California, Employment Development Department (EDD).

- **Started accepting resumes:** 1997.

- **Approximate number of resumes online April 2000:** 600,000.

- **Resume career fields:** Resumes are in all career fields.

- **Total number of corporate subscribers/ employers:** 84,000.

- **Distribution of corporate subscribers/ employers:** n/a.

- **Fee structure for corporate subscribers/ employers:** No fees are charged to employers or job seekers to use the system.

- **Methods and rules for submitting resumes:** n/a.

- **Percent of resumes submitted by Web form:** All resumes are submitted online either through self-entry or staff-assisted entry.

- **Percent of resumes received from individuals:** 100.

- **Limits on length:** May list up to four job objectives; determined by the field size and type of information entered.

- **Format:** Job seekers build their resumes by answering questions or completing pre-established fields within CalJOBS.

- **Fees for person submitting resume:** There are no fees to either the employer or job seeker for use of the system.

- **Length of time resumes remain online:** Resumes remain "active" for 60 days from the last access of the person submitting the resume. Resumes outside of the 60-day window remain on the system and are available to the author for update, but are not displayed to potential employers on a resume search.

- **Procedures for updating/renewing:** Job seekers may update their resumes at any time by selecting the "Update resume" function on the system.

- **Privacy/confidentiality:** It is possible to limit who can see a resume. It is possible to shield a resume from being viewed by a current employer.

- **Assistance provided to the person submitting a resume:** In-person assistance is available in EDD service points. Remote users may contact the Help Desk if they are experiencing problems in entering their resumes.

- **Search options available to employers viewing resumes:** Employers can search resumes by geographic location, occupational category, or job title.

- **Technology to match jobs to resumes and e-mail results to clients:** Job openings are matched to resumes by matching the job objective listed by the job seeker with the occupation listed by the employer. Job seekers may list up to four job objectives per resume, but searches and matches are made only on the primary objective.

CalJOBS allows job seekers to e-mail resumes directly to employers if the employer has indicated they are willing to accept electronic copies.

- **Average number of daily hits on resumes:** CalJOBS receives many hits daily, but they do not correspond to a single user. Rather, since it has many "pages," a "hit" may be a request by a single user to view a single page, or less than a single page if there are multiple files on the page. Consequently, a single user may generate many "hits" in a single session on CalJOBS as they view multiple pages.

- **Special features:** Job seekers have access to other employment and training Internet sites through a series of links built into CalJOBS. Sites can be selected on the basis of those that have wide appeal to a state-wide audience, but can also be tailored to find sites specific to local geographic areas.

Canadian Resume Centre

Canada
All career fields
Rating: ★ ★

The resumes at this site are from Canadians or people who want to work in Canada.

- **URL:** http://www.canres.com

- **Ownership/sponsorship:** Private company.

  The Canadian Resume Centre
  P.O. Box 81060
  Fiddlers Green Postal Outlet
  Ancaster, Ontario, Canada
  L9G 4X1
  Fax: (519) 759-1735

- **Started accepting resumes:** 1997.

- **Approximate number of resumes online April 2000:** 750.

- **Resume career fields:** Resumes are accepted in all career fields.

- **Total number of corporate subscribers/employers:** No tabulation.

- **Distribution of corporate subscribers/employers**

  Direct-hire employers: 25 percent

  Staffing firms: 75 percent

- **Fee structure for corporate subscribers/employers:** No fee.

- **Methods and rules for submitting resumes:** Fill out form on-screen, paste text/resume, and send. For a confidential resume, complete the profile: job title, years of experience, education, keywords to describe what you do (as many as you want), achievements/responsibilities, geographic preference, position desired, subject line (usually your job title or last position), salary, industry, and how you would like to be contacted when an employer wants to see your complete resume.

- **Percent of resumes submitted by**

  E-mail/Web form: 75

  Mail: 15

  Fax: 10

- **Percent of resumes received from individuals:** 100.

- **Limits on length:** None.

- **Format:** E-mail your resume directly to resume@netaccess.on.ca or use the online form. The company accepts only the following formats: .txt, .doc, .rtf, or .wp. Resumes can also be faxed or mailed.

- **Fees for person submitting resume:**

  $25 (Canadian): nonconfidential, e-mailed

  $40 (Canadian): nonconfidential, mailed or faxed

  $50 (Canadian): confidential

- **Length of time resumes remain online:** Six months.

- **Procedures for updating/renewing:** You can change or delete your resume at any time by informing the company by e-mail, fax, or mail.

- **Privacy/confidentiality:** It is possible to limit who can see a resume. Confidential resumes are recommended. It is possible to shield a resume from being viewed by a current employer.

- **Assistance provided to the person submitting a resume:** Fill out the form on-screen; fairly straightforward.

- **Search options available to employers viewing resumes:** Keyword search only. Searches a resume but sees only the profile with no personal/company information for confidential resumes.

- **Technology to match jobs to resumes and e-mail results to clients:** Permission needed to e-mail resume to clients.

- **Average number of daily hits on resumes:** 46 per month.

- **Special features:** Confidential resumes. (Employers leave contact information, and the job seeker decides whether to send a resume.)

- **Other distinguishing factors:** Primarily for Canadian job seekers and those wanting to work in Canada. Section for employers to post jobs: $25 (Canadian) for three months.

CareerMagazine

USA

Computer, engineering, manufacturing, finance, sales, and retail

Rating: ★ ★ ★ ★

Boulder, Colorado–based CareerMagazine's Web site features a magazine format and offers comprehensive employment information catering to both job candidates and potential employers. These include job listings, employer profiles, a resume bank, a career forum (for advice exchange), and a variety of articles relating to the job search process. CareerMag.com pioneered the online employment magazine format and also was one of the first Web sites solely dedicated to Internet recruitment services.

- **URL:** http://www.careermag.com

- **Ownership/sponsorship:** CareerMag is now owned by VerticalNet Inc. VerticalNet.com is a public company involved in providing B2B solutions and e-commerce through 56 vertical trade communities.

- **Started accepting resumes:** 1994.

- **Approximate number of resumes online April 2000:** Over 80,000.

- **Resume career fields:** Resumes are primarily in IT/MIS, computer/data processing, sales/marketing, accounting/finance, engineering, insurance, manufacturing, and retail.

- **Total number of corporate subscribers/employers:** 600.

- **Distribution of corporate subscribers/employers**

  Direct-hire employers: 30 percent

  Staffing firms: 52 percent

Contract/consulting firms: 7 percent

Others (products and services): 11 percent

- **Fee structure for corporate subscribers/employers:**

A single job order for $135 for 42 days

Corporate posting packages range from $3,500 to $29,000 per year and include job postings, employer profile, and resume-bank access.

- **Methods and rules for submitting resumes:** Online form; follow the instructions.

- **Percent of resumes submitted by Web form:** 100.

- **Percentage of resumes received from**

Individuals: 80

Outplacement firms: 10

Colleges or universities: 10 (This area is growing because of new programs.)

- **Limits on length:** None.

- **Format:** Use Web form.

- **Fees for person submitting resume:** None. Current promotion is free.

- **Length of time resumes remain online:** Six months to one year.

- **Procedures for updating/renewing:** Web interface with username and password.

- **Privacy/confidentiality:** It is possible to limit who can see a resume because the site now allows resumes to be confidential and contact made through blind e-mail. The site also allows storage of resumes without possible viewing by employers.

- **Assistance provided to the person submitting a resume:** E-mail/phone number if the directions do not work.

- **Search options available to employers viewing resumes:** Relational search by location, skill, and title.

- **Technology to match jobs to resumes and e-mail results to clients:** JobNotes is CareerMagazine's e-mail notification to candidates of available jobs. After being notified via e-mail, the candidates go to their Web interfaces in CareerMagazine and get the full, detailed information on the matching job openings. From a recruitment perspective, the company does not send candidate resumes. This decision is not based on a programming issue; rather, CareerMagazine feels that sending out resumes without the job seeker's permission raises ethical issues.

- **Average number of daily hits on resumes:** Of the entire site, resumes are the second most frequently hit portion.

- **Special features:** Relational database makes searching easy. Users' feedback tells CareerMagazine that this feature is very helpful when the time to find resumes is short, and it makes it almost impossible to miss opportunities in a given area instead of just a specific city.

- **Other distinguishing factors:** Articles section (called Career "Magazine") offers a range of articles about legal issues, interviewing, diversity, and so on. This section also features the On Campus section.

CareerPath

USA
All career fields
Rating: ★ ★ ★ ★ ★

CareerPath.com was co-founded in 1995 by the *Boston Globe, Chicago Tribune, Los Angeles Times, The New York Times, San Jose Mercury*

News, and *The Washington Post.* CareerPath.com brings to the Web the largest and most current database of job listings from over 90 affiliated newspapers across the United States. Over 300,000 jobs are posted and updated daily by its affiliated newspapers.

- **URL:** http://www.careerpath.com

- **Ownership/sponsorship:** *The Boston Globe, Chicago Tribune, Los Angeles Times, The New York Times, San Jose Mercury-News,* and *The Washington Post.* Financial backing is provided by Knight-Ridder, New York Times Company, Times Mirror Company, Tribune Company, The Washington Post Company, Cox Interactive Media, Gannett Company, and Hearst Corporation.

  Corporate headquarters:

  10880 Wilshire Blvd.
  Suite 600
  Los Angeles, CA 90024
  310-234-1400

- **Started accepting resumes:** Fourth quarter 1997. Within a few months, it became one of the largest sites for resumes on the Internet.

- **Approximate number of resumes online April 2000:** Over 1 million.

- **Resume career fields:** Resumes are accepted in all job classifications.

- **Total number of corporate subscribers/ employers:** Hundreds of leading companies.

- **Distribution of corporate subscribers/ employers**

  Direct-hire employers: 90 percent

  Staffing firms: 5 percent

  Contract/consulting firms: 5 percent

- **Fee structure for corporate subscribers/ employers:** n/a.

- **Methods and rules for submitting resumes:** Job seekers follow the step-by-step process on CareerPath's Resume Connection to prepare a searchable resume.

- **Percent of resumes submitted by**

  Web form: 97

  Job fairs of affiliated newspapers: 3

- **Percent of resumes received from individuals:** 100.

- **Limits on length:** No limit on employment history. The Resume Connection form prompts users to fill in necessary data.

- **Format:** Specified by the Resume Connection interactive form.

- **Fees for person submitting resume:** None.

- **Length of time resumes remain online:** Six months.

- **Procedures for updating/renewing:** Resumes can be updated by the job seekers whenever they want. Those with resumes online are notified that their resumes will be made inactive when they've been unchanged on the site for six months. If at this time job seekers want to keep their resumes in Resume Connection, they simply need to view their resumes on CareerPath to keep them actively searchable.

- **Privacy/confidentiality:** It is possible to limit who can see a resume. No employer will see a job seeker's resume unless that job seeker has given permission for it to be viewed by that particular employer. It is also possible to shield a resume from being viewed by a current employer because of the protection given by the need for permission.

■ **Assistance provided to the person submitting a resume:** Resume Connection's interactive format walks job seekers though the process, step by step.

■ **Search options available to employers viewing resumes:** For employers, the CareerPath.com Resume Connection product provides access to the industry's most precise resume search engine on the Internet to accurately identify the best candidates available from its resume database. With the CareerPath.com Resume Scout product, employers can instantly and simultaneously search virtually every Internet resume source.

■ **Technology to match jobs to resumes and e-mail results to clients:** All resume searches are performed by CareerPath staffing specialists, who contact job seekers via e-mail (to ensure privacy) and then fax qualified and interested candidates' resumes to the employer.

■ **Special features:**

Job database—Job seekers can search (by using keywords) more than 60 newspapers from across the United States. These newspapers post jobs from their classified sections on CareerPath every week, with an average of nearly 300,000 jobs per day, none more than two weeks old.

CareerPathEXTRA—Jobs listed on corporate Web sites are searchable on CareerPath, so job seekers who are interested in a particular company also have searchable access to jobs on the Web, in addition to those from newspapers across the United States.

Employer profiles—In-depth employer information is available on CareerPath, with links to corporate Web sites when applicable.

Resources—The finest job-hunting strategies and tips have been aggregated on

CareerPath for use by job seekers. CareerPath.com offers a comprehensive suite of career-management resources including individualized career counseling, salary search, technical skills certification, and online educational courses.

Other distinguishing factors: Job seeker privacy is the number-one priority for CareerPath; therefore, no resume is forwarded to any employer without the express permission of the job seeker. Also, the staffing specialists ensure that employers receive only those resumes that fit their staffing needs. A clear, concise, and intuitive design interface ensures that the job seeker can access CareerPath's information quickly and easily.

careerbuilder.com

USA and global
All career fields
Rating: ★ ★ ★ ★

CareerBuilder Inc. (Nasdaq: CBDR) is the leading provider of targeted Web recruiting and attracts about three million unique monthly visitors to its CareerBuilder Network. Using Mega Job Search℠ technology, careerbuilder.com and select affiliate network sites provide a targeted search of nearly every job on the Internet. CareerBuilder also provides personalized career services and advice. The CareerBuilder Network includes careerbuilder.com—the flagship career center—and about 30 affiliate job sites including MSN, Bloomberg, USATODAY.com, NBC, and Ticketmaster Online-CitySearch. Employer customers include AT&T, AOL, Merrill Lynch, and EDS. CareerBuilder is headquartered in Reston, Virginia, and has offices nationwide.

CareerBuilder is committed to long-term partnerships and the highest level of customer care and satisfaction. We help employers select the most effective programs and career sites based on the company's individual recruiting needs and hiring goals. Employers can create customized and creative Web recruiting campaigns.

- **URL:** http://www.careerbuilder.com

- **Ownership/sponsorship:** CareerBuilder, Inc.

- **Started accepting resumes:** Just launched Resume Database in May 2000.

- **Resume career fields:** Resumes are in all career fields.

- **Total number of corporate subscribers/ employers:** n/a.

- **Distribution of corporate subscribers/ employers:** n/a.

- **Fee structure for corporate subscribers/ employers:** Pricing varies based on length of membership, number of postings, and number of recruiters.

- **Methods and rules for submitting resumes:** Resumes submitted to the CareerBuilder Network are received through "my careerbuilder." Job seekers can find my careerbuilder on careerbuilder.com and select affiliate network sites. CareerBuilder tracks resume submissions by CareerBuilder Network Affiliation.

- **Percent of resumes submitted by Web form:** n/a.

- **Percent of resumes received from individuals:** Anyone can submit a resume to the Resume Database.

- **Limits on length:** n/a.

- **Format:** Through "my careerbuilder," job seekers can upload, or cut and paste, their resumes into the Resume Database. The system automatically converts the text to HTML.

- **Fees for person submitting resume:** None.

- **Length of time resumes remain online:** Resumes remain in the Resume Database for a year, or until they are requested to be removed.

- **Procedures for updating/renewing:** Job seekers are given a username and password. They can access and update their resumes at any given time and as often as they want. A customized cover letter can also be created and stored on "my careerbuilder." This allows for greater speed and efficiency when applying for jobs online.

- **Privacy/confidentiality:** CareerBuilder's Resume Database allows job seekers to enter their resumes as either "searchable" or "private." A searchable resume is searchable by Resume Database employer clients. Job seekers can also decide to block specific companies, including their current employer, from viewing their resume. A private resume allows job seekers to build and store resumes on careerbuilder.com so that they can apply for jobs online, but does not allow employers to access them through the resume database.

- **Assistance provided to the person submitting a resume:** Extensive online content assistance is available for job seekers.

- **Search options available to employers viewing resumes:** Employers can search resumes by date, job category, location, desired salary, education level, willingness to relocate and/or travel, years of experience, security clearance, eligibility to work in the U.S., and even keywords. Employers can create up to 250 different resume search agents, allowing them to identify specific search criteria for various positions.

■ **Technology to match jobs to resumes and e-mail results to clients:** CareerBuilder's Resume Database uses up to 250 resume search agents to match resumes with employers. The Resume Database allows employers to target their recruiting efforts, saving valuable time and money. Through my careerbuilder on careerbuilder.com and select affiliate network sites, job seekers can create up to five personal search agents to track jobs that precisely match their skills and preferences. Results for job seekers and employers are delivered by e-mail. The user can choose daily, weekly, biweekly, or monthly notifications.

■ **Average number of daily hits on resumes:** n/a.

■ **Special features:** Using Mega Job Search℠ technology, careerbuilder.com and select affiliate network sites provide a targeted search of virtually every job on the Internet. Mega Job Search℠ is the largest, most targeted search engine on the Web, providing access to virtually every online job posting.

In order to protect job seeker privacy, CareerBuilder does not sell its Resume Database to recruiting agencies or headhunters.

The CareerBuilder Network, an industry first, includes careerbuilder.com—the flagship career center—and about 30 affiliate job sites, including MSN, Bloomberg, USATODAY.com, NBC, and Ticketmaster Online-CitySearch.

CareerCity

USA
All career fields
Rating: ★ ★ ★

CareerCity was launched in 1995 by Adams Media Corporation, a publisher of job search and career books. CareerCity is a Lycos Top Five Percent Web site and is an Electronic Recruiting News "Master Site" and an Excellence in Electronic Recruiting award winner.

■ **URL:** http://www.careercity.com

■ **Ownership/sponsorship:** CareerCity, Daniel J. Hunter, president and CEO. CareerCity is a registered trademark of Adams Media Corporation.

■ **Started accepting resumes:** 1997.

■ **Approximate number of resumes online April 2000:** 80,000.

■ **Resume career fields:** Resumes are in all career fields; however, the site is specifically designed for technical and professional people.

■ **Total number of corporate subscribers/ employers:** n/a.

■ **Distribution of corporate subscribers/ employers**

  Direct-hire employers: 60 percent

  Staffing firms: 40 percent

■ **Fee structure for corporate subscribers/ employers:** n/a.

■ **Methods and rules for submitting resumes:** Go to www.careercity.com/res and submit via that Web page. Resumes not accepted by e-mail.

■ **Percent of resumes submitted by Web form:** 100.

■ **Percent of resumes received from individuals:** 100.

■ **Limits on length:** None.

■ **Format:** Use Web form.

■ **Fees for person submitting resume:** None.

■ **Length of time resumes remain online:** One year.

- **Procedures for updating/renewing:** Log in via Web by using name and password.

- **Privacy/confidentiality:** It is possible to limit who can see a resume. It is possible to shield a resume from being viewed by a current employer.

- **Assistance provided to the person submitting a resume:** E-mail assistance and sample resumes onsite.

- **Search options available to employers viewing resumes:** Keyword, occupational category, level of experience, willingness to relocate.

- **Technology to match jobs to resumes and e-mail results to clients:** n/a.

- **Average number of daily hits on resumes:** n/a.

- **Special features:** Career advice from one of the largest print publishers in the field.

CareerExchange.com

USA and Canada
Information technology, engineering, management, sales, and marketing
Rating: ★ ★ ★

CareerExchange is a recruiting Web site that has developed a specialization in the high-tech industry. The majority of the resumes come from U.S. and Canadian high-technology individuals.

- **URL:** http://www.careerexchange.com/

- **Ownership/sponsorship:** Cytiva Inc.

- **Started accepting resumes:** 1998.

- **Approximate number of resumes online April 2000:** 30,000.

- **Resume career fields:** Resumes are in all career fields.

- **Total number of corporate subscribers/ employers:** 400.

- **Distribution of corporate subscribers/ employers**

  Direct-hire employers: 30 percent

  Staffing firms: 50 percent

  Contract/consulting firms: 20 percent

- **Fee structure for corporate subscribers/ employers:**

  Single job posting, $90 for 30 days.

  Up to 10 positions, $249 per month.

  Up to 20 positions, $295 per month.

  Unlimited positions, $395 per month.

- **Methods and rules for submitting resumes:** Via Web site.

- **Percent of resumes submitted by Web form:** 100.

- **Percent of resumes received from**

  Individuals: 90

  Colleges and universities: 10

- **Limits on length:** None.

- **Format:** Text.

- **Fees for person submitting resume:** None.

- **Length of time resumes remain online:** Until removed.

- **Procedures for updating/renewing:** Log in and edit.

- **Privacy/confidentiality:** It is possible to limit who can see a resume. It is possible to shield a resume from being viewed by a current employer.

- **Assistance provided to the person submitting a resume:** None.

- **Search options available to employers viewing resumes:** Keyword, location, and date posted.

- **Technology to match jobs to resumes and e-mail results to clients:** None.

- **Average number of daily hits on resumes:** n/a.

- **Special features:** Offers employers extensive cross-postings of jobs to other career-related sites.

- **Other distinguishing factors:** Offers real-time recruiting. Employers and job seekers can immediately start chatting about a job opening.

CareerShop.com

USA
Technology, financial, engineering, management, and sales
Rating: ★ ★ ★

CareerShop.com merged with two information technology–specific sites during 1999: PlanetResume.com and SelectJobs.com are now a part of CareerShop.com.

CareerShop.com offers career management and corporate recruiting solutions by cobining the reach of the Internet with the power of television. Services include a free job search section where job seekers can search the CareerShop.com database, along with up to 42 other job databases on the Internet, all at the same time. (Sites included in the job search section include Monster.com, HotJobs, Headhunter.net, plus many others.) CareerShop.com also offers free online resume posting, online job posting and distribution to more than 150 partner sites (streaming video attached to job postings available), and a searchable resume database that includes more than 350,000 professional resumes. Additionally, it has a weekly television show called CareerTV that addresses employment, recruiting, and job search topics. CareerTV is currently airing in various local markets.

- **URL:** http://www.CareerShop.com

- **Ownership/sponsorship:** Privately owned.

- **Started accepting resumes:** 1996.

- **Approximate number of resumes online April 2000:** More than 350,000.

- **Resume career fields:** Resumes can be posted into 24 categories including accounting/bookkeeping, data processing/programming, technical, engineering, sales/marketing/advertising, financial, and management.

- **Total number of corporate subscribers/employers:** More than 650.

- **Distribution of corporate subscribers/employers**

  Direct-hire employers: 65 percent

  Staffing firms: 35 percent

- **Fee structure for corporate subscribers/employers:** Call 800-639-2060 or e-mail sales@CareerShop.com for current membership plans/rates.

- **Methods and rules for submitting resumes:** Resume posters simply enter their information in a resume posting form, and can cut and paste an existing resume directly from their word-processing software. The resume-posting process takes approximately 15 minutes if a candidate has an existing resume.

- **Percent of resumes submitted by Web form:** CareerShop.com resumes submitted by Web form. In addition, newsgroup and employer Web resume search sections have the following distributions:

  Spider search of newsgroups and Internet resume sites: 80 percent

  E-mail: 20 percent

- **Percent of resumes received from individuals:** n/a.

- **Limits on length:** None.

- **Format:** Use Web form. The body of the applicant's existing resume can be pasted directly from word processing software into the resume window.

- **Fees for person submitting resume:** None.

- **Length of time resumes remain online:** Resumes remain active in the database for up to 120 days and can be updated or deleted at any time. When a resume poster updates a resume, the expiration date automatically extends 120 days from the date of update.

- **Procedures for updating/renewing:** Resume posters can log in and update their resume at any time.

- **Privacy/confidentiality:** At this time, it is not possible to limit access to a specific resume by a particular employer. Employer customers can view any resume in the database through the employer resume search section. A membership is required to view contact information in any resume. Resumes can be entered using the name "Confidential," and the current employer's name does not have to be included in resume information.

- **Assistance provided to the person submitting a resume:** Applicants can e-mail CareerShop.com at any time for assistance: webmaster@CareerShop.com.

- **Search options available to employers viewing resumes:** Employers can search up to three resume categories at one time by using any of the following search criteria: preferred state, degree required, keywords, and/or logic, whole words only, or any part of a word.

- **Technology to match jobs to resumes and e-mail results to clients:** CareerShop.com's automated Robo Resume Match process is provided to all employers who purchase a job-posting membership. This service matches resumes entered in the database to all active job postings. Resume matches automatically e-mail directly to the posting employer. The Resume Match process runs each evening Sunday through Thursday every week and is free to all resume posters.

- **Average number of daily hits on resumes:** n/a.

- **Special features:** In addition to free resume posting and job searches, CareerShop.com also offers job seekers local job fairs that are extremely beneficial. CareerShop.com has over 40 online job fair pages that feature local and national employers' job openings.

CareerSite

USA
All career fields
Rating: ★ ★ ★ ★ ★

CareerSite's affiliate recruitment solution provides everything an Internet site needs to offer customers a full-featured e-recruiting service. This includes hosting, customer service, distribution, and access to CareerSite's database of over 200,000 candidates (recently rated number two in resume quality by the national Electronic Recruiting Index). CareerSite is also the first and only e-recruiting solution provider to offer its co-brand partners an innovative business model with a free recruiting tool for their customers.

CareerSite.com powers five industry-specific employment sites (American Bankers Association, Energy.com, EnviroXchange.com, Improvemybusiness.com, and Key Corporation) and 15 regional employment sites (Abracat, Alabama Live, Cleveland Live, Mass Live, Michigan Live, New Jersey Online, NOLA Live, Oregon Live, Penn Live, Staten

Island Live, Syracuse Online, Hire Atlanta, Hire Charlotte, Hire Dallas, and Hire San Francisco).

Using a password-protected, confidential profile that does not contain any identifying information, candidates can market themselves anonymously to employers while maintaining complete control over resume exposure. In addition, CareerSite's proprietary SmartMatch™ technology searches for jobs using concepts rather than simple words. This ensures that job seekers find all relevant positions. With one click, candidates receive automatic e-mail notification of job matches based on registered preferences, online resume storage, cover letter submissions, and the ability to search and apply for jobs. Additional services include customer service and a career resource center.

- **URL:** http://www.careersite.com

- **Ownership/sponsorship:** Private.

- **Started accepting resumes:** 1995.

- **Approximate number of resumes online April 2000:** 238,000.

- **Resume career fields:** Resumes are in all career fields.

- **Total number of corporate subscribers/ employers:** Approximately 8,000.

- **Distribution of corporate subscribers/ employers**

   Direct-hire employers: 65 percent

   Staffing/recruiting firms: 35 percent

- **Fee structure for corporate subscribers/ employers**

   Free:

   Unlimited postings

   Cross-posting to major free sites

   Job and Response Management Tool

Plus:

Plus membership gives you all the features of the Free membership plus a three-page corporate profile and a link to your Web site for $25 per three months.

Premium:

Premium membership gives you all the features of the Free membership plus a three-page corporate profile, a link to your Web site, and unlimited candidate searching for $145 per three months (recruiting agencies/headhunters $295).

- **Methods and rules for submitting resumes:** Job seekers fill out a simple profile that contains an overview of their interests, qualifications, and skills. The text they enter is matched to related concepts, and candidates are allowed to confirm the importance of the terms in their profile. They can then upload their actual resume, which is converted into an Adobe PDF and text file in real time. Resumes are not given to employers without candidate approval.

- **Percent of resumes submitted by Web form:** 100.

- **Percent of resumes received from individuals:** 100.

- **Limits on length:** n/a.

- **Format:** Web form.

- **Fees for person submitting resume:** None.

- **Length of time resumes remain online:** Job seeker profiles remain active 90 days after the last log-in date. Candidates are merely inactivated from appearing in searches. Profiles are never removed from the CareerSite database. Job seekers are usually employed and looking for the "right" job, so they continue to search and update their resumes.

- **Procedures for updating/renewing:** Online and very easy; with one click, your resume is in the system.

- **Privacy/confidentiality:** Candidates have complete control over identity disclosure. Employers view profiles that candidates create (including credentials, skills, and interests). However, personal contact information is withheld.

- **Assistance provided to the person submitting a resume:** CareerSite does not offer resume-writing services.

- **Search options available to employers viewing resumes:** Employers can search by occupation, location, industry, skills, and education. Responses to candidate profile searches are relevance-ranked for ease in viewing and comparing candidates. Employers can review profiles and request candidate resumes through the site.

- **Technology to match jobs to resumes and e-mail results to clients:** The same concept-based SmartMatch™ technology that powers the candidate profiles allows employers to enter free text and have individual terms narrowed down to concepts. A search for a "programmer" will provide candidate profiles that contain "software engineer," "software developer," "programmer," and even "programer," a common misspelling.

- **Average number of daily hits on resumes:** Over 300,000 individual visitors each month.

- **Special features:** CareerSite regularly matches candidates with the jobs they are seeking.

- **Other distinguishing factors:** CareerSite searches and matches on an 85,000-synonym knowledge base. CareerSite also powers a number of other national, regional, and industry-specific sites (over 20) that allow candidates and employers maximum exposure for their jobs and resumes.

Has a desktop recruiting-management system.

Is able to reach the passive job seeker.

Can automatically update all jobs directly from an employer's own Web site.

Cross-posts jobs to other recruitment sites.

Automatically acknowledges all replies by e-mail.

Requires no installation, upkeep, or update of software.

Accommodates multiple users with one ID and password or multiple passwords under one ID.

Casino Careers Online

Primarily USA, some international
Casino-gaming hospitality industry
Rating: ★ ★ ★ ★

This site is designed, built, and managed specifically for gaming-industry recruitment needs.

- **URL:** http://www.casinocareers.com

- **Ownership/sponsorship:** Privately owned.

- **Started accepting resumes:** 1998.

- **Approximate number of resumes online April 2000:** 6,500.

- **Resume career fields:** Resumes are in casino-gaming (slots, table games, administration, technology, pari-mutuel, poker), hospitality (food and beverage, hotel operations, housekeeping, engineering/facilities, transportation), accounting/finance (casino/hotel, internal audit, credit, collections), marketing (casino, player development, advertising, public relations, hotel/convention and retail sales, database/direct marketing), and support services (management information systems, security, surveillance, human resources, purchasing, legal/compliance).

- **Total number of corporate subscribers/ employers:** Over 65 gaming companies.

- **Distribution of corporate subscribers/employers**

  Direct-hire employers: 98 percent

  Staffing firms: 1 percent

  Contract/consulting firms: 1 percent

- **Fee structure for corporate subscribers/ employers**

  $750: Three Web pages to post open positions for a three-month period (site designs the Web pages, and the company may change postings at any time).

  $1,000: Six Web pages to post open positions for a three-month period (site designs the Web pages, and the company may change postings at any time).

  $5,000 a year: Annual Corporate Membership with unlimited access to search the database (with all special features and unlimited job posting), for facilities with fewer than 1,000 employees.

  $8,000 a year: Annual Membership for facilities with 1,000–2,500 employees.

  $10,000 a year: Annual Membership for facilities with more than 2,500 employees.

  $1,200: Separate Web page for each additional property executive who wishes to have access to the database.

- **Methods and rules for submitting resumes:** A candidate must have any of the following:

  A degree or certification from any academic, technical, mechanical, culinary, or gaming-related school, OR a minimum of one year of experience in a salaried or certified professional position (dealers, slot technicians, paralegals), OR a minimum of one year of supervisory experience, OR a minimum of one year of experience in a hospitality-related position (food and beverage, front office, housekeeping), OR a minimum of one year of managerial or above experience in the casino-gaming industry or a field related to the gaming-hospitality industry. All candidates should have a good work record, be eligible for gaming licensure commensurate with any position they are seeking, and be able to provide references to a prospective employer who requests such documentation. All candidates must have a working e-mail address and "update" their resume a minimum of once every six months (even if it is to just click on the "Update" button), to let companies know that the candidate is still interested in casino career opportunities.

- **Percent of resumes submitted by Web form:** 100.

- **Percent of resumes received from individuals:** 100.

- **Limits on length:** None.

- **Format:** Defined by specific fields.

- **Fees for person submitting resume:** None.

- **Length of time resumes remain online:** As long as candidate maintains deliverable resume and updates it as stipulated in the eligibility requirements and doesn't falsify information.

- **Procedures for updating/renewing:** Easily accomplished through the Edit menu. Access is limited to resumes to the companies who subscribe to use Casino Careers Online services; however, the candidate may post the resume in "Confidential Format" and only the ID# is visible (in lieu of any identifying information, inclusive of e-mail address).

■ **Privacy/confidentiality:** It is possible to shield a resume from being viewed by a current employer by using Confidential Format.

■ **Assistance provided to the person submitting a resume:** Online tech support and phone support is available.

■ **Search options available to employers viewing resumes:** Companies may search by title, industry, discipline, years of experience, or any combination.

■ **Technology to match jobs to resumes and e-mail results to clients:** Search fields in each resume as defined above, as well as mass e-mail (standard or customized correspondence) capabilities to all resumes that come up in a search match. Smart Search identifies new resumes posted to the database (with company notification), and resumes can be individually accessed using Resume Grabber.

■ **Average number of daily hits on resumes:** Depends on the candidate's areas of expertise (and the Job Profiles they created); however, over 65 gaming companies may search any of the above criteria, 24 hours a day, 7 days a week. Some gaming facilities are opening new casino-hotels and need candidates in every department of the property.

■ **Special features:** Any online resume can be opened with Resume Grabber using the candidate's name or ID number. These resumes can be printed or e-mailed directly to another department head for review. Job postings have a hyperlink to the company's e-mail address and to the company's Web site—they can change the position posted or the contact information at anytime. Multiple resumes can also be opened simultaneously, by searching the database by title, industry, discipline, or any combination thereof. Companies can also be apprised of new resumes added to the database for the positions they are seeking to fill. All e-mail correspondence to the job seeker from the site is customized with each company's name and title.

Christian Jobs Online

Global
All career fields
Rating: ★ ★ ★

Christian Jobs Online was founded to assist the Christian job seeker in finding employment with organizations that are also committed to Christ. Advertisers are requested to sign a Statement of Faith. Those that do display a logo in their ad.

■ **URL:** http://christianjobs.com

■ **Ownership/sponsorship:** Christian Jobs Online.

■ **Started accepting resumes:** 1996.

■ **Approximate number of resumes online April 2000:** Over 500.

■ **Resume career fields:** Resumes are in all career fields.

■ **Total number of corporate subscribers/ employers:** Christian Jobs Online has a large client base. Clients work with them as a need arises and do not have a contract with them.

■ **Distribution of corporate subscribers/employers:** n/a.

■ **Fee structure for corporate subscribers/ employers:** $75 per listing per month to advertise employment opportunities. $25 per month to access the resume database (free to current advertisers).

■ **Methods and rules for submitting resumes:** Resumes are accepted only via online submission form. Resumes can be only ASCII or HTML-formatted.

- **Percent of resumes submitted by Web form:** 100.

- **Percent of resumes received from individuals:** 100.

- **Limits on length:** None.

- **Format:** ASCII or HTML only.

- **Fees for person submitting resume:** None.

- **Length of time resumes remain online:** Six months or until the individual posting the resume removes it.

- **Procedures for updating/renewing:** Online form. Access to our resume database requires a password, which can be requested via an online form. Access to the database is $25 per month (free to current advertisers).

- **Privacy/confidentiality:** It is not possible to shield a resume from being viewed by a current employer.

- **Assistance provided to the person submitting a resume:** E-mail Customer Service with questions.

- **Search options available to employers viewing resumes:** Search by keyword or state.

Collegegrad.com

Primarily USA and Canada
Entry-level (recent college grads)
Rating: ★ ★ ★ ★ ★

Collegegrad.com is exclusively for entry-level college grads. Collegegrad.com is the largest open-access career Web site for college students and recent grads.

- **URL:** http://www.collegegrad.com

- **Ownership/sponsorship:** iCollege.com.

- **Started accepting resumes:** 1998.

- **Approximate number of resumes online April 2000:** 50,000.

- **Resume career fields:** Resumes are exclusively entry-level college graduates.

- **Total number of corporate subscribers/employers:** 6,000.

- **Distribution of corporate subscribers/employers**

  Direct-hire employers: 96 percent

  Contract/consulting firms: 4 percent

- **Fee structure for corporate subscribers/employers:** Employers pay for job postings and resume searches at the site.

- **Methods and rules for submitting resumes:** Simply register, then upload as many as five different resumes.

- **Percent of resumes submitted by Web form:** 100.

- **Percent of resumes received from**

  Individuals: 95

  Colleges and universities: 5

- **Limits on length:** None.

- **Format:** Any format that can be attached.

- **Fees for person submitting resume:** None. All candidate and college access is free.

- **Length of time resumes remain online:** Job seeker selects the time resume remains online for up to three months, which can be renewed.

- **Procedures for updating/renewing:** Updating and renewing is all done online.

- **Privacy/confidentiality:** It is not possible to limit who can see a resume. It is not possible to shield a resume from being viewed by a current employer. (All resumes are from entry-level college graduates.)

- **Assistance provided to the person submitting a resume:** Full online FAQ along with tech support.

- **Search options available to employers viewing resumes:** Geography, keyword, major, and salary.

- **Technology to match jobs to resumes and e-mail results to clients:** Automated resume and job matching along with e-mail notification.

- **Average number of daily hits on resumes:** 10,000.

- **Special features:** The site has an online library of more than 140 Quickstart entry-level resume templates located at www.collegegrad.com/resumes/quickstart. All resume templates are available for free download.

- **Other distinguishing factors:** The site has more job search material (over 500 pages) than any other site. Also includes an employer database of more than 6,000 active entry-level employers. If you are a college student or recent grad, this is the site to search for jobs and post your resume. You won't have to sort through the thousands of "experience required" positions or employers to get to the jobs that are right for you.

Colorado Online Job Connection

Colorado only
All career fields
Rating: ★ ★ ★

The Colorado Online Job Connection (COJC) was established in 1995 as a search tool for a Colorado recruiting firm. It serves the needs of Colorado job seekers and the Colorado business community.

- **URLs:** http://www.coloradojobs.com
http://www.denverjobs.com
http://www.jobsincolorado.com

http://www.peakweb.com
(All URLs point to the same place.)

- **Ownership/sponsorship:** Coloradojobs.com (Colorado owned and operated).

- **Started accepting resumes:** 1995.

- **Approximate number of resumes online April 2000:** 5,000.

- **Resume career fields:** Resumes are accepted in all career fields.

- **Total number of corporate subscribers/ employers:** More than 300.

- **Distribution of corporate subscribers/ employers**

  Direct-hire employers: 95 percent

  Staffing firms: 3 percent

  Contract/consulting firms: 2 percent

- **Fee structure for corporate subscribers/ employers:** Employers can post a single job ad for as little as $100 for 30 days. Job Bundles, which are discounted packages for buying job posts in bulk, range from $750 for 10 jobs, $1,950 for 30 jobs, and $2,700 for 50 jobs. These packages do not include resume database access. Premium packages include resume database access, company link/logo listed on the main page for more visibility, and a mini Web page describing the company, with automatic insertion of the company's jobs into the mini Web page. Premium packages range from three-month to one-year subscriptions.

- **Methods and rules for submitting resumes:** All users must abide by the posted terms of service. Users can choose a username and password and then submit their resume in real-time via a forms interface. Users without a current resume can build an online resume using the online resume builder.

173

- **Percent of resumes submitted by**

  Web form: 99.9

  E-mail: Less than 1

- **Percent of resumes received from**

  Individuals: 99

  Outplacement firms: 1

- **Limits on length:** 10,000 characters.

- **Format:** ASCII text.

- **Fees for person submitting resume:** None.

- **Length of time resumes remain online:** A maximum of six months unless renewed.

- **Procedures for updating/renewing:** Log in using a username/password combination and then just choose the appropriate option—a very simple two-step operation.

- **Privacy/confidentiality:** It is not possible at this time to limit who can see a resume. It is not possible at this time to shield a resume from being viewed by a current employer.

- **Assistance provided to the person submitting a resume:** Via e-mail or toll free 877-919-JOBS.

- **Search options available to employers viewing resumes:** Employers can execute a keyword search against the full text of the resume using Boolean search operators; or they can search for an exact phrase within the resume. Employers can also search against the user's self-defined title. Many options are given to the employer for sorting the results of the search.

- **Technology to match jobs to resumes and e-mail results to clients:** None.

- **Average number of daily hits on resumes:** Daily hits on resumes are not calculated at this time.

- **Special features:** In addition to providing employment opportunities, the site is an information portal to resume-writing sites; career sites; other job sites; Colorado real estate; Colorado news, sports, weather, and relocation info; plus many links to other Colorado sites of interest. It also provides resume-writing tips.

- **Other distinguishing factors:** The Colorado Online Job Connection was developed to serve the needs of the Colorado job seeker and the Colorado business community. Job seekers visit the site because they are interested in top-notch opportunities in Colorado with some of Colorado's most prestigious employers. Unlike large national sites, it focuses only on Colorado.

The site has joined forces with Channel 7, ABC's Denver affiliate. Channel 7 advertises the Colorado Online Job Connection more than 120 times per month as part of their 7 InTouch promotional campaign. This means more opportunities for job seekers and much more visibility for the Colorado Online Job Connection. This association also means that employers can now come to one place and choose from two very effective and powerful media to help them reach their hiring goals.

Contract Employment Weekly

USA
Temporary technical jobs
Rating: ★ ★ ★

Contract Employment Weekly has been the primary trade magazine serving the temporary technical industry since 1969. A technical temporary or contract employee is an individual who works for a contract service firm on temporary job assignment for that firm's client company. Approximately 550 contract offices advertise their current and anticipated job openings in *Contract Employment Weekly.*

- **URL:** http://www.cjhunter.com

- **Ownership/sponsorship:** C.E. Publications.

- **Started accepting resumes:** 1998.

- **Approximate number of resumes online April 2000:** 8,000–10,000.

- **Resume career fields:** Resumes are in all engineering, IT/IS, and technical job classifications.

- **Total number of corporate subscribers/ employers:** More than 500.

- **Distribution of corporate subscribers/ employers:** 100 percent are staffing firms, which include contract/consulting firms.

- **Fee structure for corporate subscribers/ employers:** Varies from $115 per month to more than $350 per week.

- **Methods and rules for submitting resumes:** You must be a *C.E. Weekly* subscriber or a ContractJobHunter member.

- **Percentage of resumes submitted by**

  Input by subscribers/members: 30

  E-mail: 25

  Diskette: 10

  Web form: 10

  Fax: 5

  Other paper (job fairs, mailings): 20

- **Percent of resumes received from individuals:** 100.

- **Limits on length:** None.

- **Format:** Open.

- **Fees for person submitting resume:** None, but you must be a subscriber/member.

- **Length of time resumes remain online:** As long as an individual is a subscriber/member (or you can deactivate the resume).

- **Procedures for updating/renewing:** Available.

- **Privacy/confidentiality:** It is possible to limit who can see a resume. Shielding a resume from being viewed by a current employer is not possible if that employer is a current advertiser.

- **Assistance provided to the person submitting a resume:** Instructions are covered in both the Subscriber's Manual and online at the Web site. Phone assistance is also available. Subscribers can input or edit their own resumes online.

- **Search options available to employers viewing resumes:** Search by keywords, location of subscriber/member, or input date of resume.

- **Technology to match jobs to resumes and e-mail results to clients:** Staffing firm can submit keywords or locations, and new or edited resumes are automatically e-mailed to them (every day); also, when online resumes are viewed by recruiters, *Contract Employment Weekly* e-mails the subscribers that their resumes have been viewed or downloaded, and by whom.

- **Average number of daily hits on resumes:** 5,000–7,500.

Contract Engineering

USA
Engineering
Rating: ★ ★ ★

Contract Engineering provides its resume service for engineers, employers of engineers, engineering organizations, and companies or individuals who offer engineering tools or software on the Internet.

- **URL:** http://www.ContractEngineering.com

- **Ownership/sponsorship:** Engineering Jobs.

- **Started accepting resumes:** 1997.

- **Approximate number of resumes online April 2000:** 609.

- **Resume career fields:** Resumes are all engineering-related: aeronautics, agricultural, automation, chemical, civil, electrical, environmental, geological, hydraulic, industrial/manufacturing, information tech/software, materials, mechanical, naval, nuclear, petroleum, solar, systems, and telecommunications/network.

- **Total number of corporate subscribers/employers:** 485.

- **Distribution of corporate subscribers/employers:** 100 percent contract/consulting firms.

- **Fee structure for corporate subscribers/employers:** Free.

- **Methods and rules for submitting resumes:** Submit at Web site.

- **Percent of resumes submitted by Web form:** 100.

- **Percent of resumes received from individuals:** 100.

- **Limits on length:** None.

- **Format:** Contract Engineering formats the resume listing from entry fields on its submission form. Actual full resumes, which are hyperlinked to the resume listings, are formatted by the job seeker.

- **Fees for person submitting resume:** None.

- **Length of time resumes remain online:** Three months.

- **Procedures for updating/renewing:** Submit new listing.

- **Privacy/confidentiality:** It is not possible to limit who can see a resume. It is not possible to shield a resume from being viewed by a current employer.

- **Assistance provided to the person submitting a resume:** None.

- **Search options available to employers viewing resumes:** Scrolling through resumes organized by engineering discipline.

- **Technology to match jobs to resumes and e-mail results to clients:** None available.

- **Average number of daily hits on resumes:** This information is proprietary.

- **Other distinguishing factors:** Probably the largest site on the Net specializing in contract engineering.

Cyberview Cvs

Canada and USA
All career fields
Rating: ★ ★ ★ ★ ★

Cyberview Cvs brings career search into the 21st century. High-technology streaming video presents a real-time video introduction to recruiters and potential employers over the Internet. No longer does an individual need to rely on a paper resume to determine interviewing success. Candidates simply record their own 30 to 60-second video presentations or visit Cyberview's studio for a fast, high-quality recording. Career seekers may select from either a searchable General Database bank for general viewing or the Confidential Database, where the file is assigned a "lock code" for maximum confidentiality. Presentations are augmented by the candidate's picture, career highlights, and a downloadable written cv.

- **URL:** http://www.cyberviewcv.com

- **Ownership/sponsorship:** Pride in Personnel Inc.

- **Started accepting resumes:** 2000.

- **Approximate number of resumes online April 2000:** 20 (new site).

- **Resume career fields:** Resumes are in engineering, sales, marketing, materials, data/telecommunications, and software.

- **Total number of corporate subscribers/employers:** n/a.

- **Distribution of corporate subscribers/employers:** n/a.

- **Fee structure for corporate subscribers/employers:** Free.

- **Methods and rules for submitting resumes:** 30–60-second video presentation via any format. Tips, samples, etc. on the site.

- **Percent of resumes submitted by**

  Mail in cassette: 40

  Visit office for video: 50

  E-mail: 10

- **Percent of resumes received from**

  Individuals: 70

  Colleges and universities: 20

  Outplacement firms: 10

- **Limits on length:** Video is limited to 30–60 seconds.

- **Format:** NTSC preferred but PAL and SECAM are accepted.

- **Fees for person submitting resume:** Currently none; standard $100 Can.

- **Length of time resumes remain online:** Three months without contact from candidate; renewed with contact.

- **Procedures for updating/renewing:** E-mail.

- **Privacy/confidentiality:** It is possible to limit who can see a resume. Confidential Bank has "lockcode" that can be supplied to potential viewers. It is possible to shield a resume from being viewed by a current employer using "lockcode" as described above.

- **Assistance provided to the person submitting a resume:** Online "Human Click"; e-mail to Webmaster.

- **Search options available to employers viewing resumes:** Search by positions, industry, and location.

- **Technology to match jobs to resumes and e-mail results to clients:** n/a.

- **Average number of daily hits on resumes:** n/a.

- **Special features:** Video resume supplemented by optional picture file, resume highlights, and downloadable written resume.

- **Other distinguishing factors:** Site requires video player, downloadable free from site. Videos best viewed with connection speeds of 56K or higher.

dice.com, High Tech Jobs Online

USA
IT or high-tech
Rating: ★ ★ ★ ★

dice.com lists contract, full-time, and contract-to-hire positions in programming, systems administration, engineering, and other high-tech fields.

- **URL:** http://www.dice.com

- **Ownership/sponsorship:** EarthWeb, Inc. (EWBX).

- **Started accepting resumes:** dice.com has two ways of obtaining information from job seekers: Announce Availability, which asks for pertinent information online and is similar to a resume bank; and ResumeOnline, which is a secure place to post resumes because it is not indexed. dice.com started to accept the Announce Availability forms in 1990 on the BBS and in 1995 on the Web. dice.com accepted resumes on ResumeOnline in 1998. dice.com's service is different from most others because of its Announce Availability.

■ **Approximate number of resumes online April 2000:** n/a.

■ **Resume career fields:** All resumes are IT or high-tech in nature.

■ **Total number of corporate subscribers/ employers:** 5,400 (as of February 2000).

■ **Distribution of corporate subscribers/ employers:** n/a.

■ **Fee structure for corporate subscribers/ employers:** Prices start at $385 for multiple offices.

■ **Methods and rules for submitting resumes:** Anyone can post a resume on dice.com. It is a secure place to store a resume because dice.com does not index it and send the information to recruiters. dice.com leaves that job to Announce Availability. The rule for Announce Availability is that the job seeker must be looking for work (either full-time or contract) within the next three weeks.

■ **Percent of resumes submitted by Web form:** 100.

■ **Percent of resumes received from individuals:** 100.

■ **Limits on length:** None.

■ **Format:** For Announce Availability, the format is specified by question. No special format is needed for resumes.

■ **Fees for person submitting resume:** None.

■ **Length of time resumes remain online:** Announce Availability is 30 days. ResumeOnline is unlimited.

■ **Procedures for updating/renewing:** Both ResumeOnline and Announce Availability can be edited from within the job seeker's JobTools account.

■ **Privacy/confidentiality:** It is not possible to limit who can see a resume for Announce Availability, but ResumeOnline can limit who sees a resume. It is possible to shield a resume from being viewed by a current employer for ResumeOnline.

■ **Assistance provided to the person submitting a resume:** Job seekers will find an FAQ sheet; they can also call in or e-mail Customer Support.

■ **Search options available to employers viewing resumes:** dice.com customers can search the Hotlist—the form that is sent out daily with the information from Announce Availability—by entering keywords, dates, contract, or full-time, among other search options.

■ **Technology to match jobs to resumes and e-mail results to clients:** Hotlist is sent out daily to the customers. In addition, an online search of the Hotlist is available to match job seekers with employers.

■ **Average number of daily hits on resumes:** Each company can look at the Announce Availability forms as much as it wants. The resumes on ResumeOnline are secure, however. Only when a job seeker wants to submit the resume is it looked at.

■ **Special features:** dice.com spends over $3,000,000 each year to advertise its service in national publications. Its service is an alternative to the newspaper classified sections.

- **Other distinguishing factors:** dice.com contains only jobs in information technology. dice.com offers a metro search capability for several cities. For more information, go to the dice.com home page and select Media Room on the left side.

employMAX.com

United States, Canada, France, United Kingdom
Technical, management, and high-tech careers
Rating: ★ ★

What began as an in-house database for one retained search firm has become one of the larger online resume databases, with over one-third of a million technical, management, and high-tech candidates. The site uses specialized "spider" technology to gather a great number of resumes in one centralized database. The site is also open to individuals seeking to post their resumes online.

- **URL:** http://www.employMAX.com

- **Ownership/sponsorship:** Privately held.

  2907 West Bay Dr.
  Belleair Bluffs, FL 33770
  Phone: 727-588-4400
  Fax: 727-588-0116

- **Started accepting resumes:** 1998.

- **Approximate number of resumes online April 2000:** 330,000.

- **Resume career fields**

  Engineering: 136,000

  IT/IS: 129,000

  Executive (nontechnical): 40,000

  Other technical: 26,000

- **Total number of corporate subscribers/employers:** n/a.

- **Distribution of corporate subscribers/employers**

  Direct-hire employers: 30 percent

  Staffing firms: 20 percent

  Contract/consulting firms: 10 percent

  Other: 40 percent

- **Fee structure for corporate subscribers/employers:** Individualized to needs. Call for a free demo.

- **Methods and rules for submitting resumes:** To submit resumes, candidates click http://www.employmax.com/jobseekers/resumes/addresume.cfm.

- **Percent of resumes submitted by**

  Spider: 40

  Web form: 35

  E-mail: 25

- **Percent of resumes received from**

  Individuals: 75

  Resume broadcasters: 23

  Outplacement firms: 2

- **Limits on length:** None.

- **Format:** Online form.

- **Fees for person submitting resume:** None.

- **Length of time resumes remain online:** One year, and then deleted.

- **Procedures for updating/renewing:** Reminder e-mailed to candidates every 60 days.

- **Privacy/confidentiality:** Only subscribers can see resumes. At this time it is not possible to shield a resume from being viewed by a current employer.

■ **Assistance provided to the person submitting a resume:** Yes.

■ **Search options available to employers viewing resumes:** Yes.

■ **Technology to match jobs to resumes and e-mail results to clients:** Yes, both clients and candidates.

■ **Average number of daily hits on resumes:** 7,500.

■ **Special features:** Powercast™ Technology; multimedia resumes free to candidates who post resumes. Also, multimedia job descriptions and company information.

The Employment Guide's CareerWeb

USA
All career fields
Rating: ★ ★ ★

The Employment Guide's CareerWeb offers a wide variety of employment opportunities ranging from hourly and entry-level to professional and managerial in over 75 different job categories. *The Employment Guide*'s CareerWeb provides employers with an effective and cost-efficient way of finding candidates, and provides job seekers with the ability to easily find jobs, post resumes online, and obtain career advice.

■ **URL:** http://www.careerweb.com

■ **Ownership/sponsorship:** Trader Publishing Company.

■ **Started accepting resumes:** 1995.

■ **Approximate number of resumes online April 2000:** More than 26,500.

■ **Resume career fields:** Resumes are in all career fields.

■ **Total number of corporate subscribers/employers:** More than 6,000.

■ **Distribution of corporate subscribers/employers:** n/a.

■ **Fee structure for corporate subscribers/employers:** *The Employment Guide*'s CareerWeb offers a range of membership opportunities, from a la carte services (single job postings, resume database access, banner/button advertising) up to comprehensive annual memberships.

■ **Methods and rules for submitting resumes:** Resumes can be submitted only by the job seeker.

■ **Percent of resumes submitted by Web form:** n/a.

■ **Percent of resumes received from individuals:** 100.

■ **Limits on length:** None.

■ **Format:** n/a.

■ **Fees for person submitting resume:** None.

■ **Length of time resumes remain online:** Currently 90 days, but this will be changing to 12 months.

■ **Procedures for updating/renewing:** The job seeker receives a notice after 80 days that he has 10 days to update his resume or it will be dropped off the site. At that point, the job seeker comes back onto the site and makes any changes or allows the resume to be deleted.

■ **Privacy/confidentiality:** It is possible to limit who can see a resume. Job seekers can opt to post their resume in the resume database only for the purpose of responding to jobs and not make it available to be searched by employers. It is not possible to shield a resume from being viewed by a current employer.

■ **Assistance provided to the person submitting a resume:** Online help.

■ **Search options available to employers viewing resumes:** Resumes can be searched by industry, metropolitan area, country, U.S. work authorization status, education, work experience, salary requirements, type of employment, the date the resume was entered into the site, and/or by keywords and more. The resume database can be searched in a normal or advanced search mode.

- **Technology to match jobs to resumes and e-mail results to clients:** Job Match and Resume Finder.

Job Match enables job seekers to create a profile of the type of job that they want to find. The computer performs ongoing job searches of new jobs entered into the jobs database, and e-mails matches to the job seeker.

Resume Finder allows employers to create up to 20 Resume Finder candidate profiles reflecting the specific skills and attributes employers are seeking. Resume Finder then searches the database automatically and e-mails the relevant resumes either weekly or three times a week to employers (employer's choice).

- **Average number of daily hits on resumes:** n/a.

- **Other distinguishing factors:** *The Employment Guide*'s CareerWeb is unique in that it is affiliated with 50 (by the end of 2000) freely distributed print publications in 46 markets across the USA. *The Employment Guide*'s CareerWeb harnesses the power of the 2.5 million distributed copies of *The Employment Guide* to drive job seekers to the Web site. Additionally, all ads placed in *Employment Guides* nationwide are posted on *The Employment Guide*'s CareerWeb, creating a robust and diversified jobs database. *The Employment Guide*'s CareerWeb also offers a comprehensive Career Resource library with career advice, resume and interviewing techniques, relevant links, and the Career Inventory test.

EngineeringJobs.Com
USA
Engineering and information technology
Rating: ★ ★ ★ ★

EngineeringJobs.Com provides free resume and job listings for engineers, employers of engineers, engineering organizations, and companies or individuals who offer engineering tools or software on the Internet. The company also offers an optional resume distribution for a fee.

- **URL:** http://www.EngineeringJobs.com

- **Ownership/sponsorship:** Engineering Jobs.

- **Started accepting resumes:** 1996.

- **Approximate number of resumes online April 2000:** 3,400.

- **Resume career fields:** Accepts only engineering and information-tech resumes, which are categorized by engineering discipline.

- **Total number of corporate subscribers/ employers:** More than 3,500.

- **Distribution of corporate subscribers/ employers**

  Direct-hire employers: 75 percent

  Staffing firms and recruiters: 25 percent (Several recruiters handle both permanent and contract positions.)

- **Fee structure for corporate subscribers/ employers:** Free access to resumes. $25 per month for keyword searching.

- **Methods and rules for submitting resumes:** Submitted by form at the Web site.

- **Percent of resumes submitted by e-mail:** 100.

- **Percent of resumes received from individuals:** 100.

- **Limits on length:** None.

- **Format:** EngineeringJobs.Com formats the resume listing from entry fields on its submission form. Actual full resumes, which are hyperlinked to the resume listings, are formatted by the job seeker.

- **Fees for person submitting resume:** None.

- **Length of time resumes remain online:** Three months.

- **Procedures for updating/renewing:** Submit a new listing.

- **Privacy/confidentiality:** It is not possible to limit who can see a resume. Shielding the job seeker's identity from a current employer is possible only by using an alias.

- **Assistance provided to the person submitting a resume:** None available.

- **Search options available to employers viewing resumes:** Employers can freely view the resumes posted on the Web, or they can do keyword searches for a fee.

- **Technology to match jobs to resumes and e-mail results to clients:** Keyword searches.

- **Average number of daily hits on resumes:** Not tracked.

- **Special features:** EngineeringJobs.Com also features listings of hundreds of recruiting agencies that specialize in engineering, IT, and high-tech employment. The company also features thousands of hyperlinks to the engineering job pages of companies that directly employ engineers.

- **Other distinguishing factors:** For $35, EngineeringJobs.Com will send an engineering resume directly to 600 headhunters who specialize in engineering and IT jobs.

Entry Level Job Seeker Assistant

USA
Entry level only, in all career fields
Rating: ★ ★ ★

This site is for people who have never held a full-time, permanent job in their field or who have less than a year of nonacademic experience. The Entry Level Job Seeker Assistant does not accept resumes; instead, it contains links to your WWW resume. This site was featured in the June 1995 edition of *NetGuide* magazine and was the only WWW Job Seeker Assistant page to have a positive rating (out of nine pages reviewed for that article).

- **URL:** http://www.dnaco.net/~dantassi/jobhome.html

- **Ownership/sponsorship:** Joseph Schmalhofer

- **Started accepting resume URLs:** 1994.

- **Approximate number of resume links online April 2000:** About 35–40 at any given time.

- **Resume career fields:** Links to resumes in all job classifications are accepted. The resumes must be for entry-level job seekers. People who are changing fields but have many years of experience in their preceding field can classify as entry-level.

- **Total number of corporate subscribers/employers:** n/a.

- **Distribution of corporate subscribers/employers:** n/a.

- **Fee structure for corporate subscribers/employers:** n/a.

- **Methods and rules for submitting resumes:**

Put your resume into an HTML document format.

Put this HTML resume on a WWW server.

E-mail the URL of your WWW resume to the administrator of the Entry Level Job Seeker Assistant.

■ **Percent of resumes submitted by individuals:** 100.

■ **Limits on length:** None.

■ **Format:** To be linked, your resume must satisfy the following criteria:

Must be readable by WWW text-only browsers.

No inline graphics images.

No nondefault background coloring or images.

No HTML 3.0+ commands or features (including TABLE).

No JAVA/ActiveX applets.

No Netscape-only/Microsoft Explorer–only features.

Must state clearly what field(s) you are interested in.

■ **Fees for person submitting resume link:** None.

■ **Length of time resume links remain active:** They remain active until the resumes can no longer be accessed; until they are changed so that they violate one of the format requirements; or until the owners tell the Entry Level Job Seeker Assistant administrator that they are no longer seeking employment.

■ **Procedures for updating/renewing:** Resume owners maintain their own resumes at their leisure.

■ **Privacy/confidentiality:** n/a.

■ **Average number of daily hits on resumes:** Not tracked.

■ **Special features:** The site has a 100 percent text-based WWW page for quick downloading by human resource departments during normal business hours. The page includes a section of links to companies and other WWW resources that provide useful information for entry-level job seekers. The second section includes links to resumes of entry-level job seekers.

■ **Other distinguishing factors:** All resumes are periodically checked. If the administrator gets a "file not found" error, the link to the resume is removed without warning. Resumes are checked before they are posted to make sure that they satisfy the required criteria. They are also spot-checked to make sure that they stay that way. If you add graphics to your resume and the administrator catches the graphics, he will delete your link without warning. Resumes will also be checked for content to make sure that only those listing little or no nonacademic experience are posted.

Federal Jobs Digest

USA and global
Professional, white-collar, and
blue-collar occupations
Rating: ★ ★ ★ ★

jobsfed.com services job candidates interested in careers with the U.S. federal government and those who may also want employment with private companies/organizations of all sizes.

■ **URL:** www.jobsfed.com

■ **Ownership/sponsorship:** *Federal Jobs Digest* newspaper.

■ **Started accepting resumes:** 1998.

■ **Approximate number of resumes online April 2000:** More than 60,000.

- **Resume career fields:** Resumes are mostly professional, computer, accounting, science, engineering, law, and many others in more than 900 white- and blue-collar occupations.

- **Total number of corporate subscribers/ employers:** U.S. federal government, state and local government, and more than 100 private companies/organizations with an emphasis on those of small and medium size.

- **Distribution of corporate subscribers/ employers**

  Direct-hire employers: 90 percent

  Staffing firms: 5 percent

  Contract/consulting firms: 5 percent

- **Fee structure for corporate subscribers/ employers:** Free job listings for employers; employers pay low fees and only for successful resume database searches.

- **Methods and rules for submitting resumes:** Anyone may submit a resume without charge. U.S. citizens are given preference for U.S. federal job openings.

- **Percent of resumes submitted by Web form:** 100.

- **Percent of resumes received from individuals:** 100.

- **Limits on length:** None.

- **Format:** Open.

- **Fees for person submitting resume:** None.

- **Length of time resumes remain online:** Six months, but can be renewed.

- **Procedures for updating/renewing:** Unlimited, online renewal and update.

- **Privacy/confidentiality:** Access to resume can be limited to federal only or all employers. The site's privacy policy is as follows: Identifying information is removed from resumes—name, street address, phone number, and e-mail address. Employers submit their e-mail messages to job candidates through jobsfed.com. The messages are then forwarded to job candidates. Job candidates decide when and if to provide identifying and contact information to employers.

- **Assistance provided to the person submitting a resume:** E-mail help provided on how to use the site.

- **Search options available to employers viewing resumes:** Occupation, date of registration, salary wanted, town/state of residence, skills, years of experience in occupation, and number supervised.

- **Technology to match jobs to resumes and e-mail results to clients:** Standing search criteria for job candidates include occupation, salary wanted, job location, and various employer criteria such as size and type. For employers, standing search criteria include occupation, date of registration, salary wanted, state/town of residence, skills, years of experience in the occupation, and number supervised.

- **Average number of daily hits on resumes:** 15,000.

- **Special features:** The only comprehensive list of federal openings on the Web. Includes all federal agencies and postal as well as private companies/organizations. Offers low-cost services to employers. Fee charged only for successful database searches.

- **Other distinguishing factors:** Job candidates can create and post as many job profiles as they wish. Each profile targets a different employment objective.

The Feminist Majority Foundation Website

Primarily USA, some international
Feminist and nonprofit
Rating: ★ ★ ★

Unlike other resume databases, feminist.org is specifically for individuals seeking feminist work, and organizations/companies seeking feminist employees. *Feminist* is defined as a person who advocates the policy, practice, or advocacy of political, economic, and social equality for women and men.

- **URL:** http://www.feminist.org

- **Ownership/sponsorship:** The Feminist Majority Foundation, a 501C(3) nonprofit organization committed to the social, political, and economic equality of women and men.

- **Started accepting resumes:** 1995.

- **Approximate number of resumes online April 2000:** 600.

- **Resume career fields:** There are no restrictions on career fields, but the job bank is directed toward feminist, nonprofit organizations and government agencies, and nontraditional sectors seeking to employ more women.

- **Total number of corporate subscribers/ employers:** n/a.

- **Distribution of corporate subscribers/employers:** n/a.

- **Fee structure for corporate subscribers/employers:** None.

- **Methods and rules for submitting resumes:** Form online at http://www.feminist.org/forms/wanted.html.

- **Percent of resumes submitted by Web form:** 100.

- **Percent of resumes received from individuals:** 100.

- **Limits on length:** n/a.

- **Format:** Online form.

- **Fees for person submitting resume:** None.

- **Length of time resumes remain online:** Six months or until the individual requests that it be removed.

- **Procedures for updating/renewing:** Individual must resubmit the online form.

- **Privacy/confidentiality:** It is not possible to limit who can see a resume. It is not possible to shield a resume from being viewed by a current employer.

- **Assistance provided to the person submitting a resume:** Tech support via e-mail is available at webmaster@feminist.org.

- **Search options available to employers viewing resumes:** Can search by any keyword.

- **Technology to match jobs to resumes and e-mail results to clients:** None.

- **Average number of daily hits on resumes:** Don't know.

Future Access Employment Guide

USA
Information technology, biotech, sales, marketing, and other
Rating: ★ ★ ★

Future Access has been providing World Wide Web information services since early 1994.

- **URL:** http://futureaccess.com/

- **Ownership/sponsorship:** Independently owned by

Future Access
PO Box 2187
Granite Bay, CA 95746

- **Started accepting resumes:** 1994.

- **Approximate number of resumes online April 2000:** 7,000.

- **Resume career fields:** Resumes are primarily from the biotech industry, hardware engineers, sales and marketing, software engineers, and miscellaneous.

- **Total number of corporate subscribers/ employers:** approximately 1,200.

- **Distribution of corporate subscribers/employers:** n/a.

- **Fee structure for corporate subscribers/ employers:** Nonsubscription; resume access is free; job postings start at $9.95 per month.

- **Methods and rules for submitting resumes:** Must supply basic information, including e-mail address.

- **Percent of resumes submitted by Web form:** 100.

- **Percent of resumes received from individuals:** 100.

- **Limits on length:** 3,000 characters.

- **Format:** Free-form.

- **Fees for person submitting resume:** None.

- **Length of time resumes remain online:** Approximately six months.

- **Procedures for updating/renewing:** Can be edited online.

- **Privacy/confidentiality:** It is not possible to limit who can see a resume. It is not possible to shield a resume from being viewed by a current employer.

- **Assistance provided to the person submitting a resume:** Online help.

- **Search options available to employers viewing resumes:** Multiple keywords, country, state, city, ZIP code, name, e-mail.

- **Technology to match jobs to resumes and e-mail results to clients:** None.

- **Average number of daily hits on resumes:** 800.

- **Other distinguishing factors:** Many applicants are non-U.S. residents, and many are willing to relocate.

GAYWORK.com

USA
All areas of professions
Rating: ★ ★ ★ ★

GAYWORK.com is a job search/job listing service for "truly equal opportunity employers." Ten percent of all proceeds from GAYWORK.com go to charitable organizations that include fighting discrimination in the workplace and HIV research and prevention.

- **URL:** http://www.gaywork.com

- **Ownership/sponsorship:** Privately owned and operated.

- **Started accepting resumes:** 1999.

- **Approximate number of resumes online April 2000:** 3,000.

- **Resume career fields:** Resumes are mostly college-graduate and high-tech.

- **Total number of corporate subscribers/ employers:** More than 100.

- **Distribution of corporate subscribers/ employers**

Direct-hire employers: 75 percent

Staffing firms: 25 percent

- **Fee structure for corporate subscribers/ employers:** Unlimited posting or links to employer's career site for an annual fee, or individual posting.

- **Methods and rules for submitting resumes:** Online via resume form.

- **Percent of resumes submitted by Web form:** 100.

- **Percent of resumes received from individuals:** 100.

- **Limits on length:** 3,000 characters.

- **Format:** Resume form into database.

- **Fees for person submitting resume:** None.

- **Length of time resumes remain online:** Unlimited.

- **Procedures for updating/renewing:** Online.

- **Privacy/confidentiality:** It is possible to limit who can see a resume. It is possible to shield a resume from being viewed by a current employer.

- **Assistance provided to the person submitting a resume:** Via e-mail or help page.

- **Search options available to employers viewing resumes:** Location, area of profession, experience, salary range, etc.

- **Technology to match jobs to resumes and e-mail results to clients:** None.

- **Average number of daily hits on resumes:** n/a.

- **Special features:** Employer logo link to their jobs WebPages directly from GAYWORK.com.

- **Other distinguishing factors:** The only gay/lesbian/bisexual/transgender job search and resume-posting Web site for the GLBT community and forward-thinking employers.

Headhunter.net

USA
All career fields
Rating: ★ ★ ★ ★ ★

Headhunter.net is a leading national online recruiting service that specializes in empowering candidates and corporations to manage the job search process. The site has more than 470,000 resumes and over 150,000 jobs representing over 10,000 of the nation's top employers across virtually every industry. The site, which receives more than three million visitors a month, distinguishes itself by providing job seekers privacy when searching and applying for jobs, and allows job seekers and job posters to manage and track the visibility and performance of their listings.

- **URL:** http://www.headhunter.net

- **Ownership/sponsorship:** Headhunter.net

- **Started accepting resumes:** 1996.

- **Approximate number of resumes online April 2000:** Over 470,000.

- **Resume career fields:** Resumes are in all career fields.

- **Total number of corporate subscribers/ employers:** n/a.

- **Distribution of corporate subscribers/employers:** n/a.

- **Fee structure for corporate subscribers/ employers:** n/a.

- **Methods and rules for submitting resumes:** Posting a resume is free and simple. Headhunter.net gives job seekers the ability to upgrade their resumes for a premium position in the search results, and they can post up to 10 different resumes.

Posting a resume on Headhunter.net is as easy as 1-2-3: Register for free by clicking on the "post resume" button. You'll quickly receive your personal password.

Log in with your new password by clicking the "My Stuff" icon. Then click the link to "My Resumes" and start posting!

- **Percent of resumes submitted by Web form:** n/a.

- **Percent of resumes received from individuals:** n/a.

- **Limits on length:** 6,000 characters.

- **Format:** Web form.

- **Fees for person submitting resume:** n/a.

- **Length of time resumes remain online:** One year. Each time you edit your resume, the expiration date is reset to one year from the date edited.

- **Procedures for updating/renewing:** Edit online.

- **Privacy/confidentiality:** Job Seekers can elect to post a "blind" resume, which will keep contact information private while still allowing potential employers to make you aware of their interest in your resume.

- **Assistance provided to the person submitting a resume:** Extensive online help as well as a "Frequently Asked Questions" section is available, or users can contact Headhunter.net at 800-891-8880.

- **Search options available to employers viewing resumes:** Employers can use our VIP Resume Search to search by date posted, job category, location, or experience from our database of over 471,000 resumes.

- **Technology to match jobs to resumes and e-mail results to clients:** n/a.

- **Average number of daily hits on resumes:** n/a.

- **Other distinguishing factors:** Headhunter.net offers job seekers a variety of services to help their career search and development. "My Stuff" allows job seek-

ers to actively manage their online resumes and keep track of their resume "stats" (such as how many times employers have clicked on their resume). Headhunter.net also allows them to upgrade their resumes so it is the first one potential employers see.

CareerBytes, Headhunter.net's monthly newsletter, delivers information on cool jobs, hot topics, and other news for job seekers. And the Career Resource Center is the one-stop shop for links to career-building tools like career assessments, company research, and interview assistance.

HealthCareerWeb

USA
Health-related industries
Rating: ★ ★ ★

HealthCareerWeb offers a wide variety of employment opportunities in the medical industry.

- **URL:** http://www.healthcareerweb.com

- **Ownership/sponsorship:** Trader Publishing Company.

- **Started accepting resumes:** 1997.

- **Approximate number of resumes online April 2000:** More than 10,000.

- **Resume career fields:** Resumes are in health-care–related fields.

- **Total number of corporate subscribers/ employers:** More than 1,100.

- **Distribution of corporate subscribers/ employers:** n/a.

- **Fee structure for corporate subscribers/ employers:** HealthCareerWeb offers a range of membership opportunities from a la carte services (single job postings, resume database access, banner/button advertising) up to comprehensive annual memberships.

- **Methods and rules for submitting resumes:** Resumes can be submitted only by the job seeker.

- **Percent of resumes submitted by Web form:** 100.

- **Percent of resumes received from individuals:** 100.

- **Limits on length:** None.

- **Fees for person submitting resume:** None.

- **Length of time resumes remain online:** Currently 90 days. This will be changing to 12 months.

- **Procedures for updating/renewing:** The job seeker receives a notice after 80 days letting them know that they have 10 days to update their resume or it will be dropped off the site. At that point the job seeker comes back onto the site and makes any changes or allows the resume to be deleted.

- **Privacy/confidentiality:** It is possible to limit who can see a resume. Job seekers can opt to post their resumes in the resume database only for the purpose of responding to jobs and not make it available to be searched by employers. It is not possible to shield a resume from being viewed by a current employer.

- **Assistance provided to the person submitting a resume:** Online help.

- **Search options available to employers viewing resumes:** Resumes can be searched by industry, metropolitan area, country, U.S. work authorization status, education, work experience, salary requirements, type of employment, the date the resume was entered into the site, and/or by keywords

and more. The resume database can be searched in a normal or advanced search mode.

- **Technology to match jobs to resumes and e-mail results to clients:** Job Match and Resume Finder.

Job Match enables job seekers to create a profile of the type of job that they want to find. The computer performs ongoing job searches of new jobs entered into the jobs database and e-mails matches to the job seeker.

Resume Finder allows employers to create up to 20 Resume Finder candidate profiles reflecting the different skills and attributes employers are specifically seeking. Resume Finder then searches the database automatically and e-mails the relevant resumes either weekly or three times a week to employers (employer's choice).

- **Average number of daily hits on resumes:** n/a.

- **Other distinguishing factors:** HealthCareerWeb is unique in that they are affiliated with 50 (by the end of 2000) freely distributed print publications in 46 markets across the USA. HealthCareerWeb harnesses the power of the 2.5 million distributed copies of *The Employment Guide* to drive job seekers to the Web site. Additionally, all ads placed in *Employment Guides* nationwide are posted on *The Employment Guide*'s CareerWeb/HealthCareerWeb, creating a robust and diversified jobs database. HealthCareerWeb also offers a comprehensive Career Resource library with career advice, resume and interviewing techniques, relevant links, and the Career Inventory test.

Hospitality Net Job Exchange

Global
Hospitality
Rating: ★ ★ ★

The Hospitality Net Job Exchange serves the global hospitality and lodging industry on the Internet.

- **URL:** http://www.hospitalitynet.org/?/jobexchange

- **Ownership/sponsorship:** Ownership by Hospitality Net.

- **Started accepting resumes:** 1995.

- **Approximate number of resumes online April 2000:** 500.

- **Resume career fields:** All resumes are in the following job classifications in the hospitality industry: Academic resources, accounting, All Demands (former Hospitality Net site), banqueting, catering/convention management, environment, human resources, sales and marketing, technology, food and beverage, front office, housekeeping, management (corporate, regional), management (hotel), miscellaneous, pre-opening staff, seasonal employment, technical maintenance, trainee opportunities, yield/revenue management.

- **Total number of corporate subscribers/employers:** 15,000 registered users.

- **Distribution of corporate subscribers/employers**

  Direct-hire employers: 70 percent

  Contract/consulting firms: 30 percent

- **Fee structure for corporate subscribers/employers:** All free of charge.

- **Methods and rules for submitting resumes:** Resumes are submitted online by using an online form; there are no special rules.

- **Percent of resumes submitted by**

  Web form: 99

  E-mail: 1

- **Percent of resumes received from**

  Individuals: 99

  Other: 1

- **Limits on length:** None.

- **Format:** Online form with name-and-address format specified; all other information is free-form text entries.

- **Fees for person submitting resume:** None.

- **Length of time resumes remain online:** Until owner removes it.

- **Procedures for updating/renewing:** Online form for updating information.

- **Privacy/confidentiality:** It is not possible to limit who can see a resume; however, there is a possibility to create a listing without contact name and address, only an e-mail address. It is not possible to shield a resume from being viewed by a current employer.

- **Assistance provided to the person submitting a resume:** Easy-to-use resume registration form. For help, contact the help desk at jobs@hospitalitynet.org.

- **Search options available to employers viewing resumes:** All parts of the resume can be found by using the Hospitality Net search engine.

- **Technology to match jobs to resumes and e-mail results to clients:** Hospitality Net's extensive search engine.

- **Average number of daily hits on resumes:** More than 15,000 per day.

- **Special features:** The Hospitality Net Job Exchange is the Job Resource for the Hospitality Industry. The Job Exchange contains two separate databases, one with resumes and one with vacancies. Registering a Job Demand or Opportunity is as simple as completing a one-page form at the Web site. When registering at Hospitality Net, you can subscribe to the weekly newsletter. Besides industry news, this newsletter includes an overview of the latest job opportunities.

Internet Job Source

USA, with focus on Silicon Valley; Los Angeles; Chicago; New York; Seattle; Boston; Texas; and Washington, D.C. Professional, Internet, computers, engineering, finance, administrative
Rating: ★ ★ ★

The site is targeted toward the nation's largest cities: New York; Boston; Washington, D.C.; Chicago; Los Angeles; and San Francisco.

- **URLs:** www.internetjobsource.com, www.statejobs.com, www.valleyjobs.com

- **Ownership/sponsorship:** Privately held.

- **Started accepting resumes:** 1999.

- **Approximate number of resumes online April 2000:** 10,000.

- **Resume career fields:** Resumes are in the computing, engineering, Internet, accounting, business, management, administrative, and design fields.

- **Total number of corporate subscribers/ employers** 100.

- **Distribution of corporate subscribers/ employers**

  Direct-hire employers: 80 percent

  Staffing firms: 20 percent

- **Fee structure for corporate subscribers/ employers:** $100 per year.

- **Methods and rules for submitting resumes:** Must be submitted via ASCII text.

- **Percent of resumes submitted by**

  Web form: 90

  E-mail: 10

- **Percent of resumes received from individuals:** 100.

- **Limits on length:** 2,000 words.

- **Fees for person submitting resume:** None.

- **Length of time resumes remain online:** Six months.

- **Procedures for updating/renewing:** Resubmit resume.

- **Privacy/confidentiality:** It is not possible to limit who can see a resume. It is not possible to shield a resume from being viewed by a current employer.

- **Assistance provided to the person submitting a resume:** n/a.

- **Search options available to employers viewing resumes:** Location, keyword, and industry.

- **Technology to match jobs to resumes and e-mail results to clients:** n/a.

- **Average number of daily hits on resumes:** n/a.

Japanese Jobs

Global
All career fields
Rating: ★ ★ ★ ★

Japanese Jobs is an Internet-based employment service that is dedicated to bringing together with hiring companies a global community of bilingual professionals who speak Japanese and English.

- **URL:** http://www.japanesejobs.com

- **Ownership/sponsorship:** A division of Fox Force Five, Inc.

- **Started accepting resumes:** 1997.

- **Approximate number of resumes online April 2000:** 11,000.

- **Resume career fields:** Resumes are in all career fields.

- **Total number of corporate subscribers/employers:** 130.

- **Distribution of corporate subscribers/employers**

   Direct-hire employers: 80 percent

   Staffing firms: 12 percent

   Contract/consulting firms: 8 percent

- **Fee structure for corporate subscribers/employers:** $495 per month, per posting.

- **Methods and rules for submitting resumes:** To submit a resume, the candidate just completes the Submit Resume form at http://www.japanesejobs.com/findjob.html.

- **Percent of resumes submitted by Web form:** 100.

- **Percent of resumes received from individuals:** Not tracked.

- **Limits on length:** None.

- **Format:** Text.

- **Fees for person submitting resume:** None.

- **Length of time resumes remain online:** As long as the candidate wants them online.

- **Procedures for updating/renewing:** Send a remove resume e-mail, then either send a new resume in an e-mail or resubmit from the Web form.

- **Privacy/confidentiality:** It is possible to limit who can see a resume. The candidate may state which companies they don't want to see their resumes. It is possible to shield a resume from being viewed by a current employer.

- **Assistance provided to the person submitting a resume:** The candidate can e-mail for assistance anytime at jobs@japanesejobs.com.

- **Search options available to employers viewing resumes:** Instead of employers searching through the resumes, the site reviews the resumes for the employer.

- **Technology to match jobs to resumes and e-mail results to clients:** All the resumes are put into a database and searched with the information provided by the client.

- **Average number of daily hits on resumes:** n/a.

- **Special features:** Japanese Jobs also features a mailing list that candidates can join at http://www.japanesejobs.com/findjob.html. By joining the mailing lists, candidates can apply to all the job openings that interest them, and they have full control over their resumes.

JobBank USA

USA
All career fields
Rating: ★ ★

JobBank USA was noted as one of the largest employment Web sites on the Internet in *USA Today,* August 26, 1996, and has received many awards, including an Excellence in the Electronic Recruiting Industry (EERI) award.

- **URL:** http://www.jobbankusa.com

- **Ownership/sponsorship:** JobBank USA, Inc.

- **Started accepting resumes:** 1995.

- **Approximate number of resumes online April 2000:** 100,000 in JobBankUSA.com database and three million using "Stealth" resume spider.

- **Resume career fields:** Resumes are in all career fields.

- **Total number of corporate subscribers/ employers:** 500–600.

- **Distribution of corporate subscribers/ employers**

  Direct-hire employers: 50 percent

  Staffing firms: 40 percent

  Contract/consulting firms: 10 percent

- **Fee structure for corporate subscribers/ employers:** $2,900 per year.

- **Methods and rules for submitting resumes:** Online via JobBank USA's Resume Builder form.

- **Percent of resumes submitted by Web form:** 100.

- **Percent of resumes received from individuals:** 100.

- **Limits on length:** 15K or five pages.

- **Format:** JobBank USA's Resume Builder form.

- **Fees for person submitting resume:** None.

- **Length of time resumes remain online:** One year.

- **Procedures for updating/renewing:** Real-time editing/updating online.

- **Privacy/confidentiality:** n/a.

- **Assistance provided to the person submitting a resume:** Online and e-mail support.

- **Search options available to employers viewing resumes:** The database is searchable by keyword, salary, geographic location, relocation status, citizenship status, and date of resume entry. Qualified resumes are easily found by using JobBank USA's QuickScan feature, which lists a candidate's employment background.

- **Technology to match jobs to resumes and e-mail results to clients:** ResumeAgent and JobAgent.

- **Average number of daily hits on resumes:** 10,000.

- **Special features:** MetaSearch pages give job seekers access to all major job databases and newspapers nationwide. MetaSearch is a convenient tool for searching various sites from one location.

JobDirect.com

Nationwide and Canada
All career fields
Rating: ★ ★ ★ ★ ★

JobDirect is specifically designed to help college students and recent graduates find internships, part-time jobs, and "real jobs."

- **URL:** http://www.JobDirect.com

- **Ownership/sponsorship:** Privately held.

- **Started accepting resumes:** 1995.

- **Approximate number of resumes online April 2000:** 250,000.

- **Resume career fields:** JobDirect.com collects and offers resumes of college students and recent graduates across all career fields and areas of interest.

- **Total number of corporate subscribers/ employers:** Several hundred. Employers subscribe to the site's full-service offerings, making JobDirect.com an integral part of their college recruiting strategy.

- **Distribution of corporate subscribers/ employers:** 100 percent direct-hire employers.

- **Fee structure for corporate subscribers/ employers:** Employer subscribers coordinate with the site's sales staff to create a package based on hiring plans. Once subscribed, employers can utilize the system for all entry-level hires.

- **Methods and rules for submitting resumes:** Students and recent grads submit resumes via the Web site. Candidates can upload an existing resume or follow an online guide to creating a resume.

- **Percent of resumes submitted by Web form:** 100.

- **Percent of resumes received from individuals:** 100. JobDirect.com offers services to and has relationships with college and university career centers. These career centers encourage students to register with JobDirect.com in a variety of ways.

- **Limits on length:** None.

- **Format:** Use online resume form or upload existing resume.

- **Fees for person submitting resume:** None.

- **Length of time resumes remain online:** Resumes are regularly reviewed for activity.

If the individual is not using the system, the site asks if they are still looking. If not, the resume is deactivated. Inactive resumes remain online for updating if the individual wishes to re-enter the job market.

- **Procedures for updating/renewing:** Log on to the site and make the needed changes.

- **Privacy/confidentiality:** It is not possible to limit who can see a resume. It is not possible to shield a resume from being viewed by a current employer.

- **Assistance provided to the person submitting a resume:** Student Help e-mail responds to student questions within 24 hours.

- **Search options available to employers viewing resumes:** The resumes are in a fully searchable database. Employers can search by major, G.P.A., degree, graduation date, location, and interest. Resumes are sorted by matching the indicated priorities.

- **Technology to match jobs to resumes and e-mail results to clients:** JobDirect.com pioneered job-matching. One of the primary reasons that students, employers, and college campuses alike choose JobDirect.com is its matching technology. More effective than a general online posting board, JobDirect.com "pre-screens" every resume to ensure that applicants are qualified for positions. This means students understand which positions are a good match for their skills and interests, and employers receive resumes from candidates who are exactly matched to fulfill their needs. Additionally, the site is easy to use and is available to every college student. Students are able to indicate their job preferences and have new jobs matching those preferences e-mailed directly to them. For the passive job seeker, there is no need to continuously search, because jobs are e-mailed directly to them. Employer clients automatically receive resumes of students meeting the qualifications for posted jobs.

- **Average number of daily hits on resumes:** n/a.

- **Special features:** Employers have the ability to utilize JD-TV, offering streaming video of employer information to students.

- **Other distinguishing factors:** Marketing efforts to students include partnerships with career centers, campus representatives at over 200 campuses nationwide, and JobDrive, which is a 32-foot RV with resume-collection features. These efforts, combined with event sponsorships and online advertising, have resulted in the largest online, searchable database of entry-level resumes.

The JobExchange

USA
All career fields
Rating: ★ ★ ★

The JobExchange Network partners with several newspapers for its job announcements. These newspapers include

California: ANG Newspapers, Eureka—*Times-Standard*, Ft. Bragg—*Advocate-News*, Long Beach—*The Press Telegram*, Los Angeles—*Daily News*, Ontario—*Inland Valley Daily Bulletin*, *San Bernardino County Sun*, West Covina—*San Gabriel Valley Tribune*, Woodland—*Daily Democrat*, Chico—*Enterprise-Record*, Vallejo—*Times-Record, Redlands Daily Facts*. **Colorado:** Denver—*The Denver Post, Ft. Morgan Times, Sterling Journal Advocate*. **Iowa:** Council Bluffs—*The Daily Nonpareil*. **Massachusetts:** Pittsfield—*The Berkshire Eagle, Lowell Sun*,

Sentinel and Enterprise. **Michigan:** Pontiac—*The Oakland Press*. **Minnesota:** *Winona Daily News*. **Nebraska:** Omaha—*The Omaha World Herald*. **New Jersey:** *South Jersey Newspapers, The Express-Times*. **New Mexico:** *Las Cruces Sun-News*, Farmington—*The Daily Times*. **Ohio:** Toledo—*The Blade*. **Oregon:** Eugene—*The Register Guard*. **Pennsylvania:** *The Express-Times*, Hanover—*The Evening Sun, Lebanon Daily News*, York Newspaper Company. **South Carolina:** Charleston—*The Post and Courier*. **Vermont:** *Bennington Banner, Brattleboro Reformer*. **Wisconsin:** *Kenosha News, La Crosse Tribune*, Madison—Madison Newspapers, Racine—*The Journal Times*, Milwaukee—*The Journal Sentinel, Janesville Gazette*. **West Virginia:** *Charleston Daily Mail and Gazette*.

- **URLs:** http://www.jobexchange.com and www.employmentwizard.com

- **Ownership/sponsorship:** Private.

- **Started accepting resumes:** 1997.

- **Approximate number of resumes online April 2000:** 60,000.

- **Resume career fields:** 27,000 occupations.

- **Total number of corporate subscribers/ employers:** 20,000.

- **Distribution of corporate subscribers/ employers**

  Direct-hire employers: 60 percent

  Staffing firms: 20 percent

  Contract/consulting firms: 20 percent

- **Fee structure for corporate subscribers/ employers:** $40 per resume download.

- **Methods and rules for submitting resumes:** You can go online and enter for free; or you can send your resume to The JobExchange or to a participating newspaper to be entered for you at a cost of $15.

- **Percent of resumes submitted by**

  Web form: 90

  Other paper (job fairs, mailings): 10

- **Percent of resumes received from**

  Individuals: 85

  Colleges or universities: 11

  Outplacement firms: 3

  Other: 1

- **Limits on length:** None.

- **Format:** Specified online.

- **Fees for person submitting resume:** None, unless you want The JobExchange to type the resume for you. This service costs $15.

- **Length of time resumes remain online:** Six months, but they can be renewed indefinitely.

- **Procedures for updating/renewing:** Respond to an e-mail message, go online and update, or mail the update to The JobExchange.

- **Privacy/confidentiality:** It is possible to limit who can see a resume; however, the limits are not foolproof because people can enter under different names or hire a recruiter to search on their behalf. It is possible to shield a resume from being viewed by a current employer, however.

- **Assistance provided to the person submitting a resume:** Online advice and references are extensive. Participating newspapers contribute editorial content for advice; an 800 number is available for people to use; and persons can mail in their resumes for assistance in typing.

- **Search options available to employers viewing resumes:** Extensive options are available. These options enable the searcher to narrow the search to very specific criteria to eliminate unqualified candidates, broaden the search to include marginal candidates, and everything in between. Searchers can see a capsule view of the resumes so that they can see how many criteria are matched before paying for a download.

- **Technology to match jobs to resumes and e-mail results to clients:** Both available.

- **Average number of daily hits on resumes:** Currently 8,000–11,000; increases daily.

- **Special features:** Classified ads are interactive with resumes online. JobBank represents classified ads from newspapers all over the country. The cost of resumes to searchers is one of the lowest on the Internet, with no large advance purchases required. New features coming online include online classified listings (not necessarily published), professional forum rooms, employee assessments, background checks, and so on.

- **Other distinguishing factors:** The JobExchange believes it is the best because of its expertise in human resources.

JobLynx

USA
All career fields
Rating: ★ ★

Resume posting to the JobLynx database hands over your resume to over 9,600 registered headhunters. Confidentiality is guaranteed because only headhunters have access to your resume. The interested headhunters contact the job seeker directly. JobLynx places a job seeker every three minutes in the "hidden job market."

- **URL:** http://joblynx.com

- **Ownership/sponsorship:** JobLynx.

- **Started accepting resumes:** 1994.

- **Approximate number of resumes online April 2000:** Many thousands.

- **Resume career fields:** Resumes are accepted in all career fields and at all levels.

- **Total number of corporate subscribers/ employers:** 9,600 headhunters.

- **Distribution of corporate subscribers/ employers:** 100 percent staffing firms.

- **Fee structure for corporate subscribers/ employers:** Confidential.

- **Methods and rules for submitting resumes:** Online registration, e-mail, postal mail.

- **Percent of resumes submitted by**

  Web form: 90

  E-mail: 8

  Diskette: 2

- **Percent of resumes received from individuals:** 100.

- **Limits on length:** None. You also can include a cover letter.

- **Format:** .txt.

- **Fees for person submitting resume:** $99.99 for three-month registration on an exclusive, confidential database searched by 9,600 headhunters with 421,938 current job openings (April 2000).

- **Length of time resumes remain online:** 90 days and are then purged automatically.

- **Procedures for updating/renewing:** You can resubmit an updated resume at no additional cost up to two separate times during a single 90-day period.

- **Privacy/confidentiality:** It is possible to limit who can see a resume. Only the 9,600-member headhunters see the resumes; they will contact the job seekers before the release of their resumes to any companies. It is possible to shield a resume from being viewed by a current employer because resumes are kept completely confidential.

- **Assistance provided to the person submitting a resume:** Online instructions and a phone number for help.

- **Search options available to employers viewing resumes:** The recruiters use keyword searches of all resume contents.

- **Technology to match jobs to resumes and e-mail results to clients:** Searchable database online for recruiter access only.

- **Average number of daily hits on resumes:** 69,000 visitors daily and climbing.

- **Special features:** JobLynx offers 10,000 free links to Web employment resources. It is currently placing a person every three minutes locally, nationwide, and internationally due to its size.

- **Other distinguishing factors:** JobLynx guarantees job search success. Use JobLynx's service for two consecutive 90-day periods. If you are not presented with available employment opportunities during this time period, JobLynx will gladly refund 50 percent of your total registration fee.

JOBNET.com

Greater Philadelphia region
All career fields
Rating: ★ ★ ★ ★

JOBNET.com started as a local, DOS-based bulletin board system in July 1992. Today it is the Philadelphia area's leading online recruitment service.

- **URL:** http://www.JOBNET.com

- **Ownership/sponsorship:** JOBNET.com,

Inc., Ward Christman, President.

- **Started accepting resumes:** 1992.

- **Approximate number of resumes online April 2000:** More than 70,000.

- **Resume career fields:** Resumes are accepted in all career fields.

- **Total number of corporate subscribers/ employers:** Approximately 180.

- **Distribution of corporate subscribers/ employers**

  Direct-hire employers: 33 percent

  Staffing firms: 33 percent

  Contract/consulting firms: 33 percent

- **Fee structure for corporate subscribers/ employers:** Quarterly or annual subscription rate, which includes unlimited access to the resume databases and a package of ads in that time period.

- **Methods and rules for submitting resumes:** Preferred method of submission is the resume submission form featured on www.JOBNET.com. They also accept resumes via e-mail at resumes@ jobnet.com. Faxed resumes are not accepted.

- **Percent of resumes submitted by**

  Web form: 70

  Other paper (job fairs, mailings): 20

  E-mail: 9

  Diskette: 1

- **Percent of resumes received from**

  Individuals: 94

  Colleges and universities: 2

  Outplacement firms: 2

  Other: 2

- **Limits on length:** None. However,

JOBNET.com encourages job seekers to emphasize content and keywords that describe their qualifications rather than create a lengthy, nondescriptive resume.

- **Format:** Job seekers copy and paste the bodies of their resumes into the Web-based resume-submission form and then give additional information such as salary preference, geographic preference, willingness to travel/relocate, current employment status, and personal information (name, e-mail, home phone). They can preview the resumes and make changes before the resumes are added to the database.

- **Fees for person submitting resume:** None when submitted through the Web site and e-mail. Paper resumes are accepted only with a $5 fee for scanning. This fee (which is waived at job fairs) is payable to JOBNET.com.

- **Length of time resumes remain online:** Indefinitely, or until the job seeker requests removal of the resume.

- **Procedures for updating/renewing:** Before actually submitting their resumes, job seekers choose a username and password that enable them to edit/update their resumes in the future.

  JOBNET.com sends out e-mails and postcards requesting an updated resume from those who have not updated or posted recently. JOBNET.com includes the usernames and passwords on the postcards and encourages job seekers to visit the Web site to edit the resumes. After a resume has been updated, JOBNET.com gives the resume an updated date to show employers that the resume has been changed. We also put the edited resumes back on top of the resume pile for employers to search.

- **Privacy/confidentiality:** Currently it is not possible to limit who can see a resume.

Any paying member employer/staffing firm can see all the resumes. It is not possible to shield a resume from being viewed by a current employer. Some job seekers choose to alter their resumes so that their current employer's name does not show.

- **Assistance provided to the person submitting a resume:** When posting the resume, the submission form fields guide a job seeker to include all important information that an employer needs to see. Other than provide this form, JOBNET.com does not help a job seeker write the resume.

- **Search options available to employers viewing resumes:** Keyword search is available for employers. They can use any combination of keywords, or they can search by such strings as ZIP codes, area codes, and so on. Explanatory examples of searching are provided on the resume-search page.

- **Technology to match jobs to resumes and e-mail results to clients:** None at this time.

- **Average number of daily hits on resumes:** JOBNET.com does not track this information.

- **Special features:** Every week, the JOBNET.com Job Butler searches the database—containing thousands of local jobs—for the latest opportunities. You select the location and criteria of the job you are looking for and the Job Butler e-mails you all the jobs matching that information. The best part is that it's absolutely free to sign up. Just provide your name and e-mail along with the job category and geographic location that interest you.

- **Other distinguishing factors:** The resumes are 80 percent from the Philadelphia region (NJ, DE, MD, and PA) and beat

out the national sites on this level because even the largest sites do not have 70,000 resumes in this area.

JobOptions.com
USA
All career fields
Rating: ★ ★ ★ ★

JobOptions.com, the next generation in employment sites, pioneered online employment services in 1991. As the Internet's top site for job listings, career tools, and HR resources, JobOptions features a searchable Employer Database and a Resume Database with Real Resume Privacy™. Through its JobOptions Network, including a wide range of partners from diversity sites to large national community sites, the aggregate traffic of the JobOptions Network Partners exceeds 35 million potential job seekers each month.

JobOptions has received numerous awards including *PC Computing*'s "MVP" finalist award, *PC Magazine*'s "Honorable Mention" (second place), *Home PC*'s "Best of the Web," *Net Guide*'s "Best of the Web," and recognition in *USA Today*'s "Hot Sites."

- **URL:** http://www.joboptions.com

- **Ownership/sponsorship:** JobOptions is a member of Gund Business Enterprises, Inc., a Cleveland, Ohio, organization.

- **Started accepting resumes:** n/a.

- **Approximate number of resumes online April 2000:** 302,000.

- **Resume career fields:** JobOptions has a diverse resume database. An employer can search for active and passive candidates in all career fields.

- **Total number of corporate subscribers/ employers:** More than 6,000.

- **Distribution of corporate subscribers/ employers**

Direct-hire employers: 85 percent

Contract/consulting firms: 15 percent

- **Fee structure for corporate subscribers/ employers:** Services range from a single job posting that remains on the site 60 days for $150 to annual packages that include unlimited use for $5,370.

- **Methods and rules for submitting resumes:** Any job candidate can submit a resume on the site for free. Resume postings from fee-based professional recruiters are prohibited.

- **Percent of resumes submitted by Web form:** 100.

- **Percent of resumes received from individuals:** Not tracked.

- **Limits on length:** None.

- **Format:** Job candidates can use the preformatted resume, or they can paste in their existing resumes.

- **Fees for person submitting resume:** None.

- **Length of time resumes remain online:** Unlimited period of time.

- **Procedures for updating/renewing:** Candidates can add, edit, and delete their resumes at any time. They can also store three formatted resumes and tailor them to a specific job.

- **Privacy/confidentiality:** JobOptions' Real Resume Privacy allows job seekers to remain completely anonymous. Unlike other sites, information is 100 percent protected and confidential.

- **Assistance provided to the person submitting a resume:** A Help section is provided on the resume-submission page.

- **Search options available to employers viewing resumes:** Employers can search by category and locations, and by skill set, industry, location, and years of experience.

- **Technology to match jobs to resumes and e-mail results to clients:** JobOptions has two special services that help both the candidates and the employers. **Job Alert:** Enables candidates to request that job openings matching their skills be directly e-mailed to them. **Resume Alert:** Enables employers to receive resumes via e-mail that meet a list of criteria they have specified for job openings.

- **Average number of daily hits on resumes:** n/a.

- **Special features:** A preformatted resume option creates a more professional, easier-to-read resume for the employer. This option also gives the passive or active job seeker a refined, formatted resume always on hand. JobOptions provides a refined job search/resume search by location, industry, skill set, experience, and so on. You can e-mail a formatted resume to an employer with the click of a button. JobOptions provides an extensive, diverse database of jobs/employers in all MSAs.

- **Other distinguishing factors:** The resume database is completely proprietary: All the resumes are from candidates who have chosen JobOptions as their employment resource. The resumes have not been pulled from other sources on the Internet. As such, the site's resume database is an exclusive collection of resumes from qualified candidates who range from entry-level candidates to professionals with years of experience.

JobOptions is the fastest-growing network of career sites on the net. It is the leader in customizable Private Label Intranet/ Extranet career site functionality for employers.

JobServe

UK and global
IT only
Rating: ★ ★ ★

JobServe is the largest source of IT vacancies in the United Kingdom. JobServe is used by over 1,800 IT-recruitment agencies to advertise more than 150,000 new contract and permanent vacancies every month. JobServe is based in the United Kingdom; however, more than 10 percent of the vacancies advertised are worldwide.

- **URL:** http://www.jobserve.com

- **Ownership/sponsorship:** JobServe Ltd.

- **Started accepting resumes:** 1994.

- **Approximate number of resumes online April 2000:** 69,800.

- **Resume career fields:** At present, JobServe accepts resumes only from IT professionals.

- **Total number of corporate subscribers/ employers (agencies):** 1,800.

- **Distribution of corporate subscribers/ employers:** 100 percent staffing firms.

- **Fee structure for corporate subscribers/ employers:** 99 per calendar month for approximately 2,000 curriculum vitae (CVs) in either Word 6.0, WordPerfect 5.x, or ASCII; and a database in dBASE III, comma-separated ASCII, or tab-separated ASCII. Individual CVs are purchased via e-mail for £5 each.

- **Methods and rules for submitting resumes:** Submit online to http://www.jobserve.com or e-mail to distribute@jobserve.com.

- **Percent of resumes submitted by Web form:** n/a.

- **Percent of resumes received from individuals:** n/a.

- **Limits on length:** None.

- **Format:** Open.

- **Fees for person submitting resume:** None.

- **Length of time resumes remain online:** CVs are not available online. Each week the agency either receives all new or updated CVs, or JobServe sends them a list of IT professionals who are actively looking for work. The agency then selects the CVs they require via an e-mail on-demand system.

- **Procedures for updating/renewing:** Same as for registering. Only agencies have access to CVs.

- **Privacy/confidentiality:** There are a number of measures to shield your CV from your present employer:

  Your CV is never displayed on the Internet.

  Employers are not allowed to view the database.

  Agencies must ask permission before using your CV.

  Alternatively, you can search for jobs and send your CV only to specific agencies for specific jobs.

- **Assistance provided to the person submitting a resume:** None specific, but the staff is always helpful and will forward any comments or advice if requested.

- **Search options available to agencies viewing resumes:** Information is provided as a database file, so agencies can search using any criteria they require.

- **Technology to match jobs to resumes and e-mail results to clients:** Information is provided as a database file, so agencies can search using any criteria they require.

- **Average number of daily hits on resumes:** n/a.

- **Special features:** JobServe provides online job searches without the need for any registration; and upon request, provides a free daily e-mail message that contains the latest vacancies, optionally "filtered" to the candidates' skills and preferences.

- **Other distinguishing factors:** JobServe is the most widely used site by IT professionals, with over 130,000 subscribers and approximately 1,700,000 page views per week (April 2000).

  A member of the staff checks every CV and converts it to a format suitable for placing on the JobServe database, which is then distributed to agencies.

jobsite.com

USA

Real estate, construction, real estate finance, engineering, architecture

Rating: ★ ★ ★

This site focuses on real estate, construction, real estate finance, and the architectural and engineering industries. jobsite.com advertises in trade publications such as *ENR, Constructor, Contractor, Commercial Property News,* and *ABC.*

- **URL:** http://www.jobsite.com

- **Ownership/sponsorship:** Privately held.

- **Started accepting resumes:** 1999.

- **Approximate number of resumes online April 2000:** 1,400.

- **Resume career fields:** Resumes are in career fields such as construction, real estate, real estate finance, architecture, and engineering.

- **Total number of corporate subscribers/ employers:** 450.

- **Distribution of corporate subscribers/ employers**

  Direct-hire employers: 70 percent

  Staffing firms: 25 percent

  Contract/consulting firms: 5 percent

- **Fee structure for corporate subscribers/ employers:** jobsite.com creates custom packages to meet a company's specific recruiting needs. Depending on the size of a company and its hiring needs, it can buy bundles of job postings along with resume database access, a company profile, banner advertising, automatic matching of jobs and resumes, cross-posting service, and links to its corporate Web site.

- **Methods and rules for submitting resumes:** Must have a work background within the disciplines jobsite.com serves. Registered companies work with jobsite.com because jobsite.com is specific to their industry.

- **Percent of resumes submitted by**

  Web form: 70

  E-mail: 28

  Fax: 2

- **Percent of resumes received from**

  Individuals: 98

  Colleges or universities: 2

- **Limits on length:** None. Job seekers can create and store different versions of their resumes.

- **Format:** Use jobsite.com's resume builder to input your resume into the system.

- **Fees for person submitting resume:** None.

- **Length of time resumes remain online:** Resumes stay online for 90 days or until the job seeker removes the resume.

- **Procedures for updating/renewing:** All job seekers have a username and password. They have access to the resume at all times to update/modify/delete.

- **Privacy/confidentiality:** jobsite.com offers job seekers confidentiality. This option hides their name, phone, address, and most current employer. It does, however, reveal the e-mail address so that employers are able to get in touch with them.

- **Assistance provided to the person submitting a resume:** jobsite.com offers live personal assistance to job seekers by telephone.

- **Search options available to employers viewing resumes:** Discipline, education level, experience level, industry, keywords, job category, job title.

- **Technology to match jobs to resumes and e-mail results to clients:** jobsite.com has a built-in matching system utilizing push technology. If a resume is entered into the jobsite.com system that matches the qualifications of a posted job, the resume is automatically e-mailed to the hiring contact for the position.

JobsNorthwest.com

US Northwest
High-tech
Rating: ★ ★

Thompson & Associates' JobsNorthwest.com specializes in personnel with practical, on-the-job experience in high-tech industries, including software-development companies, traditional industries (such as manufacturing and banking), and consulting firms in the Pacific Northwest: Washington, Idaho, Western Montana, and Oregon.

Thompson and Associates' services are paid for by its clients, which are companies with employment needs. Thompson and Associates is not an employment agency, and it is not engaged by individuals to help them find jobs.

- **URL:** http://www.jobsnorthwest.com

- **Ownership/sponsorship:** Neal Thompson, President.

  Thompson & Associates, Inc.
  2448 76th Avenue SE, Suite 212
  Mercer Island, WA 98040
  Phone: 206-236-0153
  Fax: 206-236-2262

- **Started accepting resumes:** Web site operational in 1995.

- **Resume career fields:** Resumes are strictly high-tech, including software engineers, architects, managers, project managers, program managers, programmer analysts, network engineers, and so on.

- **Methods and rules for submitting resumes:** E-mail or postal mail.

- **Percent of resumes that come from the Web site submitted by e-mail:** 100.

- **Limits on length:** None.

- **Format:** Open.

- **Fees for person submitting resume:** None.

- **Length of time resumes remain online:** Variable.

- **Procedures for updating/renewing:** Resubmit.

JOBTRAK.COM

USA
College students and graduates
Rating: ★ ★ ★ ★ ★

JOBTRAK.COM has teamed up with over 1,000 college and university career centers nationwide. JOBTRAK.COM has been listing jobs since 1988. *Forbes* magazine recently rated JOBTRAK.COM as the best site for students and graduates looking for their first job or internship.

- **URL:** http://www.jobtrak.com

- **Ownership/sponsorship:** JOBTRAK Corporation.

    1964 Westwood Blvd., 3rd Floor
    Los Angeles, CA 90025
    800-999-8725

- **Started accepting resumes:** 1997.

- **Approximate number of resumes online April 2000:** 500,000.

- **Resume career fields:** Resumes are in all job classifications. They are categorized by the following: university, job function preferred (35 classifications), industry preferred (75 classifications), years of work experience, geographic preference, degree, and major (400 classifications).

- **Total number of corporate subscribers/ employers:** Over 100,000 employers have used JOBTRAK.COM in the past year to target qualified candidates for entry-level and experienced full-time, part-time, temporary, and internship opportunities.

- **Distribution of corporate subscribers/ employers**

    Direct-hire employers: 96 percent

    Staffing firms: 3 percent

    Contract/consulting firms: 1 percent

- **Fee structure for corporate subscribers/ employers:** Employers pay to search resumes from students, MBAs, and alumni from their choice of campuses. Cost is per ad on a per-campus basis and runs from $18 for one school to $395 for all universities.

- **Methods and rules for submitting resumes:** To submit resumes, individuals must be students or alumni from one of the 1,000 universities partnered with JOBTRAK.COM. First go to www.jobtrak.com; then click on Students & Alumni; and then click on Submit Resume.

- **Percent of resumes submitted by Web form:** 100.

- **Percent of resumes received from individuals:** 100 (students or alumni from a college or university).

- **Limits on length:** None.

- **Format:** Upload document from individual's word processor.

- **Fees for person submitting resume:** None.

- **Length of time resumes remain online:** Three months; at that time, individuals must indicate whether they want their resumes to remain active.

- **Procedures for updating/renewing:** On the Web site.

- **Privacy/confidentiality:** It is not yet possible to limit who can see a resume. It is not yet possible to shield a resume from being viewed by a current employer, but the technology will be available soon.

- **Assistance provided to the person submitting a resume:** JOBTRAK.COM has created an award-winning resume guide that is located at www.jobtrak.com/jobmanual. This guide provides complete instructions for creating a resume, along with many samples.

- **Search options available to employers viewing resumes:** University, job function preferred, industry preferred, years of work experience, geographic preference, degree, major, keyword.

- **Technology to match jobs to resumes and e-mail results to clients:** n/a.

- **Average number of daily hits on resumes:** JOBTRAK has 50,000 visitors per day to its Web site.

- **Other distinguishing factors:** Established in 1988, JOBTRAK.COM is the only career site on the Internet to have formed direct partnerships with over 1,000 college and university career centers, MBA programs, and alumni associations.

  Over 300,000 job listings representing 900,000 job openings were posted on JOBTRAK.COM in 1999.

  In 1997, 1998, and 1999, JOBTRAK.COM was rated the most-visited college-targeted career site on the Internet by Student Monitor, LLC. JOBTRAK.COM was also honored as the Entrepreneur of the Year by the State of California and was a semifinalist for the prestigious Global Information & Infrastructure award.

LatPro

USA, Canada, Latin America, Caribbean, Spain, Portugal
All career fields
Rating: ★ ★ ★ ★

Started in 1997, LatPro is the leading source for Spanish and Portuguese jobs.

- **URL:** http://www.latpro.com

- **Ownership/sponsorship:** LatPro, Inc., headquartered in Plantation, Florida.

- **Started accepting resumes:** 1997.

- **Approximate number of resumes online April 2000:** 10,000.

- **Resume career fields:** Resumes are in all career fields.

- **Total number of corporate subscribers/ employers:** 3,500.

- **Distribution of corporate subscribers/ employers**

  Direct-hire employers: 60 percent

  Retained/contingency recruiters: 36 percent

  Staffing agencies/advertising agencies: 4 percent

- **Fee structure for corporate subscribers/ employers:** Free trial.

- **Methods and rules for submitting resumes:** Spanish- or Portuguese-speaking professionals can submit a resume to the site in response to a specific job posting. LatPro members receive the added benefit of having their resumes available on the site to recruiters searching the database. Up to six versions of a resume are allowed. Each version can be in English, Spanish, and/or Portuguese.

- **Percent of resumes submitted by Web form:** 100.

- **Percent of resumes received from individuals:** Nearly 100.

- **Limits on length:** 4,000–20,000 characters (depending on membership level).

- **Format:** Text only.

- **Fees for person submitting resume:** $35–$150 for 3–12-month memberships. Membership benefits include registration for an unlimited number of job listings; the ability to save three to six resume versions, each of which can be in English, Spanish, and/or Portuguese; resumes are available to recruiters searching on the resume database; e-mails announcing jobs in the field of interest in the countries of choice; one year free subscription to *Latin Trade* magazine, a leading Latin American business monthly; a personal page that tracks individual job search history, including the number of companies who have viewed your resume.

- **Length of time resumes remain online:** Varies depending on membership—between 3 and 12 months.

- **Procedures for updating/renewing:** All job seekers are given a username and password, which allows them to freely access and update their resumes.

- **Privacy/confidentiality:** LatPro has a confidentiality policy that protects the privacy of all users of the site. If requested, candidates can withhold name, address, contact numbers, and current employer from their personal profile and resume. It is possible to shield a resume from being viewed by a current employer.

- **Assistance provided to the person submitting a resume:** Members are asked to fill out a straightforward form rather than attaching their resume. The structure of the form has been designed to meet the needs and demands of recruiters. Numerous resources for resume writers are available in the advice section of the site.

- **Search options available to employers viewing resumes:** Employers can search for resumes by date, location (region, country, city), job category, and keywords.

- **Technology to match jobs to resumes and e-mail results to clients:** LatPro utilizes search agents to match resumes with employers and job openings with job seekers. The agents search postings by location, keyword, and job type and have results delivered via e-mail on a daily basis. LatPro is

the focused, time-saving solution that provides the best matches for both job seekers and employers.

- **Average number of daily hits on resumes:** 3,000 and growing.

- **Special features:** Members can post up to six versions of their resume to target different types of jobs or specific employers. Each version can be posted in English, Spanish, and/or Portuguese. A customized page for each member tracks the history of their job search activity, including the number of companies that have reviewed their resume.

- **Other distinguishing factors:** Dynamic content delivery lets job seekers customize their LatPro experience with information relevant to their job search. LatPro provides this valuable job search information through forums, news, advice, and chats.

LAWMATCH.com

Primarily USA and Canada
Law and law-practice personnel
Rating: ★ ★ ★

LAWMATCH provides employers, recruiters and job seekers in the legal community a forum designed for the specialized recruitment and staffing needs of the that community.

- **URL:** http://www.lawmatch.com

- **Ownership/sponsorship:** Baseline Recruiters Network Inc.

- **Started accepting resumes:** 1996.

- **Approximate number of resumes online April 2000:** 7,000.

- **Resume career fields:** Resumes are from attorneys, paralegals, legal secretaries, and all other law-practice personnel, whether or not professionally licensed.

- **Total number of corporate subscribers/ employers:** More than 1,000.

- **Distribution of corporate subscribers/ employers**

  Direct-hire employers: 77 percent

  Staffing firms: 20 percent

  Contract/consulting firms: 3 percent

- **Fee structure for corporate subscribers/ employers:** Resume bank is open access, free for all employers to search. LAWMATCH charges a small fee only after an employer or recruiter has reviewed a resume and wants to obtain the candidate's identity.

- **Methods and rules for submitting resumes:** Fill out form; paste resume in text box.

- **Percent of resumes submitted by Web form:** 100.

- **Percent of resumes received from**

  Individuals: 70

  Colleges or universities: 30

- **Limits on length:** None.

- **Format:** Paste only as ASCII text.

- **Fees for person submitting resume:** Range from free to $59 for three months.

- **Length of time resumes remain online:** From one month to indefinitely.

- **Procedures for updating/renewing:** Log in with name and password.

- **Privacy/confidentiality:** It is possible to limit who can see a resume. It is possible to shield a resume from being viewed by a current employer.

- **Assistance provided to the person submitting a resume:** For fee-paid profiles.

- **Search options available to employers viewing resumes:** All typical search criteria can be applied, as well as specialty criteria relating to law.

- **Technology to match jobs to resumes and e-mail results to clients:** Yes.

- **Average number of daily hits on resumes:** More than 700.

- **Special features:** LAWMATCH XT software (for multiple listing of jobs and filtering of resumes) is used by over 60 major legal institutions (law schools, bar associations, nonprofits) and dozens of law firms and recruiting agencies to power the employment/placement sections of their own Web sites.

- **Other distinguishing factors:** Open access to all employers and recruiting firms: It costs nothing to review an unlimited number of resumes. LAWMATCH also invites participation of the recruiter/search firm community.

MarketingJobs.com

USA and Canada
Marketing, sales, advertising
Rating: ★ ★ ★

MarketingJobs.com is an employment site specializing in marketing, sales, and advertising jobs. Started in 1996, MarketingJobs.com is a specialty site for marketing professionals.

- **URL:** http://www.marketingjobs.com

- **Ownership/sponsorship:** MarketingJobs.com, Inc.

- **Started accepting resumes:** 1997.

- **Approximate number of resumes online April 2000:** 7,000.

- **Resume career fields:** Resumes are in marketing, sales, and advertising.

- **Total number of corporate subscribers/ employers:** 1,200.

- **Distribution of corporate subscribers/ employers**

  Direct-hire employers: 75 percent

  Staffing firms: 10 percent

  Contract/consulting firms: 15 percent

- **Fee structure for corporate subscribers/ employers:** Standard and custom posting packages based on the client's needs.

- **Methods and rules for submitting resumes:** Online; resume must be only in marketing, sales, or advertising.

- **Percent of resumes submitted by Web form:** 100.

- **Percent of resumes received from**

  Individuals: 90

  Colleges and universities: 10

- **Limits on length:** None.

- **Format:** Text or HTML.

- **Fees for person submitting resume:** None.

- **Length of time resumes remain online:** 90 days.

- **Procedures for updating/renewing:** Simply log in and refresh resume.

- **Privacy/confidentiality:** It is not possible to limit who can see a resume. It is not possible to shield a resume from being viewed by a current employer.

- **Assistance provided to the person submitting a resume:** Yes, help link.

- **Search options available to employers viewing resumes:** City/state, category, salary, and education.

- **Technology to match jobs to resumes and e-mail results to clients:** Yes.

- **Average number of daily hits on resumes:** n/a.

MedZilla™

USA
Health care
Rating: ★ ★ ★ ★ ★

MedZilla™ was the original site on the World Wide Web to specialize in resumes and jobs for biotech, medical, pharmaceutical, and health-care professionals and scientists.

- **URL:** http://www.medzilla.com

- **Ownership/sponsorship:** MedZilla is owned by MedZilla Inc.

- **Started accepting resumes:** 1994.

- **Approximate number of resumes online April 2000:** 3,000.

- **Resume career fields:** Resumes are exclusively from professionals with expertise in biotechnology, medicine, health care, and science.

- **Total number of corporate subscribers/ employers:** More than 600.

- **Distribution of corporate subscribers/ employers**

  Direct-hire employers: 75 percent

  Staffing firms and contract/consulting firms: 25 percent

- **Fee structure for corporate subscribers/ employers:** Subscription/site license based on number of recruiters and job-posting preferences.

- **Methods and rules for submitting resumes:** Via interview form.

- **Percent of resumes submitted by Web form:** 100.

- **Percent of resumes received from individuals:** 100.

- **Limits on length:** None.

- **Format:** Resumes are free-form. Additional input is requested via interview form.

- **Fees for person submitting resume:** None.

- **Length of time resumes remain online:** Depends on the new-resume influx rate. Generally no more than 16–20 weeks from the last update.

- **Procedures for updating/renewing:** Available via MedZilla User ID.

- **Privacy/confidentiality:** It is possible to limit who can see a resume. Only MedZilla subscribers can download and view resumes. Candidates are notified every time their resumes are downloaded. They know who is reading their resumes. This service is unique to MedZilla. It is possible to shield a resume from being viewed by a current employer provided that the candidates enter their current employer's name correctly.

- **Assistance provided to the person submitting a resume:** All resumes are reviewed prior to acceptance by MedZilla. All candidates receive an e-mail confirmation when they submit their resumes, another confirmation when their resumes are accepted, and a notice every time their resumes are actually downloaded.

  Candidates are provided with extensive resources to assist in their job search, including a user-friendly resume editor to update their professional or contact information; free access to a comprehensive, interactive database of salary information; and articles about working, finding jobs, and advancing their careers.

- **Search options available to employers viewing resumes:** Any employer or recruiter can search resumes by using a simple, powerful full-text retrieval system. The system returns abstracts only, not full resumes. Abstracts are prepared by the candidates themselves via the MedZilla interview form. No contact information is allowed in resume abstracts. If the employers are licensed subscribers, they can download full resumes by using a simple form. If the employers are not subscribers, they are provided with information about obtaining a subscription.

- **Technology to match jobs to resumes and e-mail results to clients:** Voluntary by the candidates themselves. In other words, the candidates search for jobs in the resume bank and e-mail the resumes themselves. Via employer auto-referral profile: Every incoming resume is queried against the employer's set of keywords and phrases and forwarded to the employer if a match is found.

  Candidates may also include keywords or Boolean expressions to receive daily e-mail notification of new and updated jobs that match their requirements.

- **Average number of daily hits on resumes:** Approximately 90 percent of MedZilla's visitors are candidates specifically in the health-care field. The other 10 percent are employers and recruiters. MedZilla has few random visitors. Its links are carefully placed, and its search-engine terms are selected to attract only those people who are interested in the health-care field.

  Currently, MedZilla hosts around 55,000 visitors each month, as calculated from unique domains. This number does not include multiple hits from different users at the same domain, and it does not include "onlookers" (people who job-surf in groups). MedZilla often receives multiple resumes from the same domain at the same time. This activity indicates that candidates tend to use Web employment services in groups of two to five people.

Minorities' Job Bank

USA
Minorities in all career fields
Rating: ★ ★ ★

Minorities' Job Bank is a subsidiary of iMinorities.com, Inc., the publisher of *The Black Collegian* magazine and The Black Collegian Online (http://www.black-collegian.com). The Minorities' Job Bank is dedicated to all underrepresented minorities in the workforce and features the African-American Village, the Asian-American Village, the Hispanic-American Village, the Native-American Village, and the Minorities Global Village.

- **URL:** http://www.minorities-jb.com

- **Ownership/sponsorship:** iMinorities.com, Inc.

- **Started accepting resumes:** 1998.

- **Approximate number of resumes online April 2000:** 11,500.

- **Resume career fields:** Resumes are accepted in all career fields.

- **Total number of corporate subscribers/ employers:** 350.

- **Distribution of corporate subscribers/employers:** 100 percent direct-hire employers.

- **Fee structure for corporate subscribers/ employers:** Employers become members of the site. Membership includes unlimited access to the resume database, unlimited posting to the jobs database, and a company profile in the directory of members/ employers. Membership is $7,500 for one year. The Black Collegian Online has a sponsorship that also includes resume access. It does not sell resume searching as a standalone product.

- **Methods and rules for submitting resumes:** Applicant must have a college degree. A 3.0 G.P.A. is preferred but not required. Applicant must set up a user account, which has a name and contact information. Applicant can also set up an agent, which will notify him/her of job matches to their selected criteria.

- **Percent of resumes submitted by**

  Web form: 65

  Other paper (job fairs, mailings): 20

  E-mail: 10

  Diskette from universities: 5

- **Percent of resumes received from**

  Individuals: 90

  Colleges or universities: 10

- **Limits on length:** None.

- **Format:** If the job seeker wants to build a resume online, information is entered into a form. Or a resume can be cut and pasted into one text field. The job seeker can also include a cover letter to the hiring manager as a separate form field.

- **Fees for person submitting resume:** None.

- **Length of time resumes remain online:** One year.

- **Procedures for updating/renewing:** Job seekers have a username and password to access their accounts for editing, updating, deleting, or deactivating their resumes. If the resume is declined because of incomplete information or if it expires, the job seekers are notified via e-mail with a message. Expiring job seekers are encouraged to return to add their resumes or to delete their accounts if they are no longer looking for employment.

- **Privacy/confidentiality:** It is possible to limit who can see a resume. Only member employers of the sites can view resumes. It is possible to shield a resume from being viewed by a current employer. When posting resumes, applicants can choose to make personal information confidential.

- **Assistance provided to the person submitting a resume:** The database guides the job seeker along the process by explaining each and every step. Web-based help is available.

- **Search options available to employers viewing resumes:** Employers can search by discipline, location preference of applicant, G.P.A. range, ethnicity, and keywords. Employers may also set up search agents that will notify them when they have resumes matching their preselected criteria.

- **Technology to match jobs to resumes and e-mail results to clients:** n/a.

- **Average number of daily hits on resumes:** 11,000 visitors per day.

- **Special features:** Online career-development advice is also available.

- **Other distinguishing factors:** Computerworld states, "This is a standout among minority job-search sites because it creates a true sense of community for African, Asian, Hispanic, and Native American professionals." ZDNet states, "Right now, most Internet users are young, white, and have high income. But that's starting to change, and companies like The Black Collegian, which…launched Minorities' Job Bank, a job-listing Web site aimed at minority groups, should be in prime position to take advantage of the Net's diversifying ethnic user base."

Monster.com

United States, Canada, United Kingdom, the Netherlands, Belgium, Australia, France, New Zealand, Singapore, and Hong Kong
All career fields
Rating: ★ ★ ★ ★

Monster.com, headquartered in Maynard, Massachusetts, is the leading global careers Web site, with over 14.5 million unique visits per month. Monster.com connects the most progressive companies with the most qualified career-minded individuals, offering innovative technology and superior services that give them more control over the recruiting process.

- **URL:** http://www.monster.com

- **Ownership/sponsorship:** TMP Worldwide.

- **Started accepting resumes:** 1995.

- **Approximate number of resumes online April 2000:** 3,000,000.

- **Resume career fields:** Resumes are in all career fields.

- **Total number of corporate subscribers/ employers:** n/a.

- **Distribution of corporate subscribers/ employers:** n/a.

- **Fee structure for corporate subscribers/ employers:** Monster.com creates custom packages to meet a company's specific recruiting needs, which can include resume database access, job postings, a company profile, and banner advertising. Pricing varies based on length of membership and number of recruiters.

- **Methods and rules for submitting resumes:** Anyone can submit a resume to Resume City.

- **Percent of resumes submitted by Web form:** 100.

- **Percent of resumes received from individuals:** Not tracked.

- **Limits on length:** Up to five resumes and cover letters.

- **Format:** Job seekers use Monster.com's Resume Builder to input their resume. The Resume Builder walks users through the process step by step.

- **Fees for person submitting resume:** None.

- **Length of time resumes remain online:** Twelve months, or until the candidate requests they be removed.

- **Procedures for updating/renewing:** All job seekers are given a username and password. They can access and update their resumes at any time and as often as they want.

- **Privacy/confidentiality:** Monster.com's tiered resume privacy technology gives job seekers complete control over who may access their personal information:

  The Confidential option, ideal for passive job seekers, hides personal contact information and the current employer, but allows potential employers to view their skills and experience profile in Monster.com's resume database. When an employer expresses interest in your blind profile, he/she sends you an e-mail through the Monster.com confidential system. You can then evaluate on a case-by-case basis whether to grant that employer access to your full resume, including contact information.

The Public option posts your complete resume, including your contact information, in the resume database, making it searchable to Monster member companies.

The Private option allows you to build and store your resume on Monster.com so that you can apply for jobs online, but does not allow employers to access it through the resume database.

- **Assistance provided to the person submitting a resume:** Extensive online Help is available; or for assistance, job seekers can contact Monster.com at 800-MONSTER.

- **Search options available to employers viewing resumes:** Employers can search resumes by date, location, education level, job category, and keywords.

- **Technology to match jobs to resumes and e-mail results to clients:** Monster.com utilizes search agents to match resumes with employers and to match job openings with job seekers, designed to provide better matches to save time for both job seekers and employers. The agents search postings by location, keyword, job type, and job category, and have results delivered via e-mail as often as the user chooses (daily, weekly, biweekly, or monthly).

- **Special features:** Job seekers can create and store different versions of their resume in their My Monster home page, to target different types of jobs or specific employers.

- **Other distinguishing factors:** Dynamic content delivery lets job seekers customize their My Monster home page for a more personalized and meaningful online career experience. Job seekers can choose topics of interest, and Monster.com will automatically pull articles and advice related to those interests from Monster.com's

1,500-plus—and growing—pages of content. The articles, news, tips, and more are delivered to the individual's My Monster home page. The range of topics includes Career Change, Managing Your Boss, Life/Work Balance, Time Management, Interviewing, Work and Health, Self-Assessment, Relocation, Internet and E-Commerce, and more.

National Association of Broadcasters Career Center

Primarily USA
Radio and television broadcasting
Rating: ★ ★ ★

For 75 years, the National Association of Broadcasters has represented the radio and television industries. Through the Career Center, NAB helps member radio and television stations recruit qualified job candidates who reflect the diversity of the community's population.

- **URL:** http://www.nab.org/bcc

- **Ownership/sponsorship:** National Association of Broadcasters.

- **Started accepting resumes:** 1996.

- **Approximate number of resumes online April 2000:** 700.

- **Resume career fields:** Resumes are in radio, television, video, broadcasting, production, writing, producing, directing, sales, programming, on-air, and voice-overs.

- **Total number of corporate subscribers/employers:** 6,500 radio and television stations.

- **Distribution of corporate subscribers/employers:** 100 percent direct-hire employers.

- **Fee structure for corporate subscribers/employers:** n/a.

- **Methods and rules for submitting resumes:** Posted directly on Web site; e-mail address required.

- **Percent of resumes submitted by Web form:** 100.

- **Percent of resumes received from individuals:** 100.

- **Limits on length:** None.

- **Format:** Open.

- **Fees for person submitting resume:** None for members of the National Association of Broadcasters.

- **Length of time resumes remain online:** Six months.

- **Procedures for updating/renewing:** Password.

- **Privacy/confidentiality:** Only members of the National Association of Broadcasters can see resumes. It is not possible to shield a resume from being viewed by a current employer.

- **Assistance provided to the person submitting a resume:** Prompts.

- **Search options available to employers viewing resumes:** By position and geography.

- **Technology to match jobs to resumes and e-mail results to clients:** None.

- **Average number of daily hits on resumes:** n/a.

National Diversity Newspaper Job Bank

USA and international
Newspaper industry
Rating: ★ ★ ★

In 1995 *The Florida Times-Union* staff created the Southeast Diversity Journalism Job Bank, the forerunner of the current National Diversity Newspaper Job Bank, for attracting minority journalists to newspapers. *The Times-Union* provides daily staff support, site design, and maintenance for the job bank through a cooperative arrangement with the Newspaper Association of America.

- **URL:** http://newsjobs.com

- **Ownership/sponsorship:** The Florida Times-Union/Morris Communications Corp/Newspaper Association of America. Phone: 904-359-4600

- **Started accepting resumes:** 1996.

- **Approximate number of resumes online April 2000:** 1,000.

- **Resume career fields:** Resumes are in the newsroom and business side of the newspaper industry.

- **Total number of corporate subscribers/ employers:** 250.

- **Distribution of corporate subscribers/ employers:** 100 percent direct-hire employers.

- **Fee structure for corporate subscribers/ employers:** None. Fee for advertising opportunities.

- **Methods and rules for submitting resumes:** Complete fields and receive password to browse job listings.

- **Percent of resumes submitted by Web form:** 98

  E-mail: 2

- **Percent of resumes received from individuals:** 100.

- **Limits on length:** Yes.

- **Format:** HTML.

- **Fees for person submitting resume:** None.

- **Length of time resumes remain online:** Three months.

- **Procedures for updating/renewing:** Resubmit resume info.

- **Privacy/confidentiality:** Resumes cannot be seen. This job bank is designed to protect the confidentiality of those seeking employment. Employers are not allowed to see resumes. Applicants can see jobs available and contact the person for the open position. At this point, the applicant who is truly interested in that position can contact the employer about his/her interest. Applicants are not bombarded by employers they have no desire to work for, whether it be company, region, position, etc.

- **Assistance provided to the person submitting a resume:** Yes.

- **Search options available to employers viewing resumes:** None.

- **Technology to match jobs to resumes and e-mail results to clients:** None.

- **Average number of daily hits on resumes:** Cannot view resumes.

- **Special features:** Links to other newspaper-related sites.

Net-Temps

USA
All career fields
Rating: ★ ★ ★ ★

Net-Temps is the leading online job-posting service for the staffing industry. Recruiters may advertise job openings as well as search the extensive resume banks for qualified candidates.

- **URL:** http://www.net-temps.com

- **Ownership/sponsorship:** Net-Temps is a privately held company headquartered north of Boston at the following address:

  55 Middlesex Street, Suite 220
  North Chelmsford, MA 01863
  978-251-7272
  Fax: 978-251-7250

- **Started accepting resumes:** Web site was launched in 1996.

- **Approximate number of resumes online April 2000:** 211,000.

- **Resume career fields:** Resumes are accepted in all career fields. Job seekers post their resumes and search for jobs at no cost. Jobs are organized into industry-specific employment channels, making it easy to inquire about available positions and apply online.

  Through a personalized desktop, recruiters are able to post jobs and search the Net-Temps resume banks and the daily hot list of candidates. They can also check job-posting viewing and response statistics. Resume search agents can also be custom-configured to alert them to new resumes matching their criteria.

  Net-Temps pioneered the concept of cross-posting jobs and now cross-posts subscribers' jobs to over 500 Web sites including Yahoo!, Lycos, and Excite.

- **Total number of corporate subscribers/ employers:** 7,565.

- **Distribution of corporate subscribers/ employers:** n/a.

- **Fee structure for corporate subscribers/ employers:** $595 per month for posting up to 100 jobs and 50 candidate resumes (name suppressed), custom daily hot list of candidates, five resume search agents with live updates, and automatic updates of job postings to the customer corporate Web site through Net-Links. Discounts are available for multiple offices and length-of-term contracts.

- **Methods and rules for submitting resumes:** Online form in which you paste a resume.

- **Percent of resumes submitted by Web form:** 100.

- **Percent of resumes received from individuals:** 100.

- **Limits on length:** Three pages or 8,000 characters.

- **Format:** Open.

- **Fees for person submitting resume:** None.

- **Length of time resumes remain online:** 60 days and then are automatically deleted.

- **Procedures for updating/renewing:** You can edit, remove, or renew your resume online.

- **Privacy/confidentiality:** n/a.

- **Assistance provided to the person submitting a resume:** n/a.

- **Search options available to employers viewing resumes:** Five resume search agents per user with live updates.

- **Technology to match jobs to resumes and e-mail results to clients:** Open Text,

Livelink Suite, document-management software, and Verity.

■ **Average number of daily hits on resumes:** 150,000 per day.

Online Sports Career Center

USA
Sports and recreation
Rating: ★ ★ ★

The Online Sports Career Center is a resource of sports-related career opportunities and a resume bank for potential employers within the many segments of the sports and recreation industries.

■ **URL:** http://onlinesports.com/pages/ CareerCenter.html

■ **Ownership/sponsorship:** Online Sports (www.onlinesports.com).

■ **Started accepting resumes:** 1995.

■ **Approximate number of resumes online April 2000:** n/a.

■ **Resume career fields:** Only sports and recreation jobs are listed at the site. Resumes are not required to be listed in any other classification.

■ **Total number of corporate subscribers/ employers:** n/a.

■ **Distribution of corporate subscribers/ employers**

  Direct-hire employers: 80 percent

  Staffing firms: 20 percent

■ **Fee structure for corporate subscribers/ employers:** Free.

■ **Methods and rules for submitting resumes:** Post your resume (ASCII-text

format) by sending e-mail to resumes@onlinesports.com.

■ **Percent of resumes submitted by e-mail:** 100.

■ **Percent of resumes received from individuals:** 100.

■ **Limits on length:** None.

■ **Format:** Text by e-mail only.

■ **Fees for person submitting resume:** None.

■ **Length of time resumes remain online:** Six months.

■ **Procedures for updating/renewing:** Resubmit by e-mail.

■ **Privacy/confidentiality:** It is not possible to limit who can see a resume. It is not possible to shield a resume from being viewed by a current employer.

■ **Assistance provided to the person submitting a resume:** E-mail questions will be answered only by e-mail.

■ **Search options available to employers viewing resumes:** Online review.

■ **Technology to match jobs to resumes and e-mail results to clients:** n/a.

■ **Average number of daily hits on resumes:** 20,000.

■ **Special features:** The Online Sports Career Center lists career opportunities only within the sports and recreation industries and posts resumes only of individuals pursuing careers within these industries.

■ **Other distinguishing factors:** The Online Sports Career Center is a resource of sports-related career opportunities and a resume bank for potential employers. The Career Center focuses exclusively on the many segments of the sports and recreation industries.

ORASEARCH

USA
Oracle professionals
Rating: ★ ★ ★

ORASEARCH is a service that matches Oracle professionals with companies who need them.

- **URL:** http://www.orasearch.com

- **Ownership/sponsorship:** Advanced Data, Inc.

- **Started accepting resumes:** 1997.

- **Approximate number of resumes online April 2000:** More than 4,000 (with one year or more experience).

- **Resume career fields:** Resumes are limited to Oracle jobs.

- **Total number of corporate subscribers/ employers:** 80.

- **Distribution of corporate subscribers/ employers**

  Direct-hire employers: 50 percent

  Staffing firms: 40 percent

  Contract/consulting firms: 10 percent

- **Fee structure for corporate subscribers/ employers:** $2,250 for a six-month membership.

- **Methods and rules for submitting resumes:** Must have one year of paid experience in Oracle.

- **Percent of resumes submitted by Web form:** 100.

- **Percent of resumes received from individuals:** 100.

- **Limits on length:** None.

- **Format:** Open.

- **Fees for person submitting resume:** None.

- **Length of time resumes remain online:** One year.

- **Procedures for updating/renewing:** Online.

- **Privacy/confidentiality:** It is possible to limit who can see a resume. It is not possible to shield a resume from being viewed by a current employer.

- **Assistance provided to the person submitting a resume:** E-mail address to send resume to if user encounters a system error while inputting resume.

- **Search options available to employers viewing resumes:** Oracle software products.

- **Technology to match jobs to resumes and e-mail results to clients:** Employers set own screening criteria and can receive full resumes or only summaries.

- **Average number of daily hits on resumes:** 10,000.

- **Other distinguishing factors:** ORASEARCH is a dedicated Oracle resume and job site.

PassportAccess

USA
Technical
Rating: ★ ★ ★ ★

Since its inception in 1995, PassportAccess has provided industry leaders with high-quality technical talent through its user-friendly online resume database. Companies ranging from Fortune 500 IT firms to small, independent recruiting agencies depend on PassportAccess to provide world-class programmers, engineers, and network administrators.

The Wall Street Journal, Interbiznet, AIRS, and *Employment Weekly* have all praised PassportAccess as one of the premier recruiter destinations for technical resumes.

- **URL:** http://www.passportaccess.com

- **Ownership/sponsorship:** Privately held corporation.

- **Started accepting resumes:** June 1995.

- **Approximate number of resumes online April 2000:** More than 550,000.

- **Resume career fields:** PassportAccess's focus is on technical resumes. Technical resumes include IT, IS, programming, engineering, software, hardware, technical support, even sales and marketing if the candidate has a background in the technical industry. Each resume is read by one of PassportAccess's staff to ensure applicability to its database.

- **Total number of corporate subscribers/ employers:** n/a.

- **Distribution of corporate subscribers/ employers**

  Staffing firms: 50 percent

  Direct-hire employers: 35 percent

  Contract/consulting firms: 15 percent

- **Fee structure for corporate subscribers/ employers:** $995 per user license for one year of unlimited access to the database. Corporate and multi-user rates are extremely reasonable.

- **Methods and rules for submitting resumes:** A resume can be cut and pasted into the online form located on the Web site. There are no long forms to fill out.

- **Percent of resumes submitted by**

  Web form: 50

E-mail: 40

Other paper (job fairs, mailings): 10

- **Percent of resumes received from**

  Individuals: 70

  Colleges or universities: 10

  Outplacement firms: 5

  Other: 15

- **Limits on length:** None; however, PassportAccess will not upload summaries.

- **Format:** Must be full-text resume.

- **Fees for person submitting resume:** None.

- **Length of time resumes remain online:** PassportAccess believes passive candidates are key in today's recruitment strategy; therefore, they hold resumes for a maximum of 24 months. However, recruiters are able to search by any date criteria.

- **Procedures for updating/renewing:** Contact the Webmaster through the Web site.

- **Privacy/confidentiality:** Job seekers can limit some information on their resumes; but to be accepted, their resumes must have some sort of contact information.

- **Assistance provided to the person submitting a resume:** n/a.

- **Search options available to employers viewing resumes:** Subscribers to the resume database receive a complete resume-management system. This online manager allows you to perform multiple functions for quick and efficient resume processing. Features include

  Easy-to-use format: No Boolean language skills needed. Simple data entry including a separate Natural Language search engine.

  E-mail resumes: Attach resumes to an e-mail that you can send to yourself, another hiring manager, or to your resume repository.

E-mail candidates: Instead of spending all your time corresponding with one candidate, send one e-mail to hundreds of candidates at once using our broadcast e-mailer.

Notes: Keep track of candidates by making private notes on each resume. These notes can be customized for viewing by your entire organization or left proprietary for each user.

Folders/filing: Store resumes for future viewing and processing in your own virtual file. You can store resumes in folders that you designate. Only a user with your password may gain access to your saved resume files.

Reminder notification: You can set up an automated notification message to remind you of appointments, calls, and other to-do's related to recruiting.

- **Technology to match jobs to resumes and e-mail results to clients:** n/a.

- **Average number of daily hits on resumes:** Hundreds of subscribers access the database each day and perform searches.

- **Other distinguishing factors:** PassportAccess is a full-service resume-collection company. Thousands of recruiters have had success using the resume database to locate difficult-to-find candidates and legacy candidates. PassportAccess is also a perfect networking tool. It's a great companion to any database a recruiter may be using, since most resumes in the PassportAccess database system cannot be found in any other databases.

PursuitNet Online

USA and Canada
Higher-level positions in professions and sales
Rating: ★ ★ ★

PursuitNet specializes in professional, technical, sales, and management-level individuals qualified to seek jobs in the $30,000–$300,000 range. PursuitNet matches your skills and desires with compatible jobs anywhere in the United States or Canada.

- **URL:** http://www.pursuit.com/jobs

- **Ownership/sponsorship:** Corporate.

- **Started accepting resumes:** 1995.

- **Approximate number of resumes online April 2000:** More than 10,000.

- **Resume career fields:** Resumes are mostly in professional, technical, managerial, and sales areas, with annual salary qualifications in the range of $30,000–$300,000.

- **Total number of corporate subscribers/ employers:** Most of PursuitNet's efforts are in satisfaction of requirements submitted into the PursuitNet Online system by other recruiting agencies throughout the United States and Canada.

- **Distribution of corporate subscribers/ employers**

  Direct-hire employers: 10 percent

  Staffing firms: 75 percent

  Contract/consulting firms: 15 percent

- **Fee structure for corporate subscribers/ employers:** 20 to 30 percent of annual salary.

- **Methods and rules for submitting resumes:** Free through the Web site form at http://www.pursuit.com/jobs, where all instructions are provided.

- **Percent of resumes submitted by Web form:** 100.

- **Percent of resumes received from**

  Individuals: 50

  Colleges or universities: 5

  Outplacement firms: 5

  Other (recruiters/associates): 40

- **Limits on length:** Three pages.

- **Format:** Specified through the Web form.

- **Fees for person submitting resume:** None.

- **Length of time resumes remain online:** Permanently, as long as the resume is updated each month by an individual actively seeking a job and annually by someone potentially interested in advancements.

- **Procedures for updating/renewing:** Online (password for access).

- **Privacy/confidentiality:** It is possible to limit who can see a resume: The only time a resume is seen by any outside party is for a potential match with an actual job. It is possible to shield a resume from being viewed by a current employer: In the designated place on the resume form, simply indicate any employer that you don't want to receive the resume.

- **Assistance provided to the person submitting a resume:** Online guidelines are provided to assist the individual, and automatic editing is accomplished as a part of the submission process.

- **Search options available to employers viewing resumes:** None. Employers are not provided such an option. All they need to do is submit the job opening, and PursuitNet does the rest of the matching process. The employers are presented online with only the best matches, which are ranked by a complex algorithm.

- **Technology to match jobs to resumes and e-mail results to clients:** The entire system is online to match the best of the candidates to the jobs presented. Many factors are considered, and only those candidates who remain are ranked and presented online for the client to consider.

- **Average number of daily hits on resumes:** n/a.

- **Special features:** PursuitNet Online is the only known service that provides a career-long service interacting with a large number of recruiters throughout the United States and Canada to effect placements with their clients. Both direct-hire and contract placements are accommodated by this fully online system.

- **Other distinguishing factors:** According to PursuitNet Online, it is the most advanced system on the Web, now in its sixth year with an online system.

Resume Network

**Australia and New Zealand— soon to be global
Middle management to senior executives in all career fields
Rating:** ★ ★ ★

Resume Network is designed primarily as a service provider to professional recruitment agencies. The database is targeted at recruitment for professionals, middle and senior management, and executives.

- **URL:** http://www.resumenetwork.net

- **Ownership/sponsorship:** Resume Network Pty. Ltd.

- **Started accepting resumes:** November 1999.

- **Approximate number of resumes online April 2000:** 5,000.

- **Resume career fields:** Resumes are in all career fields, from middle management through senior executives only.

- **Total number of corporate subscribers/ employers:** This site is for the exclusive use of member recruitment agencies and is accessible to corporations/employers ONLY to source a recruitment agency.

- **Distribution of corporate subscribers/employers:** 100 percent recruitment agencies.

- **Fee structure for corporate subscribers/ employers:** Not available. Member recruitment agencies pay a low monthly membership fee for unlimited access to the Resume Network database and a "no win, no pay" service fee only for successful placements.

- **Methods and rules for submitting resumes:** Up to five "unidentifiable" profiles and one full resume to be completed (all based on preset templates online). Candidates are taken through the registration process by a series of user-friendly prompts.

- **Percent of resumes submitted by Web form:** 100.

- **Percent of resumes received from**

  Individuals: 90

  Colleges and universities: 5

  Outplacement firms: 5

- **Limits on length:** Templates include mandatory fields and free-text windows with capacities of up to 9,000 characters.

- **Format:** Formatted templates.

- **Fees for person submitting resume:** None.

- **Length of time resumes remain online:** Indefinitely, as long as the candidates access Resume Network and refresh their files every six weeks.

- **Procedures for updating/renewing:** Access the Registered Candidate menu and select Candidate Update & Changes. Candidates can update their profiles and/or resumes at any time. Candidates have free, unrestricted access to their files 24 hours, 7 days.

- **Privacy/confidentiality:** Candidates are in total control of the release of their resumes to requesting member recruitment agencies. The anonymous, unidentifiable profiles are available to be viewed by all member recruitment agencies. Following a request for their resume from a member recruitment agency, only the candidate can authorize the release of the resume to the requesting member recruitment agency. If the candidate chooses not to release the resume, an e-mail advising this is generated back to the recruitment agency.

- **Assistance provided to the person submitting a resume:** E-mail, telephone, and fax support available.

- **Search options available to employers viewing resumes:** Employers are not able to search for or obtain resumes. Employers' access to Resume Network is restricted to searching for and accessing the services of a member recruitment agency. Member recruitment agencies search for candidates to match their clients' recruitment needs using Resume Network's unique, patented search engine. Candidate searches are conducted using one or more of the following fields: Industry, Profession, Position, Location, Salary. There is also a Skills and Experience keyword search.

- **Technology to match jobs to resumes and e-mail results to clients:** A patented system to match and interact between candidates, member recruitment agencies, and the Resume Network system.

- **Average number of daily hits on resumes:** The unidentifiable profiles receive hundreds of hits daily. Candidates can view at any time the number of hits on their unidentifiable profiles.

- **Special features:** Any resume authorized for release by the candidate is held exclusively by the requesting member recruitment agency for up to seven days, with an option to extend.

- **Other distinguishing factors:** Resume Network is a revolutionary Internet-based network system for the exclusive use of the professional recruitment industry. Resume Network is designed for middle to senior management and executives.

ResumeBlaster.com

USA
All career fields
Rating: ★ ★

ResumeBlaster.com can e-mail your resume to as many as 3,000 recruiters nationwide. If the recruiters are interested in you for any of their positions, they will contact you directly.

- **URL:** http://www.resumeblaster.com

- **Ownership/sponsorship:** PC Pros, Inc., 800-497-6617.

- **Started accepting resumes:** 1997.

- **Approximate number of resumes online April 2000:** ResumeBlaster.com sends the resumes directly to recruiters' e-mail in-boxes. It does not have resumes in a databank.

- **Resume career fields:** ResumeBlaster.com has a General Blast, which goes to recruiters who accept resumes from all job classifications. There is also a Disciplined Blast, which goes not only to the recruiters who

accept all resumes, but also to the recruiters who have selected the same job classifications as those the candidate selects.

- **Total number of corporate subscribers/ employers:** More than 4,700 recruiters and executive search firms.

- **Distribution of corporate subscribers/ employers**

  Staffing firms/employers: 90–95 percent

  Contract/consulting firms: 5–10 percent

- **Fee structure for corporate subscribers/ employers:** Free for recruiters to receive resumes.

- **Methods and rules for submitting resumes:** Fill in the online sign-up form, which includes the type of work you do, what you're looking for, your location requirements, your salary requirements, and many other pieces of information recruiters require for matching you up with open job positions.

- **Percent of resumes submitted by**

  Web form: 99

  Fax: 1

- **Percent of resumes received from individuals:** 100.

- **Limits on length:** None.

- **Format:** Plain text.

- **Fees for person submitting resume:** $49–$89, depending on service selected.

- **Procedures for updating/renewing:** You are able to modify the resume on the Web site with e-mail and password.

- **Privacy/confidentiality:** It is possible to limit who can see a resume to some degree. You can limit the resume from going to certain firms that are in certain job classifications. It is possible to shield a resume from being viewed by a current employer. It is also possible to hide your identity through a confidential option.

- **Assistance provided to the person submitting a resume:** You can use online Help, or you can send an e-mail message for help. You can also call the customer-service line at the toll-free number, 800-497-6617.

- **Search options available to employers viewing resumes:** Employers/recruiters can subscribe to a monthly service to allow searching of past resumes sent.

- **Technology to match jobs to resumes and e-mail results to clients:** ResumeBlaster.com is a resume distribution service, so it doesn't do job matching. This is left up to the recruiters and the candidates.

- **Average number of daily hits on resumes:** n/a.

- **Special features:** As stated earlier, ResumeBlaster.com is unlike resume database sites where you can post your resume and it sits there in a database, passively waiting for someone to find it in a keyword search. Instead, ResumeBlaster.com distributes your resume to recruiters who have specifically subscribed with the site.

ResumeXPRESS!

USA
All career fields
Rating: ★ ★

ResumeXPRESS! is a service of Gonyea Career Marketing, Inc. (Formerly Online Solutions, Inc.), developed and managed by Wayne M. Gonyea, coauthor of *Electronic Resumes* (McGraw-Hill, 1996). ResumeXPRESS! distributes resumes electronically to thousands of employers, employment recruiters, and online resume-database services nationwide who have requested to receive resumes from job seekers. ResumeXPRESS! also maintains a resume database.

- **URL:** http://resumexpress.com

- **Ownership/sponsorship:** Wayne M. Gonyea.

  Gonyea Career Marketing, Inc. (Formerly OnLine Solutions, Inc.) 1810 Arturus Lane New Port Richey, FL 34655 727-375-0489

- **Started accepting resumes:** 1994.

- **Approximate number of resumes online April 2000:** 4,000.

- **Resume career fields:** Resumes are accepted in all career fields.

- **Total number of corporate subscribers/ employers:** 7,000 (increasing rapidly).

- **Distribution of corporate subscribers/ employers**

  Direct-hire employers: 20 percent

  Staffing firms: 75 percent

  Online databases: 5 percent

- **Fee structure for corporate subscribers/ employers:** Free.

- **Methods and rules for submitting resumes:** Accepted by e-mail, by Web site, on disk, or by USPS from job seekers and/ or third parties (resume writers, career counselors, and so on).

- **Percent of resumes submitted by**

  Web form: 65

  E-mail: 33

  Other paper (job fairs, mailings): 2

- **Percent of resumes received from**

  Individuals: 40

  Outplacement firms: 5

Other (career counselors, resume writers): 55

- **Limits on length:** None.

- **Format:** Prefers ASCII.

- **Fees for person submitting resume:** $39.95–$199.95 retail, which includes a six-month posting in the ResumeXPRESS! database.

- **Length of time resumes remain online:** Six months.

- **Procedures for updating/renewing:** Free update/redistribution after 30 days.

- **Privacy/confidentiality:** It is not possible to limit who can see a resume; distribution can remove current employer. It is possible to shield a resume from being viewed by a current employer by posting the resume as confidential.

- **Assistance provided to the person submitting a resume:** Free phone consultation and review of resume.

- **Search options available to employers viewing resumes:** Resumes are always fully searchable by keywords at all times—no restrictions, no cost.

- **Technology to match jobs to resumes and e-mail results to clients:** Registered employers establish the characteristics of the resumes they are seeking by using keywords. Queries can be modified, added, or deleted at any time by entering the password-protected registration area. Search criteria remain "live" on the database. These live criteria enable every resume that matches the search criteria to be selected and sent out automatically via e-mail.

- **Average number of daily hits on resumes:** 400–500.

- **Special features:** Sorted resume response, as previously described; Executive and Confidential services available.

- **Other distinguishing factors:** Also contains options for ExecutiveXPRESS! to send executive resumes to a selected list of executive/retained recruiters and venture capitalists. Portfolio presentation for executives also available.

ResumeZapper.com

Primarily USA
All career fields
Rating: ★ ★

ResumeZapper e-mails your resume and cover letter right into the e-mail boxes of thousands of America's top search, recruitment, and placement firms.

- **URL:** http://www.resumezapper.com

- **Ownership/sponsorship:** ResumeZapper.com

- **Started accepting resumes:** 1998.

- **Approximate number of resumes online April 2000:** ResumeZapper.com is a resume-distribution service only. It is not a resume database.

- **Resume career fields:** Resumes are accepted in all career fields.

- **Total number of corporate subscribers/ employers:** More than 5,000 search firms only.

- **Distribution of corporate subscribers/employers:** 100 percent staffing firms.

- **Fee structure for corporate subscribers/ employers:** Free for third-party recruiters and search firms.

- **Methods and rules for submitting resumes:** Online or via mail.

- **Percent of resumes submitted by**

  Web form: 98

  Mail: 2

- **Percent of resumes received from individuals:** 100.

- **Limits on length:** None.

- **Format:** Most formats accepted in copy-and-paste Web form.

- **Fees for person submitting resume:** Since the service is a customizable resume-distribution service, candidates can choose what type of distribution they desire, starting from a price of $49.99.

- **Length of time resumes remain online:** n/a.

- **Privacy/confidentiality:** It is possible to limit who can see a resume. It is possible to shield a resume from being viewed by a current employer as resumes are sent only to third-party recruiters and search firms.

- **Assistance provided to the person submitting a resume:** Online FAQ, plus a designated e-mail address for the candidate to ask questions; telephone personal support available on request.

- **Search options available to employers viewing resumes:** n/a.

- **Technology to match jobs to resumes and e-mail results to clients:** Resumes are filtered to the recruiters based on profile information submitted, then matched with the candidate's info, and then e-mailed to the recruiters.

- **Average number of daily hits on resumes:** n/a.

- **Special features:** ResumeZapper.com is designed with the proactive candidate in mind. Candidates use resume distribution to save them time and to get their resumes into the hands of a large quantity of search firms quickly and efficiently.

Saludos.com
USA
All career fields
Rating: ★ ★ ★ ★

Saludos.com, supported by *Saludos Hispanos* magazine, is devoted to promoting Hispanics through careers and education. The Saludos Web site and online job fairs offer excellent career and educational information and free resume posting for bilingual job seekers. Employers seeking qualified bilingual candidates are able to utilize various levels of recruitment services such as job postings, resume screenings, and multimedia job fair booths. The award-winning site received over a million hits during its first online job fair. Nearly 300 colleges and universities participate with Saludos Hispanos in promoting its services on campus.

- **URL:** http://www.saludos.com

- **Ownership/sponsorship:** *Saludos Hispanos* magazine.

- **Started accepting resumes:** 1996.

- **Approximate number of resumes online April 2000:** 6,500.

- **Resume career fields:** Resumes are in all career fields including academic, administration, advertising, computing and technology, engineering, finance/accounting/insurance, health care, human resources, marketing, media, sales, science, telecommunications, and many others.

- **Total number of corporate subscribers/employers:** Approximately 3,000 corporate subscribers advertise with Saludos Hispanos each year.

- **Distribution of corporate subscribers/employers:** n/a.

- **Fee structure for corporate subscribers/employers:** One 30-day job posting is $99.

Resume robot and database screening is available with various options in a range of package prices. Custom-designed employer profiles and links are also a regular feature of the site. Job-fair booths and banners are available three times a year.

- **Methods and rules for submitting resumes:** Must be bilingual in English and Spanish and be enrolled in a four-year college or university with expected graduation within one year of posting your resume; or have completed a two-year or four-year college program.

- **Percent of resumes submitted by**

  Other paper (job fairs, mailings): 50

  Web form: 45

  E-mail: 3

  Fax: 2

- **Percent of resumes received from**

  Individuals: 75

  Colleges or universities: 25

- **Limits on length:** None.

- **Format:** Insert answers to different sections into Web form—do not paste in existing resume. Headings include Objective, Experience, Education, Skills, and Honors, as well as field boxes for further detail such as the level of spoken and written skills in each language.

- **Fees for person submitting resume:** None. On the site, job seekers have free access to hundreds of detailed job listings. Job seekers also have the option to send their resume directly to a company themselves with one click once they are in the database. They also receive e-mail notification of jobs posted in their selected career categories.

- **Length of time resumes remain online:** As long as desired.

- **Procedures for updating/renewing:** Use a password to retrieve resume, update as desired, and click on Submit. Resumes submitted to database are privacy-protected.

- **Privacy/confidentiality:** Job seeker designates whether name and current employer can be revealed to a prospective employer.

- **Assistance provided to the person submitting a resume:** Online directions and Web-based form to fill in (or cut and paste). Or candidates can e-mail their resumes in plain-text format.

- **Search options available to employers viewing resumes:** Resume robot searches by job category and other relevant fields and sends results to employers.

- **Technology to match jobs to resumes and e-mail results to clients:** Resumes are selected by a resume robot and sent to employers when they fit the requirements of a particular job or job category.

- **Average number of daily hits on resumes:** 21,495 hits per day on the Web site.

- **Other distinguishing factors:** In order to post a resume on the Saludos Career Web, candidates must be bilingual (English and Spanish) college graduates.

Science Careers

USA
Sciences
Rating: ★ ★ ★

Science Careers is provided by The American Association for the Advancement of Science, publishers of *Science* magazine. The site is provided to scientists to find jobs in the life sciences industry. *Science* magazine typically sponsors three career fairs each year for pharmaceutical and biotechnology organizations.

- **URL:** http://www.sciencecareers.org

- **Ownership/sponsorship:** American Association for the Advancement of Science (AAAS).

- **Started accepting resumes:** October 1999.

- **Approximate number of resumes online April 2000:** 6,000.

- **Resume career fields:** Resumes are in the life sciences (agriculture, anatomy/physiology, biochemistry, biology, botany/plant science, cell biology, clinical research, developmental biology, environmental science, genetics, immunology, marine science, medicine, microbiology, molecular biology, neuroscience, nutrition/health care, oncology, pathology, pharmacology, structural Biology, toxicology, veterinary medicine, and virology) and the sciences (astronomy, atmospheric science, chemistry, computer science, engineering, geoscience, informatics, materials science, mathematics, and physics).

- **Total number of corporate subscribers/ employers:** Originally only the exhibitors in career fairs were allowed to access the resume database. In February 2000, the site was opened to any employer, and by April 2000 had 10 companies that had purchased access.

- **Distribution of corporate subscribers/ employers**

  Direct-hire employers: 90 percent

  Staffing firms: 5 percent

  Other: 5 percent

- **Fee structure for corporate subscribers/ employers:** They must advertise in certain issues and exhibit at the career fairs to have access to the databank of resumes. The rates vary depending on the size of the ad they run.

- **Methods and rules for submitting resumes:** Scientists can go online at any time to download their resumes. Go to www.sciencecareers.org and click on Resume/CV Database and follow the directions.

- **Percent of resumes submitted by**

  Web form: 50

  Other paper (job fairs, mailings): 50

- **Percent of resumes received from individuals:** 100.

- **Limits on length:** None.

- **Format:** Use Science Careers Resume/CV Entry Wizard Webform for general information; then attach a resume to the form.

- **Fees for person submitting resume:** None.

- **Length of time resumes remain online:** Seven weeks.

- **Procedures for updating/renewing:** Job seekers can edit or delete their resumes online.

- **Privacy/confidentiality:** It is possible to limit who can see a resume by submitting a confidential resume. Your resume and contact information will not be visible to employers. Employers wishing to contact you can do so via e-mail forwarded to you confidentially. Then you decide whether or not to reveal your identity. It is possible to shield a resume from being viewed by a current employer by using the confidential resume option.

- **Assistance provided to the person submitting a resume:** n/a.

- **Search options available to employers viewing resumes:** n/a.

- **Technology to match jobs to resumes and e-mail results to clients:** n/a.

- **Average number of daily hits on resumes:** n/a.

- **Special features:** Advice & Perspectives section has help for writing resumes as well as several sample resumes and cover letters.

SEEK

Australia and New Zealand
All career fields
Rating: ★ ★ ★ ★

Seek Communications is an Australian–owned-and-operated online jobs database and career-development site that is focused on the Australian and New Zealand marketplaces. SEEK also has separate areas for executives (SEEK Executive) and university students and graduates (SEEK Campus).

- **URLs:** http://www.seek.com.au (Australia) and http://www.seek.co.nz (New Zealand)

- **Ownership/sponsorship:** Private ownership.

- **Started accepting resumes:** March 1998.

- **Approximate number of resumes online April 2000:** 80,000.

- **Resume career fields:** Resumes are spread broadly across all industry/occupation categories (13 industries and more than 100 occupations).

- **Total number of corporate subscribers/ employers:** More than 1,200.

- **Distribution of corporate subscribers/ employers**

  Direct-hire employers: 20 percent

  Staffing firms and contract employers: 80 percent

- **Fee structure for corporate subscribers/ employers:** Corporations/employers pay to place advertisements on the site. Access to the resume database is given to advertisers over a specified threshold.

- **Methods and rules for submitting resumes:** Resumes are submitted online by the user through a browser interface. Users can submit multiple resumes. Users can also select whether their resume is to be private (for the convenience of using their resumes when applying for positions) or accessible by advertisers.

- **Percent of resumes submitted by**

  Web form: 95

  E-mail: 5

- **Percent of resumes received from individuals:** Virtually 100.

- **Limits on length:** Approximately 10,000 characters.

- **Format:** Format is according to a specified Web form template. Applicants enter free text into a number of areas (with most areas being optional) that include work experience, profile, education, personal interests, and so on. Users may also specify which type of work they are looking for (location, industry, occupation, and work type) to enable searching by employers. (Allowing searchable access of resume by employers is optional.)

- **Fees for person submitting resume:** None.

- **Length of time resumes remain online:** One year, but they remain accessible to advertisers for only three months. In either case, job seekers receive two expiry notices, which permits them to extend their resumes for a further period.

- **Procedures for updating/renewing:** Users can update their resumes at any time via a browser interface. To renew, users simply click on the hypertext link in the expiry notices and select the option of extending their resumes.

■ **Privacy/confidentiality:** It is possible to limit who can see a resume. Resumes can be seen only by advertisers (employers) who meet specified advertising thresholds. The advertisers can search the database to find those matches for actual vacant positions. Currently it is not possible to shield a resume from being viewed by a current employer, although SEEK is considering a move down this path. At present, users can see who the site advertisers are (and therefore who can potentially see their resumes).

■ **Assistance provided to the person submitting a resume:** Instructions on the site are clear, and an example resume is provided. Users are also informed that they can contact the customer-service staff by phone or e-mail if they have any problems. All queries are promptly attended to.

■ **Search options available to employers viewing resumes:** Employers can search for relevant potential employees by using any or all of the following: location, industry, occupation, work type, and keyword.

SEEK Campus allows far more granular searching of resumes including searching by discipline, major, subjects studied, grades, preferred employer, etc.

■ **Technology to match jobs to resumes and e-mail results to clients:** Employers can access resumes that match their searches directly through a browser interface.

■ **Average number of daily hits on resumes:** Resumes appear in a list at the rate of approximately 10,000 per day.

■ **Special features:** The site provides users with a free service that enables them to create a resume online and to lodge their resume for the purpose of attracting potential employers. Within two months of going live, a significant number of placements have been made through this process (with the first placement within three days of going live).

■ **Other distinguishing factors:** In the editorial areas of the site, there are substantial resources assisting job seekers in all aspects of the job search process.

SIRC: Shawn's Internet Resume Center

USA
Executives and experienced professionals
Rating: ★ ★ ★

Since 1995, Shawn's Internet Resume Center (SIRC) has served professional and experienced job seekers.

■ **URL:** http://www.inpursuit.com/sirc/

■ **Ownership/sponsorship:** Owned by InPursuit of Centreville, VA.

■ **Started accepting resumes:** 1995.

■ **Approximate number of resumes online April 2000:** 3,500.

■ **Resume career fields:** Resumes are in all job classifications; however, the service targets experienced professionals.

■ **Total number of corporate subscribers/ employers:** Over 1,000 subscribe for advanced features (no cost, employers/ recruiters must submit a profile). An even larger number of employers/recruiters take advantage of SIRC's basic resume searching.

■ **Distribution of corporate subscribers/ employers**

Direct-hire employers: 60 percent

Staffing firms: 30 percent

Contract/consulting firms: 10 percent

- **Fee structure for corporate subscribers/ employers:** Free. Employers/recruiters may use basic resume-searching capabilities without submitting a profile. SIRC provides the following to those who sign up for the free SIRC Employer Membership Program: company profile, unlimited job posting, advanced resume searching, and the capability for seekers to apply for jobs online.

- **Methods and rules for submitting resumes:** Online submission. To maintain the experienced professional quality of its resumes, SIRC requires that job seekers meet its criteria—more than five years of experience, Master's degree or higher, or current Master's student—to be included. This policy makes it possible for SIRC to be a niche service that targets experienced professionals.

- **Percent of resumes submitted by Web form:** 100.

- **Percent of resumes received from individuals:** 100.

- **Limits on length:** None.

- **Format:** Online form with required and optional fields. The job seekers can format their work experience and education sections as desired.

- **Fees for person submitting resume:** None.

- **Length of time resumes remain online:** A minimum of 60 days.

- **Procedures for updating/renewing:** Automated system allows job seekers to log on and update their resumes online.

- **Privacy/confidentiality:** It is not possible at this time to limit who can see a resume.

It is not possible at this time to shield a resume from being viewed by a current employer.

- **Assistance is provided to the person submitting a resume:** Submission form is self-explanatory. SIRC provides access to an online resume tutorial.

- **Search options available to employers viewing resumes:** Employers can search on more than just a keyword (state, years of experience, and job category).

- **Technology to match jobs to resumes and e-mail results to clients:** None at this time; however, the system will allow for this technology in the future.

- **Average number of daily hits on resumes:** 1,500.

- **Special features:**

  For employers:

  Unlimited job posting

  Advanced resume searching

  Company profile

  List of employers using SIRC

  For job seekers:

  Job listings

  Resume clinic

  Articles on resume writing

- **Other distinguishing factors:** SIRC launched a major set of improvements to automate the site. Job seekers have more control of their resumes and have more information to help them in their searches. Employers are able to subscribe (at no cost) to additional services, such as unlimited job postings and corporate profiles.

TCM's HR Careers

Global
Human resources/training and development
Rating: ★ ★ ★

An international company located in Canada, TCM.com specializes in the area of Human Resources. TCM's HR Careers site focuses on the human resource/training and development profession.

- **URL:** http://www.tcm.com/hr-careers

- **Ownership/sponsorship:** Wholly owned by TCM.com, Inc., Ottawa, Canada.

- **Started accepting resumes:** 1995.

- **Approximate number of resumes online April 2000:** 3,900.

- **Resume career fields:** Resumes are primarily in human resources, training and development, instructional design, organizational development, employee relations, compensation and benefits, HR planning, recruitment and employment, sales—HR/training and development products and services.

- **Total number of corporate subscribers/employers:** More than 500.

- **Distribution of corporate subscribers/employers**

  Direct-hire employers: 70 percent

  Staffing firms: 20 percent

  Contract/consulting firms: 10 percent

- **Fee structure for corporate subscribers/employers:** $200 per one-month ad; $200 per one-month resume database access; $300 for both. Banner advertising also available.

- **Methods and rules for submitting resumes:** n/a.

- **Percent of resumes submitted by**

  E-mail: 60

  Web form: 30

  Fax: 10

- **Percent of resumes received from individuals:** 100.

- **Limits on length:** None.

- **Format:** Use online form.

- **Fees for person submitting resume:** None.

- **Length of time resumes remain online:** Indefinitely, but must be maintained every six months to stay visible.

- **Procedures for updating/renewing:** Resumes must be "touched" every six months via Web, or status is changed to "hidden," and is no longer visible to database subscribers. After six months, people with older resumes are advised to update/"touch" the resume.

- **Privacy/confidentiality:** It is not possible to limit who can see a resume. It is not possible to shield a resume from being viewed by a current employer.

- **Assistance provided to the person submitting a resume:** Whatever is required: Resumes are often posted for individuals having problems. Resume critique service for $100.

- **Search options available to employers viewing resumes:** Web search; unlimited candidate folders.

- **Technology to match jobs to resumes and e-mail results to clients:** n/a.

- **Special features:** Job-notification mailing list. Proactive resume broadcasting service available for $50.

Teachers@Work

USA and Canada
Education
Rating: ★ ★ ★ ★

Teachers@Work is an innovative electronic employment service that allows schools to search resumes of current and prospective teachers nationwide and to post jobs online for candidates to view. Teachers@Work offers the opportunity to match specific teaching and extracurricular requirements with candidates' credentials, thus ensuring the most suitable prospects for each teaching position.

- **URL:** http://www.teachersatwork.com

- **Ownership/sponsorship:** Privately owned and operated.

- **Started accepting resumes:** 1997.

- **Approximate number of resumes online April 2000:** 2,500 average. More resumes are submitted during spring and summer seasons when most teaching positions are available.

- **Resume career fields:** Resumes are from teachers and administrators in the field of education, grades K–12.

- **Total number of corporate subscribers/ employers:** Average number of subscribers is 1,200, which includes individual schools and school districts.

- **Distribution of corporate subscribers/ employers**

  Direct-hire employers: 95 percent

  Staffing firms: 5 percent

- **Fee structure for corporate subscribers/ employers:** Depends on the number of schools in the subscribing district. Current fees are listed on the Web page.

- **Methods and rules for submitting resumes:** Log on and fill out resume form. Enter all information requested, especially an e-mail address, so that you can be contacted by potential employers. Select a personal username and password and click on Submit Resume. Your resume is immediately available to schools.

- **Percent of resumes submitted by Web form:** 100.

- **Percent of resumes received from individuals:** 100.

- **Limits on length:** Answers must fit into the form provided, but there is an opportunity to personalize statements of educational focus and philosophy.

- **Format:** Web form with sections appropriate to teaching, such as certifications, subject areas, etc.

- **Fees for person submitting resume:** None.

- **Length of time resumes remain online:** Resumes may remain in the database as long as desired. To keep the database current, a notice is sent at five months that the resume is about to expire; the resume is automatically deleted if not updated by six months.

- **Procedures for updating/renewing:** Using a personal username and password, job seekers edit their own resume at any time and as often as necessary. Click the UPDATE button and information is immediately updated.

- **Privacy/confidentiality:** Only registered school districts have access to the database of resumes.

- **Assistance provided to the person submitting a resume:** Technical support is available online or by phone. Teachers@Work is noted for being easy to use.

- **Search options available to employers viewing resumes:** Many options are available to locate candidates to fill specific needs, including geographic search and specific discipline search.

- **Technology to match jobs to resumes and e-mail results to clients:** Teachers can e-mail a copy of their resume to schools from the Web site.

- **Average number of daily hits on resumes:** Varies by season. The site has over 2,500,000 hits per year.

- **Special features:** Teachers can log on to view job postings without submitting a resume. The site is promoted through mailings, conferences, and advertising to ensure that large quantities of teachers and jobs are available.

- **Other distinguishing factors:** Site provides school districts an economical way to locate teaching candidates and overcome the geographic difficulties of nationwide recruiting.

TRAINING Magazine's TrainingSuperSite

USA and Global
Training and human resource fields
Rating: ★ ★ ★ ★

TrainingSuperSite is the leading Web site resource for the training and HR industries.

- **URL:** http://www.trainingsupersite.com

- **Ownership/sponsorship:** Bill Communications and *TRAINING* and *Inside Technology Training* magazines.

  > Bill Communications/
  > TrainingSuperSite
  > 50 South 9th Street
  > Minneapolis, MN 55402

- **Started accepting resumes:** 1996.

- **Approximate number of resumes online April 2000:** More than 5,000 (25–30 percent international).

- **Resume career fields:** Focuses on the training, training development, training management, and human resource fields.

- **Total number of corporate subscribers/employers:** More than 400 subscriptions have been processed.

- **Distribution of corporate subscribers/employers:** n/a.

- **Fee structure for corporate subscribers/employers:** Subscriptions are available for as low as $134 per month.

- **Methods and rules for submitting resumes:** Applicants are required to fill out an online form. Upon submission, they are granted a username and password. They are required to update their resume within six months; otherwise the resume is purged from the system.

- **Percent of resumes submitted by Web form:** 100.

- **Percentage of resumes received from**

  Individuals: 70

  Colleges or universities: 10

  Outplacement firms: 10

  Other: 10

- **Limits on length:** None.

- **Format:** It is a database-driven system that accepts only text entries.

- **Fees for person submitting resume:** None.

- **Length of time resumes remain online:** Six months from the last edit.

- **Procedures for updating/renewing:** Users can update their information using their username and password for access.

- **Privacy/confidentiality:** At press time, it was not yet possible to limit who can see a resume. This feature was to be added in 2000. It is not yet possible to shield a resume from viewing by a current employer. This was to be a feature in 2000.

- **Assistance provided to the person submitting a resume:** Links to books, software, and other reference material.

- **Search options available to employers viewing resumes:** Location, employment preferences, employment types, employment levels, preferred training/HR specialty, willingness to relocate, and keyword (full-text search).

- **Technology to match jobs to resumes and e-mail results to clients:** Resume distribution service is provided ($50 charge to job seeker, free to employers). E-mail notification of newly posted jobs sent free to employees (on request only).

- **Average number of daily hits on resumes:** Up to 500 database searches and 900 resume accesses daily.

- **Special features:** Free job-notification service (e-mail notification of newly posted job opportunities).

Transition Assistance Online

Global
Separating U.S. military, spouses, and dependents (retirees, reservists, and veterans, as well as government service personnel are welcome)
Rating: ★ ★ ★ ★ ★

Transition Assistance Online (TAO) aids the almost one million separating U.S. military service members, veterans, and military family members in finding employment in the civilian sector and federal government, and assists companies in finding and hiring these individuals. The site includes a resume database, job postings, company profiles, job hunting and resume writing advice, and so on.

- **URL:** http://www.taonline.com

- **Ownership/sponsorship:** Digital interWorks.

- **Started accepting resumes:** Late 1996.

- **Approximate number of resumes online April 2000:** More than 20,000.

- **Resume career fields:** Resumes are from separating U.S. military service members, veterans, and working spouses/dependents. The resumes are spread out into many categories that include technical and engineering fields, health care, security, communications, transportation, warehousing, purchasing, and so on.

- **Total number of corporate subscribers/ employers:** More than 150.

- **Distribution of corporate subscribers/ employers**

  Direct-hire employers: 95 percent

  Staffing firms: 2 percent

  Contract/consulting firms: 2 percent

  Other: 1 percent

- **Fee structure for corporate subscribers/ employers:** Depends on which services the employers want (resume searching, advertising, job posting); the position of the advertisement; and the length of posting, advertisement, and/or search. Current service fees are posted at the following address:

  http://www.taonline.com/generalpages/ registerform.asp

- **Methods and rules for submitting resumes:** Resume submissions can come in by e-mail, e-form (http://www.taonline.com/respages/newresume.asp), or postal mail (scanned in); or resumes can be uploaded via our Transition Assistance Software (for servicemembers) and JobMaker Plus (for military spouses and dependents). Both of these software programs can be found in all base exchanges worldwide. See http://www.taonline.com/respages/newresume.asp for more on resume-submission procedures.

- **Percent of resumes submitted by**

  Other paper (job fairs, mailings): 40

  E-mail: 30

  Web form/software: 30

- **Percent of resumes received from**

  Individuals: 60

  NCOA job fairs or similar programs: 40

- **Limits on length:** Three pages or fewer, with no cover letters, attachments, and so on.

- **Format:** ASCII-text scannable resume format, left-justified, is preferred. However, we allow resume submitters to send us their resume in a variety of ways, including faxing it to us. See http://www.taonline.com/respages/newresume.asp for details.

- **Fees for person submitting resume:** None for all U.S. military servicemembers, veterans, spouses, and dependents.

- **Length of time resumes remain online:** Three months; then they are archived for six months.

- **Procedures for updating/renewing:** Just resubmit a resume after 90 days by using

the same methods (e-mail, e-form, or postal mail). Resumes in the 3–6 month range are archived to other searchable directories.

- **Privacy/confidentiality:** Only reputable employers who have paid a fee and who have been authorized can view the resumes by using a login and password. It is not possible to shield a resume from being viewed by a current employer if the current employer is a paying corporate customer. This is generally not an issue for transitioning service members and military spouses.

- **Assistance provided to the person submitting a resume:** Extensive job-hunting and resume-writing resources are available at the online site in the Transition Information Center at http://www.taonline.com/ticpages/ticindex.asp.

- **Search options available to employers viewing resumes:** Employers can search resumes by using two search engines (Simple and Advanced) with keywords, section, service, availability dates, and so on. Resume submitters can search job postings free of charge by using an in-house search engine with keywords, occupations, and/or regions, state, and country.

- **Technology to match jobs to resumes and e-mail results to clients:** TAO has developed a system to provide employers with the most current resumes that best fit their needs on a timely basis. TAO will automatically search its resume bank for the employer's candidate specifications. When TAO finds resumes that match the employer's requirements, they are e-mailed to the employer daily, weekly, or on whatever schedule they specify. Employers can also search the resume databases themselves.

- **Average number of daily hits on resumes:** Total hits on the site are over 1,000,000 per month and increasing by about 15,000 per month.

- **Special features:**

  Military personnel are able to send their resumes electronically to TAO via e-mail or by using Transition Assistance Software (TAS), which Digital interWorks publishes. Military spouses and dependents are able to send their resumes electronically to TAO via e-mail or by using JobMaker Plus (JMP), which Digital interWorks also publishes. TAS and JMP are available at every DoD installation around the world and, in fact, are the best-selling resume-writing/job-search–organizer software programs for the 200,000 service members who transition every year, along with the 750,000 working spouses and family members who move every two to three years and must also find new jobs.

  Digital interWorks has established relationships with all of the Armed Forces transition assistance and outplacements offices and also with the Reserve Officers Association and the Non-Commissioned Officers Association, two of the world's largest military-affiliated associations. The latter is sending TAO separating service members' resumes from their monthly job fairs, which are held across the country.

- **Other distinguishing factors:** Since its introduction in January of 1997, TAO has become the fastest-growing and most popular employment-search site for transitioning military personnel on the Web. The TAO resume bank has more current military resumes than any other online service. TAO is now the military employment content site for Yahoo!Careers, and is the only military recruiting site on WebHire.

TVJobs.com

USA
Broadcast television
Rating: ★ ★ ★

This site specializes in the broadcast marketplace. It covers a broad range of broadcast-related jobs throughout North America. It has opened a new site for radio at http://www.amfmjobs.com.

- **URL:** http://www.tvjobs.com

- **Ownership/sponsorship:** Mark C. Holloway.

- **Started accepting resumes:** 1994.

- **Approximate number of resumes online April 2000:** More than 2,000.

- **Resume career fields:** Resumes are in the broadcast television career field.

- **Total number of corporate subscribers/ employers:** n/a.

- **Distribution of corporate subscribers/ employers:** n/a.

- **Fee structure for corporate subscribers/ employers:** Free.

- **Methods and rules for submitting resumes:** Requires both e-mailed and faxed resume unless e-mailed as .doc-format attachment.

- **Percent of resumes submitted by e-mail:** 100.

- **Percent of resumes received from individuals:** 100.

- **Limits on length:** None.

- **Format:** Resumes formatted by site using extensive HTML.

- **Fees for person submitting resume:** $50 for one year; $100 for two years and additional services.

- **Length of time resumes remain online:** Indefinitely.

- **Procedures for updating/renewing:** Log in and perform update.

- **Privacy/confidentiality:** It is possible to limit who can see a resume. It is possible to shield a resume from being viewed by a current employer.

- **Assistance provided to the person submitting a resume:** If requested.

- **Search options available to employers viewing resumes:** Yes.

- **Technology to match jobs to resumes and e-mail results to clients:** Yes.

- **Average number of daily hits on resumes:** Unknown.

VirtualResume

USA/Canada
All career fields
Rating: ★ ★ ★ ★

VirtualResume is devoted exclusively to resumes. Its sister Web site, CAREERspan, is an employment opportunities online service that is free for both job seekers and employers.

- **URL:** http://www.virtualresume.com

- **Ownership/sponsorship:**

  VirtualSight Communications
  11 Sterling Place
  Suite 4F
  Brooklyn, NY 11217

- **Started accepting resumes:** 1996.

- **Approximate number of resumes online April 2000:** 30,000.

- **Resume career fields:** Resumes are accepted in all career fields. Resumes are clustered into job categories.

- **Total number of corporate subscribers/employers:** n/a.

- **Distribution of corporate subscribers/employers:** n/a.

- **Fee structure for corporate subscribers/employers:** VirtualResume: $89 per month/$700 per year.

- **Methods and rules for submitting resumes:** All resumes must be submitted through the Web site. Only individuals seeking employment can post resumes; agencies cannot post candidates.

- **Percent of resumes submitted by Web form:** 100.

- **Percent of resumes received from individuals:** 100.

- **Limits on length:** None.

- **Format:** ASCII, HTML.

- **Fees for person submitting resume:** None for basic resume posting or guest access to the resume database.

- **Length of time resumes remain online:** Six months.

- **Procedures for updating/renewing:** All resume posters can update, renew, or delete their resumes any time they like by logging in to their accounts.

- **Privacy/confidentiality:** Is it possible to limit who can see a resume? Anyone can search the full database. Only VirtualResume members can view contact information. Confidential resumes are posted without name or contact information. Confidential resumes are posted blind. Recruiters can contact candidates only via a form.

- **Assistance provided to the person submitting a resume:** Customer service is always willing to assist.

- **Search options available to employers viewing resumes:** Job category, location, and/or keyword.

- **Technology to match jobs to resumes and e-mail results to clients:** VirtualResume resumes can be e-mailed directly to employers; resume posters can choose to receive e-mailed jobs.

- **Average number of daily hits on resumes:** n/a.

- **Special features:** Resume posters can choose to be posted by VirtualResume to Usenet resume newsgroups. The postings appear under the candidate's own name and e-mail address.

Your Resume Online

USA
All career fields
Rating: ★ ★ ★

Your Resume Online is a service of Southern Cross Associates, a company that provides Web page design, Web page hosting, and Web page promotion. Southern Cross Associates places your resume online and provides you with your own individual sub-domain URL, so you are the only one who has that Web address on the Internet. You give the address to interested parties and promote your URL yourself.

- **URL:** http://www.southerncross.net/rz/rz12.htm

- **Ownership/sponsorship:** Southern Cross Associates.

- **Started accepting resumes:** 1997.

- **Approximate number of resumes online April 2000:** 50.

- **Resume career fields:** Resumes are accepted in all career fields.

- **Total number of corporate subscribers/employers:** None. Individuals promote their own unique URL resume address themselves.

- **Methods and rules for submitting resumes:** E-mail, fax, floppy disk, postal mail.

- **Percent of resumes submitted by**

  E-mail: 70

  Other paper (job fairs, mailings): 15

  Diskette: 10

  Fax: 5

- **Percent of resumes received from individuals:** 100.

- **Limits on length:** None.

- **Format:** The site will fit the resume to suit its unique layout.

- **Fees for person submitting resume:** One standard price for the service. Inquire for amount at resume@southerncross.net.

- **Length of time resumes remain online:** One full year.

- **Procedures for updating/renewing:** The site allows reasonable updating for free.

- **Privacy/confidentiality:** It is possible to limit who can see a resume and to shield a resume from being viewed by a current employer. The resume owners dictate to whom they distribute the unique URL that the site allocates to them.

- **Assistance provided to the person submitting a resume:** Spelling, parsing, and general critiquing.

■ **Search options available to employers viewing resumes:** n/a.

■ **Technology to match jobs to resumes and e-mail results to clients:** n/a.

■ **Average number of daily hits on resumes:** n/a.

■ **Special features:** The site provides a service whereby job seekers can have their resumes available in a very presentable format as an Internet site. Southern Cross Associates prepares the site and hosts it for one year for a very affordable price.

■ **Other distinguishing factors:** Southern Cross Associates makes the resume fit to standard browser pages so that a printout can be made whenever required. The site also prepares much more comprehensive resumes with graphics and links to other sites. Again, this service is extremely affordable.

Sample sites:

Standard: http://www.southerncross.net/rz/rz11.htm

Vanity: http://www.southerncross.net/vj/vl01.htm

General Index

S

Y

Index of Resume Banks by Career Field

GEOGRAPHIC INDEX
OF RESUME BANKS